T0371590

# National Policy, Global Giants: how Australia built and lost its Automotive Industry

What can we tell about the future of automobiles and the industries that make them by examining their past? Wormald and Rennick trace the history of powered land transport, the rise and fall of the railways, the spectacular rise of the automobile and what might come next. Delving into the mighty and complex automotive industry, following the growth of the markets and production, this book illustrates the globalisation of vehicle manufacturers and component suppliers, giving form to the development of the industry's business model. A key factor in an industry's successes and failures is the often-difficult relationship it has with government, which varies in nature from country to country. As an illustrative case, Wormald and Rennick present and analyse the entire life cycle of Australia's automotive history – including its birth, growth, functioning and death – and its shifting relationship with the government that supported it.

JOHN WORMALD is Managing Partner and co-founder of Autopolis, which specialises in strategic assignments for actors in and around the global automotive industry, critically analysing the industry in order to understand its structures, relationships, influencing factors and dynamics. He is co-author of two major books about the automotive industry.

KIM RENNICK is Autopolis's partner resident in Australia. He also provides consulting services to business owners in the fields of governance, directorship and leadership. He has co-authored submissions and papers for the Australian Productivity Commission, the Australian Competition and Consumer Commission and various State and Federal Government Inquiries.

# National Policy, Global Giants: how Australia built and lost its Automotive Industry

JOHN WORMALD
*Autopolis Strategy Consultants*

KIM RENNICK
*Autopolis Strategy Consultants*

## CAMBRIDGE
### UNIVERSITY PRESS

University Printing House, Cambridge CB2 8BS, United Kingdom

One Liberty Plaza, 20th Floor, New York, NY 10006, USA

477 Williamstown Road, Port Melbourne, VIC 3207, Australia

314–321, 3rd Floor, Plot 3, Splendor Forum, Jasola District Centre, New Delhi – 110025, India

79 Anson Road, #06–04/06, Singapore 079906

Cambridge University Press is part of the University of Cambridge.

It furthers the University's mission by disseminating knowledge in the pursuit of education, learning, and research at the highest international levels of excellence.

www.cambridge.org
Information on this title: www.cambridge.org/9781108486064
DOI: 10.1017/9781108643948

© John Wormald and Kim Rennick 2019

First published 2019

Printed in the United Kingdom by TJ International Ltd. Padstow Cornwall

*A catalogue record for this publication is available from the British Library.*

ISBN 978-1-108-48606-4 Hardback

# Contents

# Figures

# Acknowledgements

This book has been some time in the making. We have worked with different clients in and around the automotive industry for many years. What we say to them must, of course, remain confidential. But from our long experience we have extracted a view of the industry, with its structures, relationships, modes of operation, numerous participants and competitors, successes and failings. This understanding in turn informs our work with individual clients, such that we do not begin work for them from scratch – the motto of our firm is 'We Begin with an Understanding'. This has also led us to write two previous books about the industry, published in 1995 and 2004. We had one planned about the future of the industry as a whole but decided to incorporate some of those ideas into the background section of this, a book about the rise and fall of the automotive industry in Australia. We have worked with parts of the Australian industry on various occasions since 2004 and witnessed its decline and disappearance. During that period, we felt, and more than once expressed, concern about the direction the industry was pursuing and about its relationship with government, which provided it with very significant support for decades – to no avail, in the end. We have long held the view – expressed in our first book in 1995 – that this industry, like all other sectors, is subject to going through a life cycle. Uniquely, we have been able to observe this in operation in the case of Australia. We therefore set out to record our observations and thoughts about the origins, development, decline and death of the Australian automotive industry, and about how government had worked with it through its life. Where possible, we have gone beyond the anecdotal and qualitative to find quantitative evidence for our assertions. Hence the numerous charts we have included. They are an important part of our seeking to look below the surface, especially when it comes to challenging certain public assumptions and assertions. Most of them are based on information that is available in the public domain, albeit with some searching and interpretation required. We did not approach this task as purely innocent or neutral outsiders. Our experiences and contacts in the industry and elsewhere have been essential to the task. We are grateful to all those within and around the industry whom we have had the privilege to work or be in contact with, in Australia and beyond. We owe a particular debt to Richard Johns, the creator of the Australian Automotive Intelligence Yearbook. This annual publication, which he produced for many years, is a treasure trove of information about the industry in Australia. He was also instrumental in reviewing an earlier and much more slender manuscript, and encouraging us to produce something of more consequence, notably by starting from a view of the global industry, as the context for what took place in Australia. We remain responsible for the analyses and interpretations we have made on the basis of his data and those from other sources, notably the many statistics about the industry published by the Australian government, federal and state. Books and other publications that we have accessed are referred to and acknowledged in footnotes.

# Abbreviations

| | |
|---|---|
| ACIS | Automotive Competitiveness and Investment Scheme |
| ACP | Automotive Components Producer |
| ATS | Automotive Transformation Scheme |
| BHP | Brake Horse Power |
| BP | British Preferential (Tariff Rate) |
| CAFE | Corporate Average Fuel Economy |
| CBU | Completely-Built-Up |
| CKD | Completely-Knocked-Down |
| FAPM | Federation of Automotive Products Manufacturers |
| FCAI | Federal Chamber of Automotive Industries |
| GM | General Motors |
| GST | Goods and Services Tax |
| HCV | Heavy Commercial Vehicle |
| KW | Kilowatt |
| LCT | Luxury Car Tax |
| MFN | Most Favoured Nation (Tariff Rate) |
| MMAL | Mitsubishi Motors Australia Ltd |
| MMNA | Mitsubishi Motors North America |
| MMC | Mitsubishi Motors Corporation (Japan) |
| MVP | Motor Vehicle Producer |
| NUMMI | New United Motor Manufacturing, Inc |
| PMV | Passenger Motor Vehicle |
| PPV | Police Pursuit Vehicle |
| PSA | Peugeot Citroën |
| R&D | Research & Development |
| RWD | Rear Wheel Drive |
| SKD | Semi-Knocked-Down |
| SUV | Sports Utility Vehicle |
| TAFTA | Thailand–Australia Free Trade Agreement |
| TMCA | Toyota Motor Corporation of Australia |

# Introduction

All governments have a responsibility for the economic development and well-being of their country or region. They, therefore, have to have a development strategy for it, whether implicit or explicit, laissez-faire or interventionist. An industrial strategy is an important subset of it. This is clearly a matter of great complexity and often of ideological and political controversy, particularly so in an age in which the globalisation of many economic sectors and the interests and priorities of businesses within them have created greater or lesser conflicts with governments and what is perceived as the wider public interest.

We come to this problem not as economists or politicians – we are neither – but as practitioners of corporate and business policy consulting who happen to have concentrated their efforts over many years in one particular sector of great size, importance and influence, which has undergone both huge growth and structural change: the global automotive industry. We strive to understand the structures and mechanisms of the industry, together with economic, social, technological and environmental forces that have shaped it in the past and which will continue to influence its future development. We have, on the basis of this knowledge, worked with individual corporate clients within the many sub-sectors of the industry and with institutions responsible for guiding and regulating it. Hence our by-line: 'We Begin with an Understanding'.

Automobiles are complicated products and, while they perform the same role today as they did from the outset, their complexity and sophistication has grown enormously, as a result of growing market, competitive and regulatory pressures. The complexity of the industry – invisible to its average customer – has grown with this. The industry has grown immensely in size since its inception at the end of the nineteenth century. Its social and economic impact has been huge, to the point at which it could legitimately be described as *the* industry of the twentieth century. With this have come radical internal transformations, from the individual local artisan-inventor pioneers, who had to design and make almost everything themselves, to massive interlocking oligarchical global networks of specialisms. The degree of industrial organisation, collaboration and discipline involved is unprecedented and, in many respects, still unequalled. The industry's achievements in terms of the sophistication, quality and unit cost of its products have been quite extraordinary but remain often unsung.

All this has not happened within some kind of idealised competitive paradigm of untrammelled free market economics. The safety risks involved in motoring induced government regulation from the start, with the British government's requirement for someone carrying a red flag ahead of the new-fangled horseless carriage, to warn the unsuspecting public of the approaching monster. This intrusion of the public interest has hugely expanded, to cover both the multiple dimensions of safeguarding the occupants and other users of the public road, to protecting the environment and providing much of the infrastructure on which road vehicles operate. This has set up an enduring conflict between corporate interests, which would prefer not to have costly regulations imposed on them, and governments, as guardians of the public and environmental interest. This has, of course, been made particularly evident in the case of Dieselgate in Europe, for which both sides are to blame: the industry for lack of candour about what could reasonably be achieved by way of some 'sophisticated' engineering strategies, and politicians and officials for trying to impose a Goldilocks solution without being themselves sufficiently informed. In short, a failure of dialogue.

A fully developed automotive industry is also a big part of a national or regional economy, with considerable impacts on both consumers of its products and suppliers of supporting services and goods to them and the industry itself, in both the private and public spheres. Country after country has wished to have a national automotive industry, for reasons of economic and social development, of prestige, of national security. But this in an industry whose huge growth, increasing deployment of different technologies and competitive pressures have driven an unrelenting pursuit of scale through globalisation. This has often fuelled a clash between the interests of global corporate hierarchies and guardians of the national public interest – and conflicts within the latter. The industry is desperate for growth, particularly in emerging markets, as its traditional ones have become saturated. National governments in mature markets are desperate to preserve economic activity and employment. Those in emerging markets want cheap cars for their people and a competitive exporting national industry, which, in most instances, requires scale beyond their reach. The industry has developed a considerable aptitude in begging for government support and threatening with the consequences of not providing it. Again, there is often a lack of candour on the one side and of adequate understanding on the other. None of these things is unique to the automotive industry. They are to be found aplenty in many other sectors, not least the new technology ones.

Why the automotive industry in Australia? Because it provides an almost textbook-perfect case example of policy failure. The world automotive industry changed hugely. So also did Australia, from a rather closed economy and an isolated and homogeneous society to a great degree of openness and diversity. This is a vigorous (if sometimes raucous) democracy, with an open market, not least in the automotive sector. Yet it faces real problems of how to survive as an advanced economy, which gains greatly from a large primary extractive sector but tries not to be over-dependent upon it. In the automotive sector, government policy became conflicted between opening the market to imports to benefit the consumer and trying to support and preserve an increasingly sub-scale industry. Government was unrealistic in wanting to have its cake and eat it; the industry was less than candid with government and with itself about the true options. We believe this provides a particularly strong case example, for government, for industry, within this sector and beyond it.

We start our argument from a global perspective, in order to provide a framework for our dissection of the history of the automotive industry and of government policy towards it in Australia:

- In Chapter 1, we introduce the concept of a life cycle in powered land transport, starting with the growth, maturity and partial decline of the railways in the United Kingdom (their birthplace) and the United States (their greatest extent). We track the spectacular rise of the automobile, its mature phase and possible incipient decline in its present form.
- Chapter 2 describes the development of the automobile as a product, from the first simple horseless carriages to today's highly sophisticated vehicles, with a large dose of electronic controls – and how, in its present form, it is threatened by environmental pressures and the development of new technologies. We present the spectacular growth of demand, the saturation of developed country markets, the emergence of China and the persistence of regional particularities.
- Chapter 3 relates the history of the production of automobiles: spectacular growth, the drive for scale accompanied by great waves of concentration among the vehicle builders, the emergence of new players, the globalisation of the industry. A surprising result emerges: the unbroken dominance of an oligarchy of vehicle manufacturers, with few Chinese-owned firms in their ranks, despite China's huge production volumes. We explain how the manufacturers control access to their end markets through their unique system of proprietary distribution channels.
- Chapter 4 describes the critical and growing role of the supplier sector; its own march to globalisation and interrelated sets of global oligarchies; the closed nature of the supply chains; and their highly disciplined functioning, under the leadership and tight control of the vehicle manufacturers.
- Chapter 5 discusses the influence of national governments and their long-standing role in regulating the industry, the conflicts that have arisen around safety and environmental protection. It also addresses the role of the industry in national economies, how governments have encouraged the development of national automotive sectors, the means they used to do so and the consequences for the industry. It describes the roles that different countries have sought and been able to play within this global industry.

The case of Australia is then developed against this background of a huge, complex, scale-driven, highly disciplined, oligarchic global industry:

- Chapter 6 tracks the life cycle of powered land transport in Australia, and the dominant role taken by the automobile. It follows the growth of cars in service to saturation, and the similar growth and saturation of the market for new cars. It describes the huge change in the structure of the market, with the replacement of the traditional large Australian car by more modern small cars and SUVs, driven by the immense changes in Australian society. It tracks the surge of imports, as government policy switched from protecting the national market to opening it to outside competition, and reviews pricing and the controlling effect of the tied distribution channels.
- Chapter 7 is the story of the Australian light vehicle industry from the very first developments before World War I, through the era of importing vehicles; the imposition of import controls; the decision to create a fully fledged automotive industry; and its growth, decline and end, as it lost control of its domestic market and never achieved sufficient export volumes in compensation. The principal reason for its demise is identified as lack of sufficient scale, compared to the global giants, rather than external factors such as labour costs. The impact of its departure on the balance of trade and employment is identified as relatively modest. Some unrealistic proposals for reviving it are dismissed.
- Chapter 8 relates the development of the vehicle manufacturers in Australia, focusing on their critical relationships with their parent groups. It describes the role each of the ultimate four survivors was allowed to play within these groups, and the consequences for their various attempts to build volume and scale through exports.
- Chapter 9 identifies the emergence, growth, development and ultimate failure of the supplier sector in Australia, including much of it being taken over by the global giants of the sector. Responsible, as elsewhere, for 80 per cent of the content and value of the complete car, it was never able to achieve enough local scale and was perpetually threatened by competition from imports.
- Chapter 10 addresses the role of government in Australia through the life cycle of its automotive industry, from its success in attracting manufacturers, promoting the development of the industry, protecting and

supporting, encouraging rationalisation – and then being conflicted between that purpose and opening the market to imports, losing its grip on the industry and finally succumbing to the temptation simply to subsidise it.

- Chapter 11 looks at the quality of the evidence, analysis and recommendations put forward by major reviews of the industry, and comments on their efficacy. It identifies the need for better definition of present and desired future states, objectives and paths to them, and management, controls and incentives. It emphasises the need for proper sectoral analysis in support of government intervention – not only in the automotive industry.

# I  The Triumph of the Automobile: and Its Incipient Decline

## THE POWERED LAND TRANSPORT REVOLUTION STARTED IN BRITAIN

The First Industrial Revolution was born in Britain. It was based on two seminal innovations, which interacted and mutually reinforced each other. The blast furnace enabled the production of iron in large quantities by using coke made from coal to reduce iron ore, in the place of charcoal obtained from wood (at the cost of many of Britain's ancient forests). The steam engine made it possible to pump water efficiently from deep mines and thereby greatly facilitated the production of coal in much larger quantities and at lower cost. At first coal was moved from the mines by heavy horse-drawn carts. The idea soon emerged of reducing wheel-track friction by running the cars on rails, imitating the crude systems that already existed within the mines, using wooden rails. These were superseded by the use of iron wheels running on iron rails, offering better load-carrying capacity and lower friction. These early iron roads were used to move coal from the mines to ports or to the canals which had expanded significantly in the seventeenth and eighteenth centuries as a means of moving goods efficiently. By the beginning of the nineteenth century, stationary steam engines were widely used not only for pumping out mines but to spin machinery and power looms in the textile industry – the first example of large-scale industrial mechanisation.

The first commercially successful steam engine was built by Thomas Newcomen in 1712 and relied on the curious principle of spraying water on the cylinder to condense steam inside it, thereby creating a partial vacuum. The piston was driven by the pressure of the outside atmosphere, creating a linear force that pumped water from

7

the mine shaft. Not until 1781 did James Watt launch his engine that used an external condenser to create the vacuum and drove a crank to produce rotary motion. There is a splendid working example of a James Watt engine to be seen in the Power House Museum in Sydney, which originally provided power to a London brewery for decades. Working pressures and the power produced were low, and the engines were hugely bulky. It took almost a century of develop ment of the steam engine before it could successfully be applied to transport. Richard Trevithick built the first high-pressure steam machine in the form of a locomotive and produced a series of locomo tives from the end of the eighteenth century. In 1825 George Stephenson opened the Stockton and Darlington Railway, the world's first public railway, with his Locomotion No 1. His son's Rocket of 1829 won the Rainhill Trials, a competition to choose the motive power for the new Liverpool and Manchester Railway. Powered land transport became a practical reality for the first time. The application of steam engines to ships took place in parallel.

The British population, 10.5 million in 1801, almost doubled to 20.8 million in 1851 and almost doubled again to 40.4 million in 1901 as this first Industrial and Transport Revolution created fast economic growth, though this then slowed, to 48.9 million in 1951 and just under 59 million in 2001. Figure 1.1 tracks the growth of GDP and of transport and communications from 1855 to 1980. GDP multiplied sevenfold but transport and communica tion (T&C in the diagram) twenty-one-fold. This series reaches only from 1851 to 1981 but still gives a fascinating picture of the explosive development of powered transport.[1] The transport and communication intensity of the economy increased threefold during this period. Rapid economic development (the 'take off' described by economists) has thus both been supported by a huge increase in mobility and also been an enabler of it.

---

[1] Taken from *British Historical Statistics*, B. R. Mitchell, Cambridge University Press, 2011. A 2010 project to extend this work seems not to have come to fruition yet.

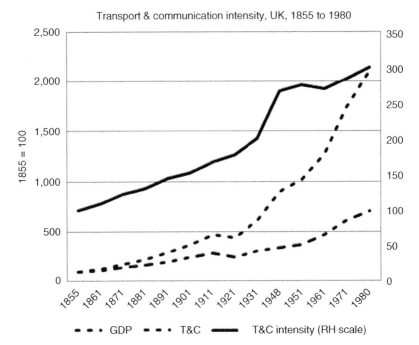

FIGURE I.I The UK transport revolution
Data source: British Transport Statistics

Before the invention of the railway, passenger transport was overwhelmingly by road, with a rapid improvement in infrastructure and journey times beginning in the eighteenth century, thanks to the use of macadam surfaces and the institution of turnpikes.[2] Rail very rapidly took over medium- and long-distance travel, as the network expanded. Horse-drawn local transport remained but trams and powered omnibuses took over from the close of the nineteenth century.

The advent of the railways transformed Britain.[3] The railway network grew dramatically during the nineteenth century, with most of the main lines completed by the middle of the century. There was

---

[2]  For a fascinating discussion of this, see *The Rise and Rise of Road Transport, 1700–1990*, Theo Barker & Dorian Gerhold, Macmillan, 1993.

[3]  For a lucid and well-researched account of this, see Christian Wolmar's *Fire & Steam, How the Railways Transformed Britain*, Atlantic Books, 2007.

considerable duplication and waste through the railway mania that led to the building of a good number of lines that never repaid the investment in them. The heavy cuts to the network, recommended by Dr Beeching in the 1960s and forever associated with his name, attracted much sentimental opprobrium but mainly made sense, especially as the railways in Britain had suffered from persistent under-investment and technological lag, compared to those in the rest of Europe and in North America. Britain still retains a substantial and reasonably well-balanced railway network. It has undergone a technological transformation with the elimination of the steam engine, with its lamentable thermal inefficiency, huge maintenance requirements and harsh working conditions for those who operated and cared for it. Not to mention the grime it spread all around it. Modern signalling and power-operated doors have greatly reduced the incidence of accidents to passengers, making the railways a very safe form of transport.

## THE RAILWAYS IN BRITAIN ROSE TO DOMINATION AND THEN RETREATED INTO NICHES

Railway passenger transport in fact reached its apogee, in terms of the number of passenger journeys made, just after World War I – see Figure 1.2. The apparent collapse for 1914 to 1919 is the result of no statistics having been published in wartime, perhaps to conceal them from the enemy. After that, the number of journeys made declined until 1980, apart from a brief revival during World War II, with many lightly used rural lines closed. Since then, there has been a remarkable revival of passenger rail travel, as shown (using the more telling metric of passenger-kilometres) in Figure 1.3. The 1939 to 1943 gap is again caused by the absence of published statistics. While the number of journeys declined on trend from 1945 to 1985, the passenger-kilometres held constant, reflecting a growth in average journey length. This was caused by rail virtually disappearing from the market for short journeys and re-concentrating on longer inter-city trips and commuting. The trend reversal seems to

FIGURE I.2  Growth, decline and resurgence in rail passenger journeys
Data source: Transport Statistics GB[4]

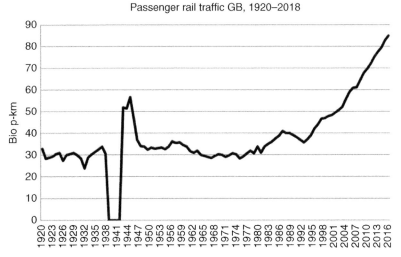

FIGURE I.3  Renewed growth in rail passenger traffic
Data source: Transport Statistics GB

have started in about 1985, as the refurbishment of British Rail –
poorly begun with the inept 1955 Modernisation Plan – finally
became effective. The disruption caused by the politically inspired

4     www.gov.uk/government/statistics/transport-statistics-great-britain

and over-complicated privatisation of British Rail initially reversed this trend but growth soon resumed. Tory Secretaries of State for Transport like to claim that it was privatisation that led to the reversal of the declining trend but the statistics do not support this. In reality, this return to growth is attributable to growing congestion on the road network and to the railways' creative use of airline-style yield management and pricing. The intended, very belated, construction of a limited high-speed network can be expected to produce some more growth in rail travel but its impact on the overall numbers will be very minor.

Passenger rail has not, in the end, declined in absolute terms, although it has clearly done so relative to road transport. It has moved from being the dominant, quasi-universal, mode into a set of specialised niches: a few long-distance routes and, dominantly, commuting into large urban areas, primarily London. Qualitatively, too, the glamour has gone out of rail travel. Most of the famous named expresses have disappeared. No more magnificent engines and handsome carriages, painted in distinctive colours. Comfortable compartments with plush seats have been replaced by plasticky airline-style cramped seating, except in a very few retro tourist trains. Dining cars with table settings and proper meals have been replaced by bland buffets, except for a few trains. Little boys no longer dream of becoming engine drivers. Travel by rail has become a commodity, more marked by frustration at delays and cancellations than by excitement. There are portents in this for the future of the automobile.

Rail freight in Britain grew, declined and revived only modestly – see Figure 1.4. It reached its peak before World War I, stagnated between the wars, revived during World War II (although annual statistics were not available), held up for ten years thereafter, went into a secular decline from 1953 to 1995, and has enjoyed a modest recovery since. The 1955 Railway Modernisation Plan included a major investment in large new marshalling yards to speed up traditional wagon-load rail freight – which was then lost to road haulage after this was denationalised. The primitive technology of British

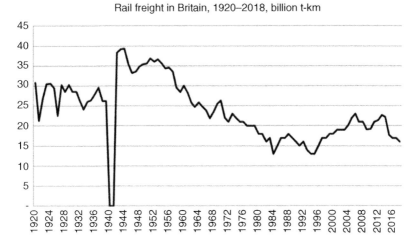

FIGURE 1.4  The rise and fall of rail freight in Britain
Data sources: Inland Transport Statistics GB 1900–1970, Transport
Statistics GB

freight trains – mainly steam-hauled, loose-coupled and unbraked
apart from the engine and guard's van – was no help either.

This recovery was essentially attributable to the railways concentrating on the market sectors in which they have a real comparative advantage, to wit hauling bulk commodities and intermodal
(containers). Coal movements – mainly to power stations – grew but
then declined, as Britain moved from coal- to gas-fired thermal electricity generation. Intermodal freight grew to compensate. Once
again, the quasi-universal transport mode became a specialised one,
quite limited in scope in a country of short distances and high population densities, unfavourable to rail freight. Hopes of rail freight regain-
ing a share in the ever-growing cross-Channel trades by means of the
Channel Tunnel accessing longer hauls were dashed. The British rail
gauge is the same as that in most of Europe (except for Spain, Russia,
Finland and the Baltics) but the British loading gauge is significantly
smaller, such that normal-sized European rail vehicles cannot run in
Britain. This, therefore, means investment in special wagons able to
run in Britain, which has happened only for some specific market

segments, such as new car carriers and company trains – for example, Ford's movement of parts between its British and continental plants. The special fresh fruit and vegetable trains from southern France and Spain that used to run via the train ferries have been displaced by trucks, many of them using the freight shuttles through the Channel Tunnel. There is limited intermodal freight movement through the tunnel, to and from more distant destinations.

## ROAD BECAME AND REMAINS THE DOMINANT LAND
## TRANSPORT MODE

Even though 1946's demobilisation peak volume was surpassed in 2007, rail – the great mobility enabler of the nineteenth century – has been completely dwarfed in significance by the growth of road transport, retaining a significant market share only for commuter and long-distance travel. As Figure 1.5 shows, the use of light four-wheel road vehicles – cars, taxis and vans – has grown enormously and now completely dominates passenger transport within Britain. The flexibility and universality of the automobile has caused it to win hands down, despite greatly increased traffic densities and congestion. While rail travel has enjoyed a revival, the steady decline in travel by bus and coach is notable. Motorising the individual has enormously increased our range of choices, in terms of where and how we live, work and play, and has had a powerful influence on economic development. The motor car hugely boosted the trend to suburbanisation (which was started by the railways) and suburbanisation hugely supported the growth in the use of cars. This symbiosis has turned into a powerful mutual dependency. Which is not to say that it is eternal, as we shall see later.

Similarly, road has captured the major share of freight tonnage, thanks to its inherent flexibility – see Figure 1.6. Water transport also expanded for a time, mainly based on coastal shipping of bulk commodities, principally coal, which then declined as power generation switched away from it. Britain built a comprehensive canal network from the seventeenth century but which only allowed for very narrow

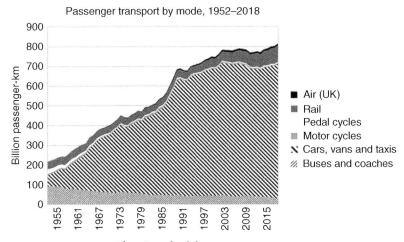

FIGURE 1.5 The triumph of the car
Data source: Transport Statistics GB

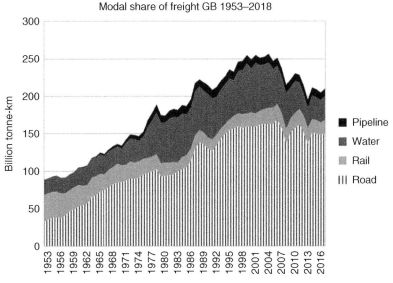

FIGURE 1.6 The growth of road freight
Data source: Transport Statistics GB

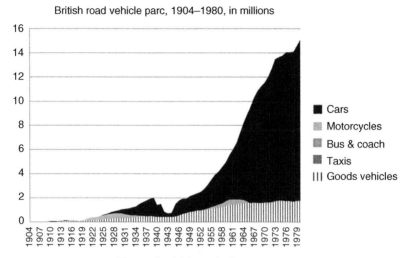

FIGURE 1.7  The road vehicle explosion
Data source: British Historical Statistics

barges, so that it has fallen into disuse other than for recreational purposes, in contrast to the continuing extensive traffic on rivers and wide-gauge canals in continental Europe.

## THE ROAD VEHICLE PARC GREW EXPLOSIVELY
### AFTER WORLD WAR II

Figure 1.7 shows the rise in the number of vehicles operating on British roads from 1904 to 1980. A very modest start was made before World War I. It is interesting to note that motorcycles were as popular as cars until the late 1920s, as they were more affordable in terms of both acquisition cost and fuel consumption, and required less space for garaging. They enjoyed a brief revival as a serious means of personal transport in the 1950s and early 1960s but are now essentially used for recreational purposes. Goods vehicles grew steadily in number, with only a slowing during the two world wars. Note that here they include both light and heavy commercial vehicles. The growth of the passenger car parc (or fleet) started in earnest in the 1930s – Britain, with France, was an early motoriser among European countries. Most

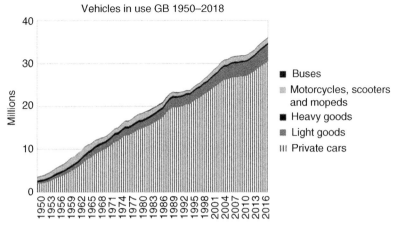

FIGURE 1.8 Continuing growth – and the van phenomenon
Data source: Transport Statistics GB

private cars were taken off the road during World War II, as fuel for personal use became almost unavailable. The parc really took off in the early 1950s, with the end of fuel rationing and growing real disposable incomes.

Figure 1.8 shows the number of vehicles in use on British roads from 1950 to 2016, excluding special vehicles, taxis and Crown vehicles (the categories used in the statistics behind Figures 1.7 and 1.8 are not compatible). Buses are relatively few in number. The population of two-wheelers (motorcycles, scooters and mopeds) has fluctuated. The population of heavy goods vehicles has remained fairly steady. They have grown in weight and – above all – been used more intensively to shift a steadily increasing tonne-kilometres of road freight, thanks to IT and telecommunications support which enables much more efficient routing. Light goods vehicles (mainly vans) and private cars have shown the fastest growth, which has continued with the growth of courier vehicles (propelled first by the abolition of the Post Office monopoly and then by on-line shopping) and the increased ownership of second cars. The car is truly king of the road and an integral and fundamental part of daily life.

## US RAILROAD PASSENGER TRAFFIC BOOMED
## IN THE NINETEENTH CENTURY BUT THEN ALMOST
## VANISHED

The United States provides the contrasting example of the development of transport in a new country, with vast expanses and distances, and, on average, low population density. The United States rapidly followed Great Britain in the development of railways. As in Britain, the railroads developed at an astonishing speed, and had an immense impact on American society.[5] They were instrumental in the opening up of the West, the Manifest Destiny of the early United States. Initial growth was rapid, with a veritable railroad mania developing and the use of rail transport intensified by the Civil War.[6] By the 1880s, most of the national rail network was in place. The railroad was the stuff of romance well into the twentieth century.[7] At its peak, the network was immense, reaching virtually every important city and town, although thinner in the lightly populated West than in the more densely populated East. As in Britain, there was a veritable railroad fever and many marginal lines were built. Even today, after rationalisation and the closure of many small branch lines, the US rail network is 250,000 km in length, the longest in the world, followed by China, Russia and India, but with only 35,000 km of the network used for passenger traffic (Amtrak plus commuter lines).

Passenger transport by rail in the United States has gone from experimental to dominant (flanked by local horse-drawn vehicles) and back to niche. This is an almost perfect example of a category life cycle as shown quantitatively in Figure 1.9. Passenger rail traffic continued to increase rapidly after the Civil War but had begun to plateau by the late 1910s. Apart from a short-lived boost in 1917–18 from World War I mobilisation, the trend was flat. A decline in fact began in the 1920s, with the rapid growth of personal motorisation. It became precipitate

---

[5]    This is well related in Christian Wolmar's *The Great Railway Revolution: the Epic Story of the American Railroad*, Atlantic Books, 2013.

[6]    Ibid.

[7]    Well described with numerous illustrations in *Hear the Train Blow*, Lucius Beebe & Charles Clegg, Grosset and Dunlap, 1952.

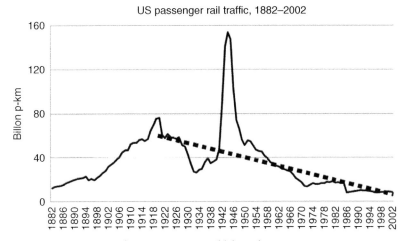

FIGURE 1.9  The US passenger rail life cycle
Data source: International Historical Statistics

with the Great Recession, with some recovery until the massive
boost provided by World War II and a small blip from the Korean
War. But the downward trend resumed in the late 1940s (the trend is
the dashed line in the figure), until by 1972 passenger traffic was back
down to the level of 1882. It has remained at a low level since. Apart
from the modernised and electrified North East Corridor from
Washington, DC, to Boston via New York, the rest is a skeleton of
long-distance Amtrak services patronised by enthusiasts and tourists, plus a limited number of commuter networks in major metropolitan areas, notably New York and Chicago. Long-distance rail
travel is now for tourists and nostalgics.

## IN CONTRAST, RAIL FREIGHT IN THE UNITED STATES
## HAS NEVER STOPPED GROWING

The contrast with the continuing development of US railroad freight
transport could not be greater. Rail freight has just grown and grown. It
was instrumental to the development of the economy in the nineteenth century, as can be seen in Figure 1.10, which shows how the
transport intensity of the economy developed over 130 years. Using

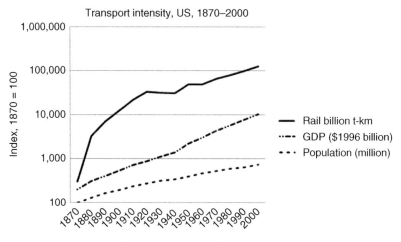

FIGURE 1.10  Transport intensity, United States
Data source: International Historical Statistics, the Americas, 1750–2005

only rail freight tonne-kilometres neglects the role of water and horse-powered transport at the start of the series and of trucks at the end. Nevertheless, population grew 7-fold from 1870 to 2000, real GDP 97-fold and rail freight 1,155-fold. The transport intensity of the economy therefore increased at least tenfold from 1870 to 1920, after which rail freight grew in parallel with the economy.

Figure 1.11 shows the development of the absolute level of rail freight in the United States. The ceaseless-growth trend was only disrupted by the Great Depression and the World War II bounce-back caused by the country's massive mobilisation and production of military equipment. It has, in fact, accelerated since 1990. US freight railroads have invested massively in technology and modernisation (they were pioneers in diesel-electric traction and centralised train control from the 1930s), accompanied by a major consolidation of lines through mergers and acquisitions, and a clear separation between long-distance and local companies. Rail vehicles are completely standardised and interchangeable between the different railroads. Huge trains laden with bulk minerals (especially coal) run to power stations and export ports. Equally huge trains laden with containers

FIGURE I.II  The relentless growth of US rail freight
Data source: International Historical Statistics

(often stacked two-deep thanks to the generous loading gauge) and trucks on flat cars cover immense distances. New automobiles are delivered in special car carriers. These railroads are profitable private companies that have transformed themselves from universal general carriers into long-haul specialists with robust business models, seemingly impervious to life cycle effects. The contrast with the United Kingdom could not be stronger and is mainly attributable to the very different sizes of the two countries and consequent length of hauls. The other difference has been between pervasive and often detrimental state intervention in Britain's railways (including nationalisation in 1948) and the United States's free enterprise approach (apart from the US Rail Road Administration taking charge in wartime).

## IT REMAINS THE LARGEST MODE FOR LONG-DISTANCE FREIGHT

Rail has lost share of long-distance freight in the United States since 1940, as Figure 1.12 shows, but has continued to grow and remains the largest mode. This may seem surprising, given that road is usually

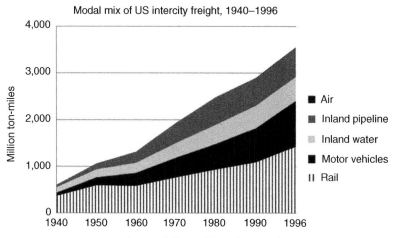

FIGURE 1.12  A high rail share of long-distance freight
Data source: Historical statistics of the United States

assumed to dominate the scene. Of course, it does so for local haulage and is larger in aggregate. There is simply a rational division of labour, with rail dominating bulk freight (notably coal, upon which the United States is still heavily reliant for electric power generation) and long hauls. The US railroad industry has been a major beneficiary of containerisation and of the country's increasing dependence on manufactured imports. Air freight has grown vigorously but remains very small in terms of ton-miles. So here we have a different manifestation of the lifecycle one in which a particular activity is partly but not wholly superseded by a newer one, a segmentation of the market and of the means of satisfying its needs. As in passenger transport, road freight wins on flexibility but not on cost over long distances.

## RAIL TRANSPORT PROVOKED THE FIRST INSTANCES OF GOVERNMENT INTERVENTION AND REGULATION

Rail is interesting not just as the first form of powered land transport, with its own life cycle. It was also the first non-military industrial sector to provoke government intervention and regulation, for reasons of economic development, financing, protection of property, safety, standardisation and anti-trust. This took very different forms in the nineteenth century heyday of railway development in different countries: largely laissez-faire in Britain, state-interventionist from the start in France and initially interventionist at the State level then changing to rules-based regulatory in the United States.[8] Large-scale industry usually forces governments to intervene in some or all of these aspects. Most relevant from the perspective of this book is Dobbin's argument that industrial policy is rooted in the nature of the national polity itself, and that this can radically change from one approach to another, as in the US example, as that polity changes.

## ROAD OVERWHELMED RAIL IN PASSENGER TRANSPORT FROM BEFORE WORLD WAR II

The development of passenger transport has been the diametrical opposite, as can be seen in Figure 1.13. Cars (including light trucks, vans and SUVs used for passenger transport) have absolutely dominated the fast-growing overall volume of traffic since before 1940, the

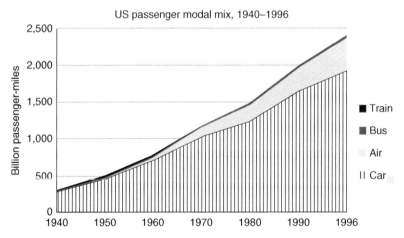

FIGURE I.I3 Dominated by the car – and the airplane
Data source: Historical statistics of the United States

---

[8]   All this is thoroughly described in *Forging Industrial Policy*, Frank Dobbin, Cambridge University Press, 1994.

result of the United States's early mass motorisation. Air transport has made significant inroads since the 1950s. Bus and train are completely marginal today. Rail was squeezed from both ends – by the flexibility of the car for short distances and by the speed of the airplane for long ones. The passenger rail life cycle in the United States took about 100 years to run its course. Rail now only enjoys a significant share of passenger traffic in the North East corridor and in commuting into New York and Chicago. A major reversal is highly unlikely under present circumstances, despite various attempts to develop high-speed routes, in imitation of Japan, Europe and China.

## THE US LIGHT VEHICLE PARC REALLY TOOK OFF
## AFTER WORLD WAR II

The US light vehicle parc grew continuously for 100 years – see Figure 1.14 – with a slowdown caused by the Great Depression and World War II. The discontinuity in the chart reflects a reclassification that recognised that many light commercials (light trucks) were being used as alternatives to passenger cars. This was an unintended consequence of poorly thought out CAFE (Corporate Average Fuel Economy) rules instigated in the early 1980s, in response to the 1973 and 1979 oil price shocks. The parc

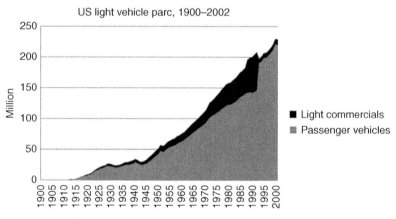

FIGURE 1.14  100 years of continuous growth
Data source: International Historical Statistics

has continued to grow since, more or less in line with population growth.

Passenger transport is thus dominated by the car in the large-area developed countries (the United States, Canada, Australia) and also in Europe, despite a much higher average density of population. Limits are really only encountered at very high densities, as in Japan. This is a possible harbinger of things to come, as more and more of the world's population moves into mega-cities.

## MASS MOTORISATION TOOK PLACE IN MANY COUNTRIES BUT TO DIFFERENT DEGREES

Mass motorisation remains a phenomenon of the developed world, as shown in Figure 1.15. The low-population-density developed countries are most highly motorised, although the correlation with per

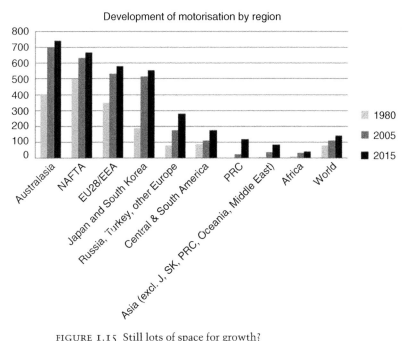

FIGURE 1.15 Still lots of space for growth?
Data source: MVMA 1982, OICA

capita GDP is not perfect – New Zealand had 819 vehicles in use per 1,000 population in 2015, sustained at low cost by having opened its market to massive imports of used cars. These mainly come from Japan, which also drives on the left, and has very stringent vehicle inspection standards, such that cars are retired from service unusually early. Japanese motorists also drive fewer kilometres per year than those in North America, Europe or Australasia, which further ensures a steady supply of good quality low-mileage used cars. Australia has always resisted this solution but keeps its cars in operation for a long time, aided by the dry climate. The US figure for 2015 was 821 cars (or car equivalents) per 1,000 population but the NAFTA average is pulled down a little by Canada and more so by Mexico. Rich but more densely settled regions, such as Europe and industrialised Asia (mainly Japan and South Korea) have slightly lower levels. All other regions remain considerably behind. The People's Republic of China has been motorising fast but still lags the OECD countries by a long way. The big question, of course, is whether it and other fast-developing Asian economies will follow the West along the road to mass motorisation. The automotive industry does, of course, wish this to be so. But will it really happen?

## DESPITE APPEARANCES, THE GROWTH IS NOT ENDLESS

The number of vehicles in service throughout the world has indeed increased hugely, from very small beginnings, as shown in Figure 1.16. The difference between passenger cars (PCs) and all motor vehicles (MVs) is principally made up of non-PC light vehicles (LVs). These include not only light commercial vehicles (LCVs – notably pickup trucks, vans and 4x4s used for commercial purposes) but also many of these, including SUVs, used as substitutes for passenger cars, notably in North America but also increasingly so elsewhere. This seems to convey a picture of unending growth, heading for 2 billion vehicles in use or even more. But the story is more nuanced than that. Careful examination of the chart shows the beginnings of a change in the pace of growth in the later years.

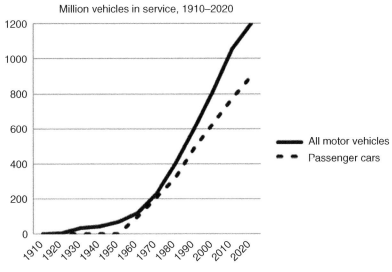

FIGURE I.16  Seemingly endless growth
Data sources: OICA statistics, Autopolis

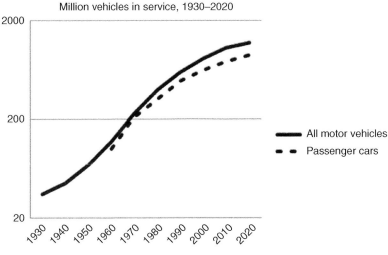

FIGURE I.17  Growth apparently stalling
Data sources: OICA statistics, Autopolis

Figure 1.17 narrows the time frame, starting in 1930, by which time the industry was almost wholly operating on a mass production rather than a craft basis. The vertical axis is now a logarithmic one, emphasising growth rates rather than absolute numbers. The growth rate of vehicles in service (known as the parc) increased after World War II but began to slow again after 1980, which we would argue was the midpoint of the industry's life cycle and also marked the end of post-war reconstruction. But that would still leave it with another ninety-five years to go. The brake is simply market saturation: the mobility needs of people in the developed economies are now largely catered to. The expectation that newly emerging markets will take up the baton and race towards mass motorisation in the same way is, in fact, a false one, for a number of reasons. It is dangerous simply to extrapolate from past experience.

## CHINA HAS RELAUNCHED MARKET GROWTH — BUT WILL NOT NECESSARILY FOLLOW THE SAME PATH

By 2005, the world vehicle market was no longer growing significantly. Figure 1.18 shows its development since then. The NAFTA region,

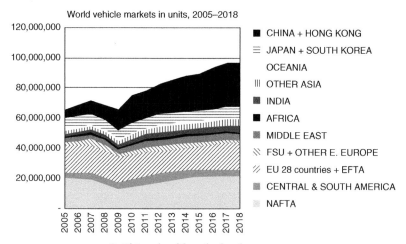

FIGURE 1.18  China shoulders the burden
Data source: OICA statistics

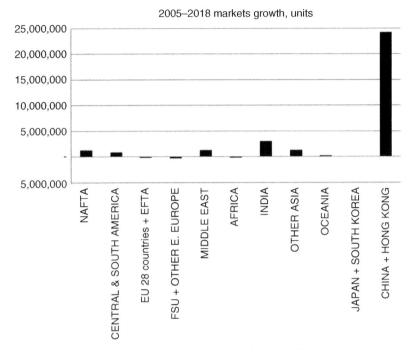

FIGURE 1.19  76% of recent growth has been in China
Data source: OICA statistics

dominated by the United States, took a bad knock from the Global
Financial Crisis but has since recovered. Central and South America is
small in comparison and suffers from the fluctuations of its largest
market, Brazil, which continues to go through cycles of social and
economic optimism followed by disappointment. The EU suffered less,
largely thanks to government support schemes (scrappage incentives)
and has also recovered. The market in the FSU (former Soviet Union) and
neighbouring countries has been affected by the problems in Russia and
is small. Everything else is also small, including India, with the huge
exception of China, which has been responsible for the overwhelming
majority of all the growth in the global vehicle market. These numbers,
incidentally, are for all motor vehicles, as heavy and light commercial
vehicles are irrationally lumped together in the statistics. This is

particularly problematical for North America, where large volumes of light trucks are used as substitutes for passenger cars. Heavy commercial vehicle volumes are small, however, so that the overall picture for light vehicles is not much distorted.

The point is reinforced by Figure 1.19: 97 per cent of all net market growth between 2005 and 2017 came from the emerging markets, and 76 per cent of it from China alone. The mature markets contributed very little at all. Will this growth continue at such a pace, particularly in China, until the emerging markets achieve mass motorisation as in the West, Japan and South Korea? There are serious reasons to doubt this.

## FOUR FACTORS ARE NOW STARTING TO CONSTRAIN THE FURTHER GROWTH OF MOTORISATION

The answer is that headlong growth will most probably not continue, at least not for the automobile in its present form, although there is some growth yet to come. Events outside the automotive industry have overtaken it. Its environment has changed from favourable to increasingly hostile. There are four factors that will increasingly limit its future growth:

- The cost of fuel
- Urbanisation
- The environment
- The telecommunications revolution

First of all, the cost of fuels for cars will inexorably rise. The initial symbiosis between coal production and the steam engine was described earlier. The steam locomotive was superseded not only because of its inflexibility but also because of its hideously poor thermal efficiency (of the order of 4 per cent, compared to 30 per cent for a diesel engine). Coal production continued to grow enormously to feed the production of steel, cement and electricity. The cost of producing it, in fact, fell, in part through the mechanisation of deep mines but mostly through the large-scale development of open cast mining. World coal production is huge: 1 billion tonnes per year in the United States, 3 billion in China, plus Australia, South Africa, etc. The vast growth in the use of road vehicles powered by petroleum-based fuels was the largest factor in the development of the oil industry.

CHEAP OIL NO LONGER HELPS DRIVE MASS
MOTORISATION

Figure 1.20 shows the history of crude oil prices from 1861 to 2018. In the first years of production, oil was expensive to extract. As production built up and techniques of well drilling improved, the price fell by 80 per cent. For the first seventy years of automotive history, from 1900 to 1973, it remained remarkably low and stable. Since then, it has fluctuated wildly around a much higher level. Beyond the political events in the Middle East, which have brought actual or feared shortages, two factors are in play. First, the industry has considerable difficulty in adjusting to downturns, in large part because many of the producing countries are so economically reliant on oil production. Secondly, and underlying it all, are the huge disparities in production costs. Delivered to the refinery, oil from traditional fields such as those in Saudi Arabia,

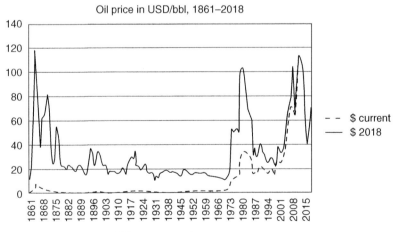

FIGURE 1.20  Oil gets expensive
Data sources: Oil industry, Autopolis

Iraq or Iran, costs about $10 per bbl to produce. That from deep-sea fields can cost over $50 per bbl. This is a source of short-term pricing instability. But, more fundamentally, as the lower-cost fields become exhausted, oil has to be found from ever-more-difficult and costly sources, notably deep-sea fields, such as those off Brazil. The risk of accidents that are very damaging to the environment and very costly is all too real – witness BP's 2010 Deepwater Horizon 'spill', which almost broke the company and caused huge damage to the US Gulf Coast. Road transport – dominated by passenger vehicles – is the largest and one of the fastest-growing consumers of oil. Fuelling cars will, on trend, continue to become more and more expensive, reducing their relative attractiveness.

## THE GROWTH OF URBANISATION MAKES DRIVING CARS LESS ATTRACTIVE THAN BEFORE

Second, urbanisation is an inexorable global trend. Car use in cities is declining while urbanisation continues. It is well known that the ownership and use of private cars in the centres of large metropolitan areas is well below average. Look at Tokyo, Manhattan, London or Paris. The share of journeys made by car in more densely populated metropolitan areas has been falling – 30 per cent down from its peak in London, for example. Car use in German cities started to decline twenty years ago. The larger the city, the smaller the role of the private car. Increased traffic congestion and the rising cost of motoring are one factor in this. An increasing number of cities are restricting access to city centres for private cars, often imposing entry tolls and making parking very expensive. Many city and town centres have already been made car-free. As a result, there is increasing recourse to other modes of transportation, from walking and cycling to taxis and car sharing and to buses, light rail and heavy rail. Access to and the convenience of using alternative transport modes has been greatly increased through IT, notably apps on smartphones. The free use of individually owned cars will be increasingly inhibited. Driving – not only in cities – is subject to increasing congestion and constraints. It's simply not the fun or convenience that it used to be. The day is not far off when we shall have to file a journey plan and book a slot, just as has long been the case in aviation.

## GLOBAL WARMING POSES AN EXISTENTIAL THREAT TO AUTOMOBILES IN THEIR PRESENT FORM

Third, the environment. This has been the subject of so much writing and discussion that it need not be repeated in detail here. The scientific consensus is clear: if we do not cut greenhouse gas emissions deeply and rapidly, we risk catastrophe. The urgency and the measures required are starkly presented in a recent book:[9] one measure is to ration car use to 3,000 km per year, one-third of today's average in Europe, let alone the United States. Road transport is one of the largest sources of toxic emissions and of $CO_2$, and the fastest growing. It is clear that the world cannot afford for the emerging markets to motorise en masse, as did the OECD countries. Allowing them to achieve a sufficient level of mobility as they develop economically, and sustaining one in the already developed countries is impossible with the present pattern of road vehicle use and the technologies employed. We are not going to see 2 billion vehicles or more of today's type of cars on the world's roads. Simply electrifying existing types of vehicles provides no real solution either, while most electricity is generated from fossil primary energy sources. This ultimately has to mean the end of the automobile and of the automotive industry, as we know it today. We return to this in Chapter 2. The public is in general unaware of how deep and rapid the cuts need to be. There is much resistance, for example, to attempts by governments to restrict motoring directly or indirectly via increased taxes. The Gilets Jaunes protest movement in France against increased taxes on motor fuels, particularly diesel, and supported by 78 per cent of those questioned in attitude surveys is a case in point. Universal road tolling, with rates varied by time of day

9    *Change! Warum wir eine radikale Wende brauchen*, Graeme Maxton, Komplett VEDA, 2018.

and journey, is already technically feasible but politically very hard to implement. Change will have to come but socially and politically it will be very difficult to achieve. But this is no excuse for inaction. Nor is it enough to load the whole responsibility onto the supply side, i.e., the automotive industry and the vehicles it delivers. As an admirably lucid former CEO of PSA Peugeot Citroën put it some years ago, if people want less pollution from their cars, they have will to drive them less. So much for the untrammelled freedom afforded by the automobile.

### HAVING SUBSTITUTED FOR RAIL, THE AUTOMOBILE IS ITSELF STARTING TO BE SUBSTITUTED BY VIRTUAL MEANS

Fourth, a fundamental factor working against the growth of the automobile has been the enormous expansion in data and telecommunications services of every variety, at steeply declining real costs. In hindsight, the start of this trend was already evident in 2000. Figure 1.21 illustrates how

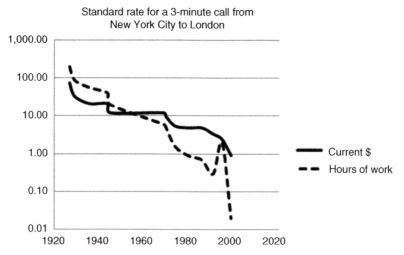

FIGURE 1.21  A staggering decrease in telecoms prices
Data source: Internet Pricing and the History of Communications
Andrew Odlyzko, AT&T Labs Research, 2001

the cost of a telephone call went into steep decline with the advent of fibre optics and satellite communications, plus digital switchgear. Much more was to follow, as we now know, but this was one of the precursors. The explosion in digital electronics has been literally life changing. One hundred years ago, the great majority of those who emigrated across the oceans could not expect to see their original homes and families again. Cheap airfares then made an occasional visit affordable for most. Now a virtual visit can be made as often as desired, at virtually no cost. It is a real revolution, of the most fundamental kind. We are only just beginning to appreciate its scope and impact. This is a clear and spectacular example of a substitutional life cycle effect. Lower-cost water transport by canal wiped out the cart-and-horse haulier. The railway wiped out the stagecoach and the post chaise, and also water transport for freight, except for bulk commodities. The car and the truck wiped out the railway, except in specific market segments. Now telecommunications is wiping out the car (but not the truck), or at least improving the efficiency of their use, except in specific demand segments. In every case, it's a matter of faster, cheaper, more convenient – and, today, less environmentally damaging. And this is an effect on the demand side of the equation, which causes a reduction in the need and desire for physical mobility, a market-driven natural response to innovation, unlike retroactive restrictive constraints placed on physical mobility.

## THE AUTOMOBILE IS NOW NO LONGER THE ICON THAT IT ONCE WAS

The consequence of all these increasing pressures is that the private car is no longer the icon of growth and personal fulfilment that it once was. A deeply threatening trend for the automotive industry is the loss of interest in driving and owning cars on the part of millennials. This represents a fall in demand, rather than a regulatory constraint, whether on driving or on the specific fuel consumption of cars. US Department of Transportation statistics for driving licences show that only half of teens now drive. This is a huge change from the past, when every American kid wanted a car as soon as possible. The car has lost its prime social role among the young. No more cruising up and down Main Street in the evening. A 2014 survey by Schoettle and Sivak of the University of Michigan examined why a substantial percentage of young adults currently do not have a driver's licence and the future plans of this group concerning obtaining a licence.[10] The top eight reasons for not having a driver's licence were as follows: (1) too busy or not enough time to get a driver's licence (determined by personal priorities), (2) owning and maintaining a vehicle is too expensive, (3) able to get transportation from others, (4) prefer to bike or walk, (5) prefer to use public transportation, (6) concerned about how driving impacts the environment, (7) able to communicate and/or conduct business online instead and (8) disability/medical/vision problems. Of the respondents, 22 per cent indicated that they plan never to obtain a driver's licence. On the other hand, 69 per cent expect to get a driver's licence within the next five years. It's rather different once you have a job, a family and a house in the suburbs. But 69 per cent is still a historically low figure. It may all seem rather anodyne and modest but in fact it reflects a profound change in attitude towards individual motorised mobility.

A 2011 study by the same authors examined the recent changes in the percentage of persons with a driver's licence in fifteen countries as a function of age. The countries included were Canada, Finland, Germany, Great Britain, Israel, Japan, Latvia, the Netherlands, Norway, Poland, South Korea, Spain, Sweden, Switzerland and the United States. The results indicate two patterns of change over time. In one pattern (observed for eight countries), there was a decrease in the percentage of young people with a driver's licence, and an increase in the percentage of older people with a driver's licence. In the other pattern (observed for the other seven countries), there was an increase in the percentage of people with a driver's licence in all age categories. A regression analysis was performed on the data for young drivers in

---

[10]   *A survey of public opinion about autonomous and self-driving vehicles in the U.S., the U.K., and Australia,* Brandon Schoettle & Michael Sivak, University of Michigan Ann Arbor, Transportation Research Institute, 2014.

the fifteen countries to explore the relationship between licensing and a variety of societal parameters. Of particular note was the finding that a higher proportion of Internet users was associated with a lower licensure rate. The results of the analysis are consistent with the hypothesis that access to virtual contact reduces the need for actual contact among young people. A smartphone matters to them more than a car. They can do more with it, at much less effort and cost.

Car brands – volume ones at least – have also fallen far behind other product brands in the esteem of consumers. An analysis of the 2017 Forbes ranking of brand values is revealing in this respect. Only eleven automobile manufacturer brands made it into the top 100: Toyota #8, Mercedes-Benz #17, BMW #21, Honda #26, Audi #37, Ford #39, Chevrolet #57, Porsche #60, Nissan #67, Hyundai #68, Caterpillar #82. Note the preponderance of German up-line and Asian brands. The automotive cohort in the top 100 achieves half the brand value relative to brand revenue of the non-automotive brands, despite spending 30 per cent more on advertising as a proportion of revenue, and gets less than half the brand value per advertising dollar. This is a sinister development for an industry that relies so much on branding and advertising its products in order to achieve differentiation and hopefully increased sales. We return to the industry's failing business model in Chapter 3.

## IN SUMMARY, THE AUTOMOBILE IS SUBJECT TO ITS OWN LIFE CYCLE PHENOMENON

The railways were the great transportation innovation of the first half of the nineteenth century, an unprecedented and epoch-making upheaval in human lives. They rapidly became the dominant, indeed near-universal mode of passenger transport. They did not disappear with the arrival of the automobile but were relegated to specific niches within the overall market. They often hold on to these only with the help of government subsidies. It is the tail end of a long life cycle. The same will hold for the automobile, even if its life cycle ends up spanning more than two centuries. Already, the overwhelming mass of person-to-person contacts is enabled by telecommunications and electronic media. Physical mobility will never wholly disappear but it will be reduced in scale and achieved by different means. But it will be a very long and difficult disentanglement, given how much the automobile is imbedded in developed and developing societies. Until now, everything has been done to encourage and facilitate an increase in physical mobility, and the automobile has been the greatest ever instrument of that. We need to understand that from now on the trend has to reverse, with physical mobility reduced or accomplished in ways that are less damaging to the planet. There are no silver bullets for this. Technological fixes to automobiles won't do it and it is unreasonable to expect the automotive industry (the supply side) to solve the problems on its own. The initiative has to come from the demand side. Individual consumers generally have neither the immediate motivation nor the means to do so. This is the role of government, through the political process. It will be neither quick nor easy. They will be bitterly resisted and progress may be fatally slowed.[11] This massive industry has a great depth of sunk investment in highly developed existing products, technologies and processes, along with very strong internal disciplines and a great deal of pride. Unless some environmental catastrophe forces a change of heart and very possibly panic measures, it will continue to struggle with replacing these with something else, in all likelihood less attractive to consumers and more expensive.

---

[11]   The Gilets Jaunes movement in France in 2018 is a case in point, supposedly triggered by the reduction of the national speed limit from 90 to 80 km/hour.

# 2 From Revolution to Revolution: a Changing Automotive Industry

Automobiles still do today what they did from their very beginnings with Karl Benz's Patent Motorwagen of 1885, shown in Figure 2.1, considered to have been the first practical motor car: they transport people and goods under their own power, free from the constraints of guiding rails and able to be driven by ordinary citizens. Their level of sophistication and their complexity have, however, increased by orders of magnitude since then. Their performance, safety, fuel economy, convenience and comfort have also increased spectacularly, as have reliability and durability. Their appearance has been transformed. Like most of its myriad successors, the one shown has an internal combustion engine driving the wheels through a clutch and gearbox arrangement, fuelled by a liquid hydrocarbon (petrol or gasoline) with a spark ignition. It is light and flimsy, called in French a *voiturette*. The brakes and steering are primitive and the occupants are unprotected against the weather or impacts.

Figure 2.2 shows a beautifully restored 1910 Fiat. By now it is recognisably what we would call a car, with a steering wheel, brakes, comfortable seats, suspension and steering systems, pneumatic tyres (courtesy of Dr Dunlop, who pioneered them for bicycles) and headlights. It is still started by hand cranking and also note the frame. But it drives like a car, handling remarkably well. At this time, vehicle manufacturers often supplied the chassis, while the owner – a daring pioneer or rich enthusiast – had a body built for it by a professional coachbuilder.

FIGURE 2.1 The Benz Patent Motorwagen of 1885
Picture credit: Daimler AG

FIGURE 2.2 1910 Fiat in Australia
Author's photograph

FIGURE 2.3 1926 Sunbeam in the United Kingdom
Author's photograph

Figure 2.3 shows a 1926 Sunbeam. The constructional principles are still pretty much the same, with a separate body placed
on a frame to which are attached the engine, gearbox and axles.
There are improvements, such as a self-starter and a folding top.
The driver still has to control the ignition timing. As with the
Fiat, the engine drives the rear wheels through a manually operated gearbox, without synchromesh, which requires some dexter-
ity in gear changing.

This basic design then continued for four decades in the United
States, where mass motorisation first took hold, albeit with considerable improvements: all-steel enclosed bodies, the first automatic
transmissions in the 1940s, etc. It found its culmination in spectacular
monsters, such as the pink Cadillac convertible in Figure 2.4, pre-
served in the Gosford Motor Museum in New South Wales.

Europe did not mass-motorise until after World War II but was in
some respects more innovative in its products:

FIGURE 2.4 The ultimate traditional American car
Author's photograph

- Earlier adoption of the Budd principle of the load-bearing integrated sheet steel bodyshell, dispensing with a separate frame.
- Front-wheel drive, first deployed on a large scale by André Citroën and pursued later in the semi-agricultural but affordable 2CV.
- Two stroke engines, used by DKW in Germany before World War II and continued in East Germany, notably in the Trabant, and by Saab for a period thereafter. They proved a technical and ecological dead end.
- The very innovative 1938 VW Beetle, with its rear-mounted aluminium alloy air-cooled flat 4 engine, magnesium transmission casing, integral body and all-independent torsion bar suspension.
- The same layout but with a conventional water-cooled in-line 4 engine in the Renault 4CV, Dauphine, R8 and R10.
- The wholesale move from rear-wheel to front-wheel drive that took place in Europe in the 1970s, particularly at VW after the old Beetle and at Renault, in search of both more compact packages for a given interior space (the old BMC Mini was the pioneer in this respect) and better road holding.

## AMERICAN AND EUROPEAN DESIGNS DIVERGED:
### AND THEN PARTLY RE-CONVERGED

American and European practice diverged substantially as a result of higher fuel prices and less road space in Europe compared to the United States. Motor fuels have always been more highly taxed in Europe, as there was not much domestic oil production, until the discovery of the North Sea oil fields. Governments strove to limit imports and thereafter found this to be a major and enduring cash cow, along with alcohol and tobacco taxes. There was also a conscious attempt to prevent the motor car from wiping out public transport, as it largely did in the United States. This situation persisted until the late 1970s, when the second oil shock, caused by the Iranian revolution, led to Americans queuing at gas stations and a severe scare over massive dependency on imported oil. The response was a wholesale product downsizing and shift to front-wheel drive packages forced upon the US automotive industry (the supply side of the equation) by the US government through the CAFE (corporate average fuel economy) programme. There was no political appetite for controlling fuel consumption from the demand side through increased gasoline taxes, nor is there to this day. Detroit's first attempts at smaller FWD cars were not a startling success and led to two unplanned results:

- A flood of imports from Japan, whose manufacturers were already building smaller but reliable and cheap cars.
- A flight of many American consumers from conventional passenger cars to light trucks, vans and SUVs used as substitutes for these. This whole family of products was not subject to the same CAFE standards and furthermore was protected from imports by a much higher tariff barrier, which remains in place today – the same prevailing in Europe.

We have seen a Europeanisation of product designs and standards within Europe, as a result of the creation of the European Economic Communities and later the European Union, and in part globalisation, with passenger car designs, in the high-volume categories at least, becoming essentially similar across the Triad of the United

States, Europe and Japan, and later followed by South Korea and China. Some differences do remain: European drivers are generally more interested in styling and driving performance than Americans, whereas the attitude towards cars in crowded Asia is often more functional, with more variety in body styles.

## CONTINUOUS IMPROVEMENT WITH PRUDENT TECHNOLOGICAL INNOVATION WAS THE NORM FOR DECADES

Throughout all this, the technological foundations of the automobile have changed but gradually and only in part. At its heart, it keeps the internal combustion engine, a device for converting the chemical energy latent in the combination of a hydrocarbon fuel and atmospheric oxygen into mechanical energy. A multi-ratio transmission, manual or automatic, is required to overcome the fundamentally poor adaptation of the ICE's power and torque curves to traction applications. The power and torque are transmitted by means of shafts to usually two but sometimes four out of four road wheels, which are equipped with pneumatic tyres. There is usually a brake fitted to each wheel, hydraulically operated from a central master cylinder. The body shell is suspended on the wheels by arrangements of springs and dampers (shock absorbers). The front two wheels (rarely, all four) swivel to allow steering, controlled by the driver through a steering wheel and column, increasingly with the help of hydraulic or electric power assistance. The body is fitted with doors, hatches or lids over the engine compartment and luggage space, plus windows with glass that moves up and down to open and close them, often with electric lifters. There are lights fore and aft, and instruments to measure speed, engine revolutions per minute, remaining fuel, etc. A heating, ventilation and often air-conditioning system is provided, as is some form of in-car entertainment.

Little of this is new and indeed the automotive industry's history is replete with the efforts of inventors to improve the basic machine, starting with Kettering's invention of the self-starter, a

major early convenience feature. The industry has always been innovative – but in small, prudent steps. Major leaps are risky in a sector
that is so sensitive to the market with respect to cost, ease of use and
reliability. But much has changed over the years. These are examples,
not an attempt at an exhaustive list:

- The reliability and durability of engines has been hugely improved. Their life
  expectancy has doubled even within the last twenty years, thanks to the use
  of better materials and to more precise machining, to closer tolerances – for
  example to 1 micron in cylinder bores. Four valves per cylinder instead of two
  have improved the engine's breathing and thus its responsiveness and fuel
  efficiency. This first appeared in a Mercedes racing car of 1914 but took over
  fifty years to achieve mass deployment. Variable timing in valve trains has
  had the same effect. Overhead camshafts, single or double, are almost
  universal, often driven – for smaller engines at least – by a notched rubber
  belt, which saves cost and weight compared to a chain drive
- Gasoline/petrol engines now almost all use fuel injection, single- or multi-
  point, as carburettors cannot deliver the precision fuelling required to meet
  the consumption and de-pollution standards of today and tomorrow
- Electronic engine management systems, controlling both fuel injection and
  spark timing, are now universal
- European development of small high-speed diesel engines produced a
  breakthrough in the compromise between drivability and fuel
  consumption, especially in larger cars. This required major innovations in
  fuelling systems, notably the very high pressure and highly precise common
  rail diesel injection systems. But there remains a difficult problem of
  reconciling performance with the control of both particulate and nitrogen
  oxide emissions, which has got several European vehicle manufacturers
  into trouble with the regulatory authorities, as we shall see later
- Stop-start systems, which shut down the engine when the vehicle is at rest
  and restart it when the driver depresses the accelerator to move off, have
  become common, with the aim of reducing fuel consumption and
  emissions
- Toyota pioneered hybrid drives, combining an ICE and a battery-electric
  motor combination, through some very clever engineering. Almost all other
  manufacturers have followed – at a distance. There is now a wide variety of
  hybrids, from using the starter motor as a generator to provide electric

braking and store energy from that in the battery; to the Toyota-type mild hybrid, combining an ICE and a battery-electric drive train, with a quite limited all-electric range (typically around 10 km); to plug-in hybrids, where electric range is greater (up to 50 km) but with an ICE recharging the battery on the move

- Gearboxes have added ratios, now up to nine in automatics and six in manuals, to try to ensure that the engine is always operating at the optimal part of its performance curve. Sophisticated automatic transmissions now provide very smooth and efficient driving, and fuel economy as good as with a manual gearbox. The combination of a diesel engine and a sophisticated automatic transmission has enabled both agreeable driving and remarkable fuel economy in large premium European cars
- Suspensions have become more sophisticated and independent suspension of all four wheels is now very widespread
- Anti-lock braking systems have spread from their initial application in large, fast up-line cars to become quasi-universal. The wheel rotation speed sensors are also used to feed into anti-slip systems, which reduce the risk of wheel spin. The two are combined in automatic stability systems, which reduce the risk of loss of control and ensure directional stability in critical situations
- Power steering has also spread down from up-line cars, with the help of electric systems partly replacing the traditional hydraulic ones. This is very helpful in smaller front-wheel-drive cars
- Air-conditioning, once a rarity in Europe, is now almost universal
- The body changed from a housing put on a chassis, to an integrated shell. Huge efforts have gone into ensuring the protection of occupants in case of a collision, by the use of stiff protective cells, with energy-channelling pathways and crumple zones around them. All new car models are tested through a variety of simulated crashes. Much more attention has been paid of late to the protection of vulnerable other road users, i.e., pedestrians and cyclists. Serious attempts have been made to replace sheet steel in bodies with lightweight materials, principally aluminium alloys, in order to reduce fuel consumption and emissions
- Seat belts were introduced and improved with pre-tensioning systems, and supplemented by airbags, increasing in number, to provide side as well as frontal protection

## THE ELECTRIFICATION OF INDIVIDUAL FUNCTIONS
### AND ELECTRONIC CONTROLS HAVE SPREAD HUGELY

Across all these functions of the vehicle, the requirement for better controls has become ever stronger. Initially, the control of some functions was taken out of the hands of the driver by means of mechanical feedback loops. The classic early one was centrifugal and vacuum-operated retardation of the spark. Automobiles have increasingly become based on electrical engineering, from the cooling fan, no longer driven by a belt off the crankshaft, to window winders and seat position adjusters, to the point at which the wiring harness is now one of the largest, most complex and heaviest components. To cope with the extra load, alternators replaced the early dynamos, which, with coils and distributors, had replaced the early magnetos. Six-volt DC distribution was replaced with twelve-volt. There have been attempts – none really successful so far – to move to higher voltages and to separate the power and control circuits through smart actuators and multiplexing. Almost everything is now under electronic control, requiring a multiplicity of sensors, logic circuits and actuators. The sophistication of information, navigation, entertainment and communications systems grows almost daily, mirroring the trends in the wider world. The latest direction is to move away from the individual vehicle being fully autonomous to making it able to communicate with other vehicles, the road infrastructure, emergency services (in the case of a crash), and maintenance and repair workshops. All of this, however, complex and sophisticated though the new systems and their architectures are, has taken place within the framework of what remains the traditional automobile.

## THE DISRUPTIVE THREAT OF NEW TECHNOLOGIES
### IS NOT AS IMMEDIATE AS IT MAY SEEM

The industry has always been a deployer of new technologies, rather than a creator of them, with the exception of some that are specific to itself, such as engine-fuel injection and management systems, and novel lightweight body structures. The relentless pace of change coming from outside it is in conflict with its historically prudent approach to innovation, very much conditioned by the immense pressures from both market and regulators for the industry to deliver safe, attractive and remarkably cheap products, given their extraordinary sophistication. These days, however, there is much uncertainty in the air, about how we shall cope with a much more difficult environment, with the idea of replacing the internal combustion engine with electric motors, and the driver with automated driving systems. The problem being that the industry's existing solutions, which may sometimes appear curious (Heath Robinson or Rube Goldberg could have invented the piston engine) but they work and work very well – for the driver at least. Cars have never been so attractive, pleasant to drive and reliable. And yet there is uncertainty. During an interview with the *Financial Times*, Carlos Ghosn, the former chairman and chief executive of the Renault-Nissan Alliance, expressed the feeling: 'It's an industry that's a bit in the dark, fundamentally disrupted because of connectivity, artificial intelligence, because electric cars are going to be part of the future, because also consumers are changing, they don't want to only own a car, sometimes they want to share it. The industry is asking itself how it will catch up.'[1]

There is, in fact, a great deal of nonsense talked about the electrification of cars. The extra cost of a battery pack able to propel a vehicle for anything like the distance available from a tankful of fuel remains prohibitive, despite some cost reduction. Batteries are not made from low-cost materials by automated machining and assembly, as are engines and gearboxes, but from expensive and already scarce metals, such as lithium and cobalt. Inorganic chemistry and mechanical engineering are very different disciplines. Reversible energy storage is inherently very expensive. Despite the progress, a charged battery still costs, weighs and bulks well above a metal or plastic tank full of petrol or diesel fuel. Greater energy

[1]    Lunch with the FT, 15 June 2018.

density in batteries is achieved by packing the positive and negative charges ever more tightly together, down to the molecular level. This ominously mimics the close packing together at the molecular level of fuel and oxidant in high explosives. The risk of catastrophic battery fires has not been removed by any means. Fast charging – in twenty minutes, compared to five minutes to fill a fuel tank – is only possible at few locations. Changing this will require massive investments in charging stations, which the industry expects governments to pay for. Slow charging from a conventional electricity socket at one's place of work or home is not universally possible and imposes a huge inconvenience. Speeding this up with reinforced chargers will overload domestic and local electricity distribution circuits.

## ELECTRIFYING CONVENTIONALLY BODIED AUTOMOBILES MAKES NO SENSE

It doesn't even make ecological sense to replace the ICE with battery electric drives in conventional vehicles. Figure 2.5 shows the results of an analysis conducted in the United States. ICE-powered vehicles are on the left, including HEVs (hybrid electric vehicles, typified by the Toyota Prius, with very limited electric

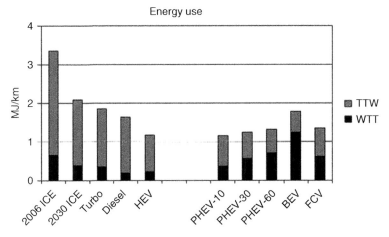

FIGURE 2.5 Comparative fuel economy by propulsion type
Data source: Kromer, MIT, combined, adjusted HWFET/FTP cycle

range), electric powered one on the right, with PHEVs (plug-in hybrid electric vehicles) in order of increasing all-electric range. BEVs are pure battery electrics, FCVs are fuel cell powered vehicles. This is a US analysis and the most spectacular improvement is from 2006 ICEs (which still form a fair proportion of vehicles in service) to 2030 ICEs – on the presumption of a radical downsizing and down-weighting. Although, as we know, the US motoring public to a large extent circumvents this by buying light trucks, vans and SUVs, there is a powerful indicator here. ICE-powered vehicles are poor on TTW – tank to wheels efficiency – because of the inherent characteristics of the ICE as an energy converter. But they are good on WTT – well to tank – as the process of refining crude oil into motor fuels is not all that energy intensive. Electrically powered vehicles show the reverse characteristic: the electric motor is a very efficient and controllable converter of electric energy to mechanical but it requires a highly refined 'fuel' which is costly and energy-intensive in its production. The claimed consumer benefit of paying much less for electrical energy than for liquid motor fuels blissfully ignores the awkward fact that in most jurisdictions the latter are much more heavily taxed – a huge fiscal cash cow that governments will not readily surrender. Fuel cell vehicles (FCVs) look generally better but there remain huge problems of cost and durability with fuel cells and of how to provide hydrogen on a local basis.

The results of the simulations for greenhouse gas emissions (GHG), shown in Figure 2.6, are not very different. All these results were computed using the then-current US electrical energy generating mix, with its heavy reliance on coal. They would of course improve dramatically for electric drives if most electricity could be generated from renewables. A very few countries have massive hydro-electric resources – Canada, Norway, Brazil – but wind in particular is intermittent. Electric car batteries could provide massive storage capacity but the availability and inconvenience problems would remain.

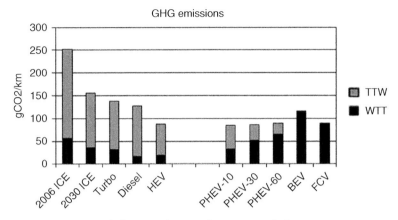

FIGURE 2.6 Comparative greenhouse gas emissions
Data source: Kromer, MIT, combined, adjusted HWFET/FTP cycle

## THE ERROR LIES IN PLACING THE BURDEN OF CHANGE ON THE AUTOMOBILE, NOT THE DRIVER

The trouble with all these approaches is that they attempt to fix the problems via the supply side, i.e., the vehicles and the industry that builds them. The ultimate solution is to work on the fundamental problem, the demand for physical mobility and how it is satisfied. It's here that we run into attitudes and expectations. Figure 2.7 neatly encapsulates one of them: traditionally cars, however compact, should have effectively infinite range and be permanently available. Most people also want their vehicle to be multi-functional, which provides an incentive for many to buy the largest one possible within the limits of their budget. This inhibits the true specialisation of vehicles, which would require a clear distinction between long-distance ones, presumably still running on liquid fuels, and urban/suburban small ones, which could be electric, given that the great majority of daily trips are under 100 km. This is not a new debate. Up to the 1920s, some in the United States believed that battery electric vehicles (which were widespread in the early days of motorisation there) would continue to prevail in short-range urban applications, complemented by ICE-powered vehicles

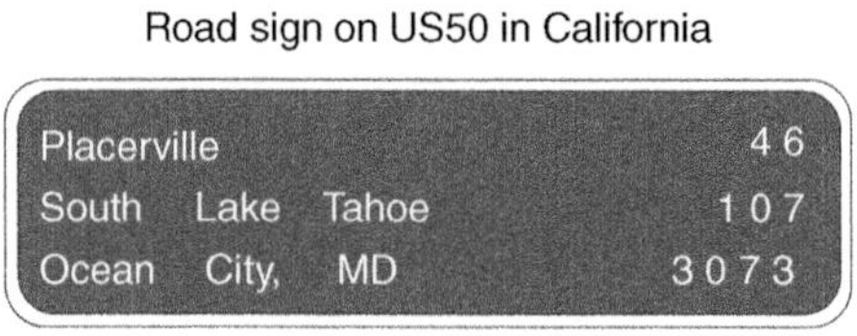

Road sign on US50 in California

| Placerville | 4 6 |
| South Lake Tahoe | 1 0 7 |
| Ocean City, MD | 3 0 7 3 |

FIGURE 2.7 I'll drive as far as I want to
Source: author's image

for longer-range duties[2]. They were mistaken: as people at the time could usually only afford one vehicle, they chose the more flexible one.

## A MORE SENSIBLE AND RADICAL APPROACH WOULD BE TO TACKLE THE DEMAND FOR MOTORISED TRANSPORT, IN STAGES AND OVER FIFTY YEARS

The sensible approach therefore is not to try to lean on the supply side alone but progressively to modify attitudes and expectations on the demand side. Figure 2.8 shows possible stages in seeking a really big long-term drop in GHG emissions, first to 80 per cent, then to 50 per cent of current levels and finally to 20 per cent of them. The key is to combine a reduction in demand for physical mobility with achieving each passenger-kilometre with less vehicle mass, accelerated and decelerated less often and less sharply, and with less rolling and wind resistance – without compromising safety. In Stage 1, existing vehicle technologies continue to be used but there is a modest down-rating of their performance with respect to top speed and acceleration. This has in fact been incentivised for several years already in Europe, through $CO_2$-related taxation but remains a political no-no in the United States. Mobility starts to be more actively managed, with more car sharing and modest modal shifts in favour of shared or public transport, greatly facilitated by the Internet as a vehicle for information and booking. Modest restrictions are placed on the use of individual vehicles in urban

---

[2]   For a penetrating and fascinating description of the rise and fall of the electric vehicle in the United States (and a good example of a life cycle see *The Electric Vehicle: The Burden of History*, David A. Kirsch, Rutgers University Press, 1964.

|          | Stage 1 | Stage 2 | Stage 3 |
|----------|---------|---------|---------|
| Now      | 5–10 years | 10–20 years | 20–50 years |
| 100%     | 80% | 50% | 20% |
| Vehicles | • Existing technologies<br>• Modest down-rating | • Strong specialisation<br>• New technologies | • Active safety supplants passive<br>• Radical lightening |
| Mobility | • More car sharing<br>• Small modal shifts<br>• Modest restrictions<br>• e-commerce | • New transportation packages<br>• Tighter restrictions<br>• Road tolling<br>• Planning & control | • Much reduced primary need<br>• Extensive substitution by virtual means |
| Habitat  | | | • New habitats and work habits<br>• Decoupling mobility from GDP |

FIGURE 2.8 Possible future stages
Source: Autopolis

areas. Both of these last two actions are already underway in Europe. They have been in place in Japan for a long while already. E-commerce is starting to have a serious impact on the need physically to go shopping, but some rationalisation of the means of delivery is needed, given the explosion of competing delivery services, often with very poor load factors. All this is readily achievable, given the right political consensus and will. But the United States is increasingly looking like an outlier, except with respect to e-commerce.

Stage 2 gets altogether more serious, aiming at a 50 per cent reduction in GHG emissions compared to present levels in a longer time frame, up to twenty years. This requires a serious degree of specialisation of vehicles by purpose, with the aim of sharply reducing the unnecessary use of over-sized and over-weight vehicles, and reducing vehicle speeds. New technologies start to break through, notably electric propulsion for small urban vehicles, but also automatic driving, made much easier to implement as driving becomes less individualistic and uncontrolled. New transportation packages are on offer, enabling customers to plan their travel needs and access the most appropriate solutions to them. All these measures have the explicit objective of greatly improving the ratio between load and empty weight. Restrictions on individual mobility become tighter, together with universal road tolling, the most effective and equitable way to allocate access to the public infrastructure. Planning and control become the dominant functions: it is this which has such an enormous potential impact on the automotive industry, as the providers are more likely to be systems houses than vehicle manufacturers. Some suppliers with a strong base in the new technologies will gain but many traditional ones will lose out. But that has happened in the past and it will not change the basic nature of the automobile.

## THE ULTIMATE SOLUTION IS A LONG-TERM REVOLUTION IN TRANSPORTATION ITSELF

Stage 3, starting twenty years out, completes the transportation revolution. This means a real revolution in how we achieve mobility and in the vehicles that will convey us. It is this that determines the later stages of the life cycle of the current automotive industry. At the product level, active safety (avoiding collisions of all kinds in the first place) takes precedence over passive safety (mitigation of the consequences of an accident that is already happening). This enables a radical down-weighting of vehicle structures and a consequent reduction in power requirements. Electric propulsion now becomes dominant, at least for short ranges – the great majority of journeys and of vehicles. The primary need for physical mobility is much reduced, largely compensated by virtual mobility. But the whole pattern of living also changes, with a move back from suburban sprawl to more urban patterns. This is, of course, a long-term prospect, given all the sunk investments in transport infrastructure, housing and places of work. Mobility is increasingly decoupled from GDP, which becomes less based on physical consumption. The whole concept of this latter radical qualitative shift and the urgent necessity to undertake it are discussed by Maxton and Randers.[3]

How soon could this happen? This is hard to predict, as there are so many extraneous variables – environmental, economic, social, political – at play. Will it happen smoothly or abruptly? Again, it's hard to predict. But happen it will, in some form. And this means the beginning of the end for the automobile, as we have known and loved it. Make no mistake about that: the whole nature of the proposition will have changed. There will no longer be automobiles, defined as operating as independent units or monads, under the ultimate control of their individual drivers, however many on-board functions are automated. Now we shall have units that operate under central control, that are no longer autonomous. They will therefore no longer be automobiles. What we shall have is a new decentralised form of public transport. This has enormous implications for the long-term structure of the industry. To be blunt, it is likely to disappear in its present form.

## A SERIES OF REVOLUTIONS IN HOW AUTOMOBILES ARE BUILT HAS TAKEN PLACE OVER DECADES

As the automobile has come to dominate land passenger transport, so the automotive industry has grown prodigiously since its inception. It now produces over 80 million individual passenger vehicles per year, plus some 15 million light commercials and similar vehicles, plus over 3 million heavy trucks and buses. This is in effect the breadth of production. What it does not reveal is the hugely increased depth of it, the ever-growing complexity of road vehicles, as we have described. In value terms, the industry grew not eightfold but eightyfold from

---

[3]  *Reinventing Prosperity: Managing Economic Growth to Reduce Unemployment, Inequality and Climate Change*, Graeme Maxton & Jorgen Randers, Greystone Books, 2016.

1950 until today. In many respects, it was *the* industry of the twentieth century.

The building of road vehicles was initially the work of individual pioneer inventors, who designed and produced on a craft basis, making each car individually on an artisan scale. They emerged almost simultaneously in virtually all the industrialised countries of the late nineteenth and early twentieth centuries, in a very similar fashion to the birth of the aircraft industry. Their early customers were mainly enthusiasts and the wealthy. Cars became objects of absolute fascination, drawing the limelight from the railways. Enthusiasm for car racing – much of it on public roads – was enormous. Cars at the beginning of the twentieth century were well beyond the pocket of the ordinary citizen. But they unleashed a desire for individual mobility that yearned to be quenched.

## HENRY FORD'S MASS PRODUCTION OF A SINGLE PRODUCT BROUGHT THE AUTOMOBILE WITHIN REACH FOR MILLIONS

The industry's first major production revolution was that instigated in the United States with the Model T by Henry Ford, who both saw the huge market potential of the car and deployed the mass production techniques – using standard interchangeable parts and production line assembly – which made it accessible by radically cutting unit costs. His example was followed to a lesser or greater degree almost everywhere.

The whole emphasis was on driving costs down by maximising scale and experience effects with a single product, which users could customise if they so wished. 'Available in any colour, as long as it's black' was the aphorism that described this. The cost effect is summed up by Figure 2.9. In constant dollars of 2018, i.e., with inflation removed, the real price of a Model T fell by three quarters between 1909 and 1923. The slope of the line on the log-log scale is equivalent to a 15 per cent reduction in real price for every doubling of cumulative production experience – a fairly typical experience effect. This steadily

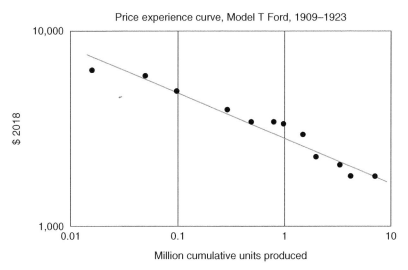

FIGURE 2.9 At an ever-lower real price
Data source: IIASA

increasing affordability contributed mightily to the motorisation of the United States. The same experience curve effect was visible in the real prices of the VW Beetle, the Renault 2 CV and Dauphine and the Citroën 2 CV in post–World War II Europe, similarly enabling an increasing number of ordinary citizens to own an automobile. This scale-driven cost and price reduction, based on high-volume production of a single product had, of course, been one of the explicit motivations for the foundation of VW in the 1930s.

This approach stimulated the development of automatic machinery, for those production processes that could be mechanised. Transfer lines were developed to move an item from one automated process step to the next. Notable examples were in the successive machining steps required for an engine block, or progressive press-forming steps for deep-drawn sheet steel parts, which would tear were the whole forming operation to be attempted in one single blow. Progressive improvements enabled steady decreases in cycle times and thus in unit cost in this kind of inflexible automation. It still works well for items such as engines, which have long life cycles because of their very high cost of development. Other processes, such as welding together pressed steel parts into a bare body shell (the so-called body in white) were for a time automated in the same fashion but this required massive multi-point welders, completely limited by geometry to the production of one model. 'We'd never do this again', commented a plant engineer to one of the authors, who was admiring one of these monster machines in the mid-1970s. Retrospective comparative cost analyses embarrassingly revealed that it would have been cheaper to stay with manual spot-welding, adding and closing smaller capacity lines as the model went through its life cycle at a much lower investment cost. Processes such as painting the body in white or those of the trim and mechanical assembly lines could not at this time be automated. Their real unit costs did not decline as steeply.

## EVOLVING MARKET DEMAND FORCED A WIDENING OF THE PRODUCT RANGE

The second revolution was that of diversifying the product offering. This was pioneered by General Motors, under the leadership of Alfred P. Sloan, in the 1920s. GM had been put together by acquiring a number of the early pioneers, such as Chevrolet and Oldsmobile, so that it started with a much broader product base than Ford's. Sloan's genius lay in bringing this diversity under control through the invention of the multi-divisional corporation, with scale sharing across brands where possible, notably through the creation of specialised internal components supplier divisions. This fortunately coincided with a time of fast-increasing real incomes, in the years before the Wall Street crash of 1929. The relentless downward trend in real unit cost and price was lost but consumers were willing to pay a premium for more diversity. Exactly the same phenomenon was to be seen in Europe, as national markets emerged from post-war austerity and consumers demanded more choice. The downward real price trend was broken and prices drifted upwards from it. The industry has been managing the balance between maintaining price competitiveness and the extra costs imposed by greater product diversity ever since. The extra costs of diversity often manifest themselves in indirect and overhead costs – the costs of changeovers, of extra stock items, of additional lines in IT systems – which traditional standard cost systems buried in uniform overhead allocations. Thus there was every incentive for designers to design a unique new part for a new model rather than carry over a previous one. This is, of course, most flagrant when large expenditures are involved, such as a new engine, a new gearbox or a new car model. Hence, the use of platform strategies, pioneered by the VW Group, as its product diversity hugely increased with its acquisition of SEAT, Škoda and other manufacturers. The idea is to use invisible common underpinnings – platforms or modules – and common parts as much as possible, while maintaining and indeed broadening the visible richness and distinctiveness of the individual brands' offerings. Today, the highest volume platforms are produced at the rate of several millions per year across the globe.

## JAPANESE VEHICLE MANUFACTURERS UP-ENDED RELATIONSHIPS ON THE SHOP FLOOR AND BETWEEN PRODUCTION UNITS

The third revolution came from Japan, in the form of lean production, pioneered in the Toyota Production System, which was influenced by the work of W. Edwards Deming, the American engineer, statistician, professor and consultant in the field of quality management. In essence, lean production required:

- Delegation of responsibility for quality back down to shop floor operatives, so that problems could be identified at the source, rather than fixed through ex-post-facto inspection and rectification of the assembled vehicle. Stopping the assembly line changed from a heinous crime to a requirement, should a problem be spotted. This also saved much expensive reworking – witness VW's advertising boast in the US press in the 1960s that it had more quality control inspectors than assembly line workers!
- Linked to this was the philosophy of continuous improvement, or *kaizen*, which required operatives to take charge of their process, understanding

how it worked (or failed to work properly), and develop their own measures for measuring and controlling it.

- The introduction of flexibility into hitherto rigid processes, where possible. A notorious example of this involved the changing of dies on press lines making body parts, particularly large and complex ones. Presses have a short cycle time and can produce many thousands of a given part in a day, whereas the body-in-white assembly lines normally produce 1,000 a day. The mismatch was resolved by running the press line in a 'campaign' until an inventory of a given part had been built up, after which the dies were exchanged to produce another inventory of another part. This not only generated inventory carrying costs but also the risk of accumulating a large stock of defective parts, should there be an unnoticed problem. Press dies for large parts are massive and very heavy. Large hydraulic presses were originally not designed for ease of die changes, which could take up to 24 hours. Imagine the shock experienced by European automotive manufacturer executives visiting Japan in the late 1970s and witnessing Japanese press shops changing die sets in ten minutes, under the direction of whistle-blowing supervisors, thereby enabling them to run much shorter campaigns. The whole philosophy was to move away from 'push', in which the upstream stages generated inventories of their product for the downstream stages to use alter, to 'pull', in which they responded more accurately to actual demand from downstream.
- Multiple automatic machine tools clustered around a single operator, rather than having one operator per machine tool.
- A general attention to the elimination of all forms of waste, such as superfluous process steps, procedures and accompanying investments.
- And – last but not least – a cooperative rather than confrontational relationship with suppliers, grouped into *keiretsu* or supplier families, mainly linked to a single vehicle manufacturer customer. *

Deming is generally credited with being at the origins of this movement but the Japanese craft tradition and frugality, coupled with post-war shortages of every kind, also contributed. The results were spectacular: unit costs of anything up to 30 per cent lower than those in the West; and – perhaps most tellingly for Western customers – much more reliable cars, based on expected failure rates of parts per million rather than parts per thousand. Some of the gains were reinvested in increased levels of standard equipment, such as heaters and radios, which had often been extra-cost options in Western cars. It made sense to 'standardise upwards', given the length of the supply route from Japan.

## FLEXIBLE AUTOMATION, ROBOTISATION, PLATFORMS AND MODULES HAVE REDUCED THE COST BURDEN OF PRODUCT DIVERSITY

The fourth revolution came through flexible automation and robotisation, together with invisible standardisation. The advent of solid-state digital data processing, sensors and power electronics made it possible for machine tools – lathes to start with – to execute multiple different cycles, through calling up libraries of tool positions and movements, through CNC (computer numerical control). This was extended from machining operations themselves to handling parts between such processes and to such activities as the spot welding of body shells and painting them, by means of multi-axis manipulators, or robots. This not only eliminated much process labour but also reduced the number of difficult or even hazardous jobs and improved consistency and quality. Together with this went the use of platforms or modules invisibly shared between models, brands (as pioneered by the VW Group, the world champion of multiple brands), and even manufacturers. These innovations removed a good deal of the cost penalty involved in producing multiple products, although it is inherently more difficult to reduce cycle times with these complex systems. They have been used to stage a deliberate shortening of model lifecycles across the industry. Major mechanical components, such as engines and transmissions, have much longer life cycles than car models, as development costs and investments in highly mechanised production facilities are huge. These items are also much less visible, although obviously critical to performance. In pure economic logic, there ought to be more sharing of engines between manufacturers. But they have almost always refused to treat them as standard plug-compatible items. Automatic transmissions in Europe represent an exception, most coming from outside suppliers, as they remain the minority solution on that continent.

## PRICE COMPETITION AND HUGE INVESTMENT
### REQUIREMENTS HAVE FUELLED AN UNRELENTING
### PURSUIT OF SCALE

The benefits of all these improvements have mainly been handed over to customers, given the intensely competitive nature of the new car business. This has fuelled a seemingly unending drive to achieve greater scale. While there were numerous early pioneers, manufacturers started to consolidate quite soon, through eliminations, mergers and acquisitions on a national basis. But the larger firms quickly started to seek extra volume abroad. Henry Ford started to globalise his business before 1914, setting up assembly plants outside the United States, but the first globalisation was halted and then reversed by World War I and its effects, culminating in the Great Depression. Despite this, Ford continued to invest abroad, notably in Europe, but on a localised basis, with products that increasingly diverged from American models. GM followed suit, although somewhat later and mainly by acquiring existing European manufacturers (Opel and Vauxhall) plus Holden in Australia. Chrysler did much the same, acquiring Rootes in the United Kingdom and Simca in France. The huge investments required to meet growing market demand forced a brutal shake-out of the pioneers, such that by the 1930s the US car industry was effectively an oligopoly of the Detroit Big Three, with some marginal players such as AMC still hanging on, together with a fringe of imports. The same scenario played out in Europe a generation later, after World War II.

## MARKETS HAVE COALESCED, FIRST WITHIN REGIONS,
### THEN GLOBALLY

The second big transition went with market coalescence. European markets started to interpenetrate with the creation of the EEC, later the EU. This effectively killed the British car industry, which had remained insular and complacent, and became increasingly uncompetitive on both product design and quality, not helped by faltering government policy and interventions. The German and French governments were much more percipient and coherent in this respect.[4] Thirty years ago, a major national manufacturer enjoyed a 10 per cent market share advantage in its home market. This attachment to national brands has all but disappeared today in Europe, although it still prevails in Japan, South Korea and the more rural parts of the United States.

Intercontinental coalescence began with the Japanese attack on foreign markets. European markets were difficult to penetrate, as they were protected by tariffs on imported cars and by governments defending their national car manufacturers. But the United States inadvertently opened the door by forcing a downsizing required by CAFE (Corporate Average Fuel Economy) regulations on its industry, following the 1973 and 1979 oil shocks. Fortuitously, the Japanese MVPs, led by Toyota, had perfected lean production, which enabled them build price-competitive and reliable cars, which proved attractive to American customers. After an initial surge of Japanese penetration of European countries without a car industry, European MVPs got their act together on productivity and quality and fought back with products more interesting to European motorists. Japanese penetration in the European Union as a whole never went beyond the 10 per cent penetration ceiling that had been voluntarily agreed upon, as compared to 30 per cent in the United States. But two crucial changes had occurred: the interpenetration of product markets and the beginnings of global manufacturing reach. Within the passenger car market segment, designs converged, driven by converging government regulations on emissions, fuel economy and safety. All major mainstream players needed to be global in their design approach, deploying common platforms and models across all markets, which tended to remove major design distinctions.

[4]   Despite its sensationalist title, Simon Reich's 1990 book *The Fruits of Fascism: Post-War Prosperity in Historical Perspective*, Cornell University Press, 1990, is in fact a thorough comparative review of the British and German governments' support to their automotive industries.

## PRODUCTION VOLUMES IN THE WEST CEASED GROWING AND ASIA TOOK THE LEAD

As Figure 2.10 shows, by 1990 production volumes for light vehicles as a whole had virtually stopped growing in Europe and NAFTA (the free trade area comprised of the United States, Canada and Mexico). South America continued to grow – irregularly, thanks to recurring crises in Brazil, by far its biggest market and producer. But it grew enormously in Asia-Oceania, to reach half of all world production by 2017. Everyone was hit by the Global Financial Crisis of 2008–9, none more so than manufacturers in North America. Europe had a blip but the worst was averted with the help of government scrappage incentives, which took many older cars off the road by giving their owners cash incentives to buy new ones, ostensibly to reduce emissions and improve crash safety. Asia-Oceania suffered a brief standstill but quickly resumed vigorous growth. The era in which VW Beetles were built in Wolfsburg and shipped to all the world is long over. Being able to react to local market demand with great product diversity, and to avoid unnecessary exchange rate exposure, plus political pressures, have caused the large-scale production of volume cars to be localised.

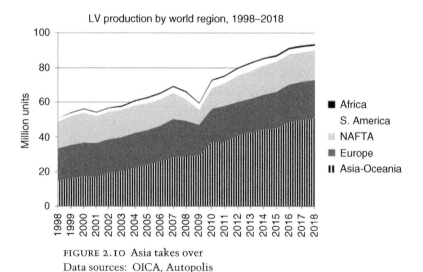

FIGURE 2.10  Asia takes over
Data sources: OICA, Autopolis

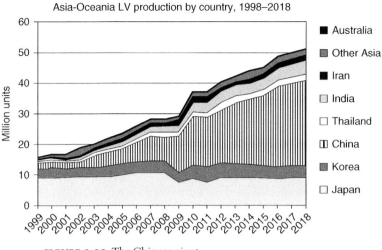

FIGURE 2.11  The Chinese giant
Data sources:  OICA, Autopolis

CHINESE LIGHT VEHICLE PRODUCTION HAS GROWN
ENORMOUSLY AND NOW DOMINATES ASIA

Figure 2.11 shows the further breakdown of Asia-Oceania production by country. Japanese production, which had only been growing very slowly before the GFC, never quite recovered from the shock of it, because so much of Japan's production is exported to the United States. South Korean production recovered better but is now no longer growing. The ever-growing giant is of course China. Thailand, India and other Asian countries have continued to grow but from a much smaller base.

BUT THERE IS A DIFFERENCE BETWEEN THE PRODUCTION
STRUCTURES BETWEEN CARS AND NON-CAR LIGHT
VEHICLES

Splitting light vehicles (LVs) into passenger cars and the family of light trucks, light commercials and SUVs shows two quite different patterns – see Figure 2.12 for passenger cars. Today, Asia-Oceania builds 60 per cent of all of these, led, of course, by China. Superficially, it

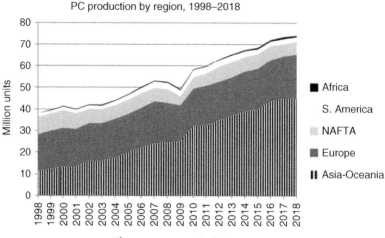

FIGURE 2.12  The passenger car is Asian
Data sources: OICA, Autopolis

looks as though Chinese manufacturers have managed a dramatic entrance onto the world automotive stage, just as their Japanese and Korean competitors did in previous generations. This, in fact, not at all the case, as Chapter 3 will demonstrate.

The pattern in light trucks, etc. is entirely different. See Figure 2.13. Here is the American exception in all its might. Sixty per cent of global production of these vehicles takes place in North America, largely because of very low US motor fuel taxation but also protected by a particularly high tariff rate of 25 per cent on imports. European production is similarly protected but the European market for these vehicles is much smaller, as the light trucks and vans are predominantly used by commercial operators there, whereas the SUV segment, although fashionably growing, remains fairly limited. Asia-Oceania is not a huge producer, in contrast to the situation in passenger cars. China represents only 30 per cent of production in the region, although it has been growing. Chinese light commercial producers have always been very fragmented in the past and the sector is still far from consolidated today. Global growth has been slower than for passenger cars and

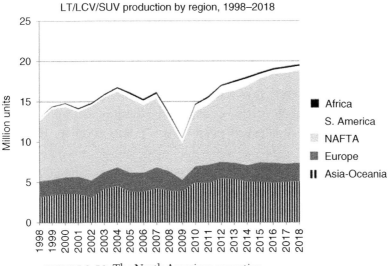

FIGURE 2.13  The North American exception
Data sources: OICA, Autopolis

the NAFTA market took a big temporary hit from the GFC and the bankruptcies of GM and Chrysler.

We, therefore, now in effect have three automotive worlds: part of the market in the large developed countries, with their predilection for larger vehicles, increasingly met by the light truck, van and SUV family; a large part satisfied by a range of traditional passenger cars; and a micro-vehicle market in crowded Asian mega-cities. Product coalescence is thus not total, reflecting different physical environments and driving conditions. Environmental pressures should favour a drift downwards in size, except where they and it are actively resisted, as they notably are in the United States, with its low fuel prices. As environmental pressures increase, the different regions of the automotive world are likely to respond in different ways. But the cost pressures and the drive for maximum scale are likely to intensify further. Yet a Stage 3 revolution in how much and how we physically transport ourselves could render all of this obsolete.

## IN SUMMARY, THE CONVENTIONAL AUTOMOBILE
### IS REACHING THE END OF ITS ROAD

Until now, automobiles have continued to deliver what they did from the start but have become much more sophisticated, through huge but progressive product innovation. American and European designs diverged – and then partly re-converged. Continuous improvement with prudent technological innovation was the norm for decades. The electrification of individual functions and electronic controls have spread hugely. But the disruptive threat of new technologies is not as immediate as it may seem, and electrifying conventionally bodied automobiles makes no ecological sense. The error lies in placing the burden of change on the automobile (the supply side), not the driver (the demand side). A more sensible and radical approach would be to tackle the demand for motorised transport, in stages and over fifty years. Really biting into demand would start ten years out, and the ultimate solution is a long-term revolution in transportation itself. A series of revolutions in how automobiles are built has taken place over decades. Henry Ford's mass production of a single product brought the automobile within reach for millions. Evolving market demand forced a widening of the product range. Japanese vehicle manufacturers up-ended relationships on the shop floor and between production units by introducing lean production. Flexible automation, robotisation, platforms and modules have reduced the cost burden of product diversity but not eliminated it. Price competition and the industry's huge investment requirements have fuelled an unrelenting pursuit of scale. Markets have coalesced, first within regions, then globally. Production volumes in the West ceased growing as the developed markets became saturated, and Asia took the lead. Chinese light vehicle production has grown enormously and now dominates Asia. But there is a difference between the production structures between cars and non-car light vehicles. China builds 60 per cent of all passenger cars, while the United States dominates the light truck sector.

# The Vehicle Manufacturers: a Controlling Global Semi-oligarchy

Figure 3.1 shows the development of world light vehicle production from the beginning of post-World War II recovery to 2017. With the return to a peace-time economy in the United States, given a huge Keynesian boost by war-time government spending, and reconstruction and a return to prosperity in Europe and Japan, production struggled to keep up with pent-up demand. It grew at almost 6 per cent per year from 1950 to 1973, the year in which the first oil shock brought everything to a juddering halt. Reconstruction was over, developed country automotive markets were getting saturated, and the industry struggled to achieve even 1 per cent annual growth for the next twenty-two years. Then Deng Xiaoping liberated the Chinese People's Republic from the throttling grip of Maoism and its economy took off. This, as we saw in Chapter 2, rekindled global demand for cars and generated twenty-two years of production growth at a very respectable 4.5 per cent per year, with only a slight temporary down-draft caused by the Global Financial Crisis. In 2017, production was almost sevenfold that in 1950.

## FROM NATIONAL TO GLOBAL OLIGARCHIES

While vehicle manufacture remained a craft affair, numerous pioneers set out to make cars in almost every developed country. Scale effects were minimal, as each manufacturer had its own idiosyncratic designs. ICE-, steam- and electrically-powered cars co-existed. Investment requirements and barriers to entry were low. Almost

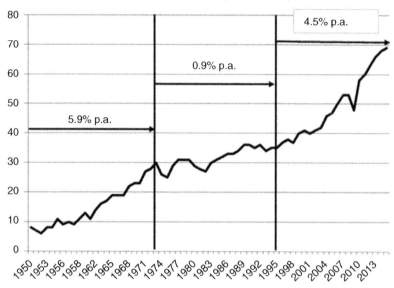

FIGURE 3.1 Fast-slow-fast
Data sources: Autopolis, OICA

anyone could try their hand. Henry Ford's revolution changed all that. Massive plants were required, involving huge investments, and deploying very large labour forces. Ford in particular continually forced real costs and prices down by maximising the scale of its operations. The gasoline-fuelled ICE rapidly wiped out its steam and electric competitors. Ford took product standardisation to its extremes with the Model T. All this forced an early consolidation of the industry, starting in the United States. Many marques were driven out of business. Others were taken over: for example, Chevrolet and Oldsmobile became brands within GM. The process happened again in Europe, a generation later, reflecting that continent's later mass motorisation. This started at the national level, particularly in the United Kingdom and in France. It should logically have continued at the European level, once the EEC was created. National governments, however, resisted this, seeking to protect their national champions, so the process was never entirely completed.

Despite that, the motor vehicle industry is inherently oligarchic in nature. It does not obey the laws of classical micro-economics. Forty-five years ago, Bruce Henderson, the charismatic founder of the Boston Consulting Group, laid down the rules of corporate and business strategy as a competitive sport. You had to outwit and defeat your opponents. But he was under no illusions as to the nature of competition, identifying some sectors, notably those involving large physical networks, such as telecommunications in those days and utilities as natural monopolies, which required effective public regulation. The then-still-national American automotive industry he described as a natural oligopoly. GM had 50 per cent of the United States market and, given is size, made up to 70 per cent of its products, sourcing mainly from its own component divisions. Ford had 25 per cent and was about 40 per cent integrated. Chrysler had 10–15 per cent and lived by its ingenuity (inventing the van and buying Jeep from Renault, when its acquisition of American Motors failed) and relied extensively on outside suppliers. AMC and the imports hung on the fringes. If GM, which was cost advantaged by virtue of its large scale, cut prices too much, the Justice Department would pursue it for predatory pricing. If it charged too much, it stood to lose out to its competitors. Thus the system was stable, until the oil price shocks and the Japanese came along.

Figure 3.2 shows what happened between 1964 and 2005: the number of independent major producers in the world fell by 75 per cent, from sixty-two in 1985 to forty, finally leaving fifteen in place, in a still-imperfect global oligarchy. Imperfect in the sense that, even today, we have not reached a state in which three or four global groups rule the world in high-volume cars. The failure to consolidate completely is attributable to two major inertial factors: government intervention in the competitive dynamics of the industry (further developed in Chapter 5) and the vehicle manufacturers' highly protective distribution system, which seriously inhibits the ability of new entrants to penetrate established markets.

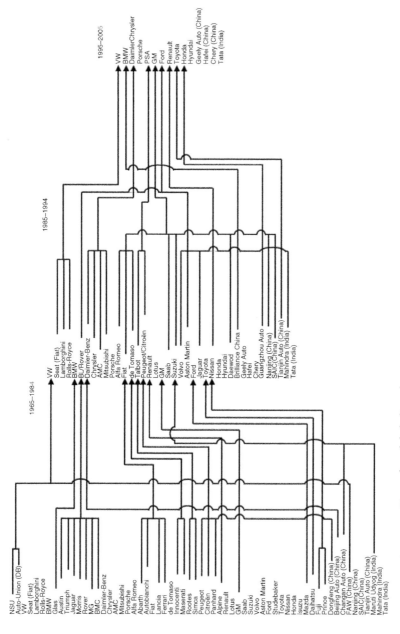

FIGURE 3.2 Towards a global oligarchy

Source: Autopolis

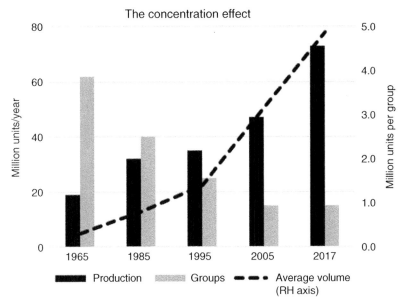

FIGURE 3.3  A mighty gain in effective scale
Data sources: OICA, Autopolis

## GLOBALISATION HAS ENABLED HUGE GAINS
### IN EFFECTIVE SCALE AND THEREFORE IN UNIT COSTS

If we take the number of groups at different points in time in Figure 3.2 and divide them into annual production, we get a simple measure of scale in terms of million units produced by each group per year on average. The results are portrayed in Figure 3.3. The black columns are production, the grey columns are the numbers of groups and the dotted black line average volume per group. What we see is a huge gain in effective scale, multiplied fifteenfold over forty years. As we explained earlier, there were no significant new entrants after 2005, despite the huge growth in Chinese production, so the gains continued to accrue.

Of course, this is a simplified measure. The effects will have been diluted by the need to disperse production across the globe. They will have been reinforced by the use of platform strategies, which allow scale to be maintained per unique underlying design, while

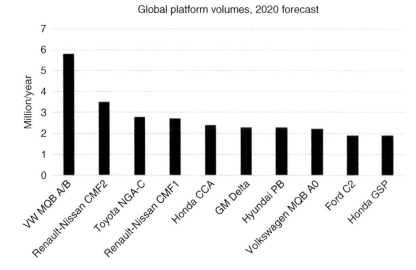

FIGURE 3.4 Gigantic platform volumes
Data sources: IHS Automotive, AAI 2017 Yearbook

allowing a more diverse offering in terms of models. A 2020 volume forecast for the ten most produced platforms and some of the models built on them is shown in Figure 3.4:[1]

- Volkswagen, confronted with exploding product diversity following its acquisition of Audi, SEAT in Spain and Škoda in the Czech Republic, pioneered platform strategies. Its mid-range MQB A/B platform (QB stands for Querbau, i.e., transverse engine layout) underpins the Golf, Jetta, Tiguan and Passat. Its entry-level MQB A0 platform is used in the Polo, Ai and Rapid.
- Renault-Nissan launched cross-brand platforms, following Renault's taking control of Nissan. CMF2 is used for the Clio, Juke, March and Note. CMF1 for the Qashai, Rogue and Megane.
- Toyota uses its NGA-C platform in the Auris, Corolla, RAV4 and Prius. Use of a high-volume platform helps to contain the costs of the Prius, made inherently expensive by its dual-drive system.
- Honda employs its CCA platform in the Civic, CR-V and Accord, and its GSP platform for the Fit, City and Brio.

---

[1]    These are only partial listings of models that are built on these platforms, the ones with the highest volumes.

- GM's Delta platform is used in the Astra, Cruze and Equinox.
- Hyundai's PB platform is under the Accent, Pride, Rio and i20.
- Ford's C2 platform is used in the Focus and Escape.

## FROM EXPORTING CARS TO TRANSPLANTING FACTORIES

Import duty tariffs on built-up cars were high in the United States but low in Europe before World War I but reversed thereafter, with European countries strongly protected and the United States tariff dropping to 10 per cent by 1929, where it remained until 1950 – a curious exception to the general increase in protectionism – before gradually declining to under 3 per cent by the 1980s. Individual European countries generally had high tariffs on built-up cars but tariffs were eliminated within the EEC, which the United Kingdom joined in 1983, by a common 10 per cent external tariff which was placed around the whole EEC (later EU).[2] Almost all other countries had high import tariffs or quotas and many of them have been kept. Thus exporting complete vehicles was a rarity in the initial decades of the industry.

Ford, as the first mass producer, established a small assembly plant in the United Kingdom before 1914 and a full operation later, with local product development, engine production and a large assembly plant in Dagenham (opened in 1931), east of London, followed by another at Halewood after World War II. A parallel operation was set up outside Cologne in Germany and one at Poissy in France, which was later to become Simca before being sold to Chrysler and then PSA, which still operates it. GM acquired Opel in the 1920s and then Vauxhall in the United Kingdom. Chrysler bought Rootes in the United Kingdom as well as Simca. All of the Detroit Big Three established manufacturing operations in Canada and Mexico, long before NAFTA (the North American Free Trade Agreement). So localisation of manufacturing became the norm early on in the majority of markets.

---

[2]  For details from 1913 to 1983, see *The Future of the Automobile*, Alan Altshuler et al., MIT Press, 1984, p. 17.

The reduced US tariff enabled VW to ship Beetles into the United States in quantity, as they became a cult object among college students in the 1960s. Volvo cars were similarly popular among faculty and other professionals. Both were making a statement of opposition to Detroit's gas guzzlers. Renault also tried with the 4CV and then the Dauphine but failed because of poor product quality. Japanese imports started very timidly at the same time but became a flood following the 1973 and 1979 oil shocks and the first CAFE programme. Political pressures (employment and the balance of trade), however, soon led to demands for import quotas and forced the Japanese into a voluntary restraint agreement on built-up imports into the United States. With continuing strong demand for their products there, this caused them to establish the so-called transplant factories. Honda set up the first Japanese-owned car assembly plant in Marysville, Ohio, in 1982. Toyota, Nissan and Mazda followed suit. The political pressures to do so were reinforced by the risks involved in achieving huge sales across currency zones and by the inflexibility of a long physical supply chain in responding to short-term changes in market demand.

Japanese cars started to have similar success in parts of Europe to that which they had enjoyed in the United States, thanks to low prices and a good reputation for reliability. In some import markets, such as Norway and the Netherlands, the Japanese makes collectively reached up to 40 per cent market share at one point. Quota protection varied considerably from country to country: a very low annual volume allowed into Italy.[3] A 3 per cent market share ceiling was imposed in France, the Spanish market was virtually closed, others were wide open. These measures were replaced by a 10 per cent EEC-wide quota – another voluntary restraint agreement. There was a closing of ranks and a tacit understanding to discourage the Japanese from repeating their US transplant approach. But the United Kingdom, having largely lost its own industry to European competition after it joined the EEC

[3]   Ironically based on a post–World War II voluntary restraint agreement designed to protect the Japanese market from Fiat!

in 1973, broke ranks and opened its doors to Japanese transplants. Nissan was the first, with a large plant in Sunderland in England's depressed North East. Toyota followed. So did Honda, despite having been gracelessly deprived by the British government of its partnership in Rover when this was sold to BMW. There was some strong resistance on the part of France in particular, with an attempt to include exports to other EEC countries from the Japanese plants in the United Kingdom in the import quota figures for completely built-up units (CBUs) but this failed. The transplants succeeded and effectively recreated an automotive industry for the United Kingdom. The European manufacturers and their suppliers, however, made major efforts to catch up with Japanese quality and reliability and held the invaders at bay, such that they never hit their 10 per cent Europe-wide quota ceiling. South Korea essentially followed in Japan's footsteps, following unsuccessful first attempts in North America and the United Kingdom. The Asian Financial Crisis of the 1980s forced a rationalisation of its manufacturers, with Daewoo sold to GM and the fledgling Samsung to Renault, with the sole independent survivor Hyundai taking over Kia and breaking through into the ranks of the global majors.

The general pattern in volume cars is to produce as close to the point of market demand as is practically and economically feasible, subject to scale versus logistical trade-offs, even in markets open to imports. Tariff barriers and import quotas artificially reinforce this tendency and interfere with the normal drive to scale. Premium, niche and special vehicles still tend to be produced in one location and exported.

## A SURPRISING OUTCOME: THE JAPANESE AND EUROPEANS STAY ON TOP

Forcing one's way into foreign markets, whether freely into open ones or by invitation into closed ones, normally requires a previous build-up of scale-driven competitiveness in one's starting domestic market. Ford and GM had a head start in this, thanks to early and massive motorisation in the United States. Japanese manufacturers crashed the party thanks to the combination of their development of lean production and of the US CAFE regulations. South Korea forced its way in by sheer determination. Back in 1998, we asked a South Korean delegate to the World Trade Organisation in Geneva how he thought his country could achieve it. The answer was that they had done so in shipbuilding and electronics, so why not in automotive? It happened, at unrecorded financial cost to the South Korean exchequer, and not without false starts. There were four runners at the start – Hyundai, Kia, Daewoo and Samsung. Only Hyundai-Kia got through as a surviving independent, but get through it did, in spectacular fashion, without the benefit of a massive home market.

As we saw in Chapter 2, China has been the great growth story of recent years, with its national production of cars now widely outstripping that of North American and Europe. From this, we might have expected at least two Chinese mega-manufacturers to have emerged onto the global stage. In fact this has not happened. The results in Figure 3.5 come as a surprise. These are annual production figures for all light vehicles, sorted

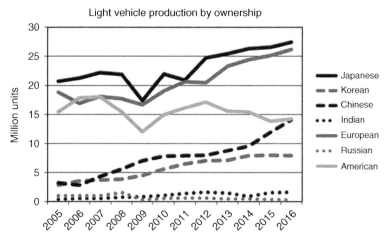

FIGURE 3.5  A surprising outcome
Data sources: OICA, Autopolis

not by where they were made but by the national ownership of the groups that built them. The Russians remain firmly in the doldrums, their score having fallen even further when Renault took control of their largest manufacturer Avtovaz, owner of the vast Togliattigrad assembly plant (set up with the help of Fiat and named after the Italian communist leader Palmiro Togliatti). Indian-owned manufacturers are struggling to take off – Maruti, a big producer in India, is owned by Suzuki. Chinese manufacturers are roaring away. Or so it seems, until one realises that they only produce half the total volume built in China. The rest is made by the joint ventures with foreign manufacturers. The Chinese-owned manufacturers have grown fast but collectively are far behind the group of Japanese or European producers. They are, however, now as big collectively as the Americans, although individually far more fragmented – today there are only two major American-owned groups, GM and Ford, but tens of Chinese light vehicle manufacturers. The Korean-owned Koreans have plateaued – but this isn't so bad, given there is only one of them. The big dip caused by the GFC and the bankruptcies is overlaid on a trend of stagnation if not decline for the US-owned manufacturers, accentuated by Fiat's acquisition of Chrysler and – more recent than these statistics, GM's sale of Opel and Vauxhall to PSA. Triumphant are the Japanese and – perhaps unexpectedly – the Europeans.

## THE INDUSTRY IS SPLITTING BETWEEN ASIAN-EUROPEAN PASSENGER CARS AND AMERICAN LIGHT TRUCKS

Figure 3.6 repeats the same analysis but this time for passenger cars alone. OICA data for these were only available to 2014 at the time of writing. Yet the messages are clear. Europe still leads, having surged ahead of the Japanese following the GFC, which badly hit the latter in the North American market. The US manufacturers have almost given up on passenger cars. Indeed, Ford is explicitly doing so, and is retreating from production in Brazil and Argentina, while the overall US figure has been further weakened by over 1 million units per year by GM's sale of GM Europe to PSA. The Chinese-owned manufacturers are, as a

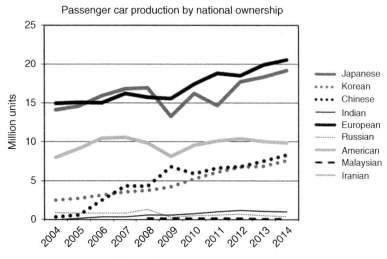

FIGURE 3.6  The vanishing Americans
Data sources: OICA, Autopolis

numerous group, barely ahead of the one single Korean and still behind even the two Americans.

The corresponding time series for light trucks, etc. is shown in Figure 3.7. It highlights the heavy dependency of the American producers on their national market anomaly. The GFC blow to them is clearly visible. No wonder GM and Chrysler had to file for bankruptcy, given that these were – and still are – far and away their most profitable products. The Europeans appear to have bounded up from 2013 but this is merely the result of Fiat acquiring Chrysler, for whom the whole light truck category was always a forte. Chrysler is strong in pickups, is credited with inventing the van as a passenger vehicle and owns Jeep – ceded to it by Renault, following the dissolution of its misadventure with American Motors. It does not show here but the Americans' products – other than Jeep – are virtually unsellable outside North America, owing to their crude designs. The Japanese remain quite strong. The Chinese are collectively sizeable but very fragmented between numerous, mainly small, producers. The rest have got nowhere.

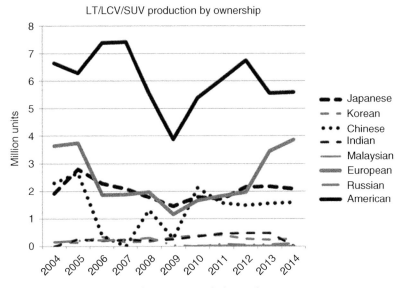

FIGURE 3.7  Long live American light trucks?
Data sources: OICA, Autopolis

And the whole sector is virtually stagnant. Note that this sector consists of 'real commercials', which includes light trucks extensively used in North America as substitutes for passenger cars, but not crossovers (passenger cars dressed up as SUVs) – the passenger car manufacturers' latest product ploy.

Figure 3.8 dramatically underlines these observations and is full of portents for the future. The OECD Triad countries of Europe, Japan and the United States totally dominate automotive innovation, whether in R&D spend or patents issued. The United States has fallen well behind its two main competitors and China barely registers. China is, in essence, a very large production satellite for foreign automotive groups. Europe includes its peripheral automotive producing countries, notably Turkey. Automotive R&D spends are at least 80 per cent devoted to the normal cycle of product replacements, i.e., D rather than R. While this can cause problems with inter-sectoral comparisons, it doesn't for international comparisons within the automotive sector.

|              | R&D spend 2016<br>Euro billion | Patents 2017 |
|--------------|--------------------------------|--------------|
| Europe        | 54 | 4,935 |
| Japan         | 29 | 2,382 |
| United States | 18 | 1,016 |
| China         | 5  | 156   |
| Rest of world | 6  | 243   |

FIGURE 3.8 The innovation rankings
Data source: ACEA automobile industry pocket guide, 2018–2019

## THE AMERICAN MANUFACTURERS WERE THE FIRST TO GLOBALISE PRODUCTION

Figure 3.9 shows where the different vehicle manufacturers (VMs) grouped by national ownership built their cars in 1999. 'Other Asia' includes China, whose production was very limited at this time. The Europeans mainly produced in the EU, with limited volumes built in 'Other Europe' (which includes Russia) and Turkey (TR), a small presence in China and some in the Americas. No great globalisation for them at this point in time. In contrast, the Americans, for passenger cars at least, were almost balanced between the United States and the EU. This was, of course, the result of their much earlier acquisitions and investments in Europe, starting well before World War II. It should, however, be pointed out that this was done with very different products on the two continents. They also had a small presence in Other Asia and Oceania (Australia). The Japanese still mainly built at home but already had a significant transplant presence in the Americas and also in Other Asia (mainly South-East Asia). The Koreans very largely built at home, the others were mainly the Comecon manufacturers, almost wholly in their home countries. So whatever was sold abroad was mainly exported from the home country – except for the Americans.

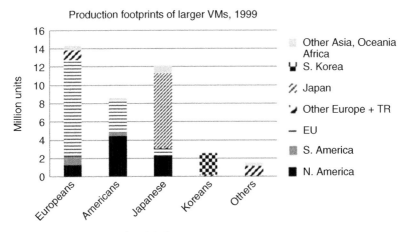

FIGURE 3.9  The global Americans – once upon a time
Data sources: OICA, Autopolis

## VW LED THE EUROPEANS IN GLOBALISING ITS OPERATIONS

Figure 3.10 looks more closely at the European manufacturers at the same date. VW still produced principally in Europe but had a long-standing presence in the Americas – Mexico and Brazil – in Other Europe through its acquisition of Škoda and, most crucially for the future, in Other Asia, i.e., China. Fiat had its long-standing manufacturing presences in Brazil and Eastern Europe. PSA was almost wholly European. Daimler was half American but only by virtue of its ill-starred acquisition of Chrysler. Renault was almost wholly European. BMW, together with its doomed acquisition of Rover, and Volvo were also built in Europe. So only VW, already much larger than the other Europeans was the only one 'out of the blocks' on globalisation. How ironic that such an icon of German nationalism at the time of its creation, and the youngest of any of these competitors, should have taken the lead! Germany really persisted with its national champion in volume cars and was making it into a true international one, shifting gears from build-in-Germany-and-export (as with the old Beetle) to transplanting its manufacturing operations overseas.

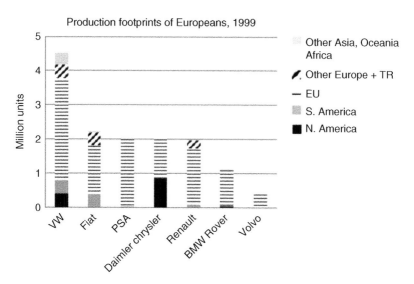

FIGURE 3.10 European outposts
Data sources: OICA, Autopolis

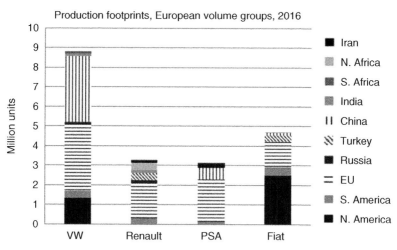

FIGURE 3.11 VW out in front
Data sources: OICA, Autopolis

By 2016 much had changed. We can see from Figure 3.11 that VW's bold early bet on China has paid off hugely, propelling it into the class of Super Majors, although it is still under-weight in North America.

Renault is still preponderantly European, having largely missed out on China. But the balance is in theory redressed by its alliance with Nissan, in which it holds a 44 per cent stake. So is PSA, although with a bigger Chinese manufacturing presence. Fiat, with its acquisition of Chrysler, replicates Daimler of 1999. Will this marriage be any happier?

## THE GERMAN OLIGOPOLY IN PREMIUM CARS REMAINS UNSHAKEABLE

German makes dominate the world market for premium cars, forming an almost perfect oligopoly. And they still mainly build them in Germany (see Figure 3.12) and export them to the world, their premium pricing allowing them to override tariffs and quotas. Foreign governments also have no national champions to defend in this sub-sector. One exception is China, which limits imports – and Audi long ago established itself there as the make of choice for senior party officials and managers of state enterprises. BMW and Mercedes have also put their assembly plants for SUVs in the United States, as this is far and away the leading market for these. Not, note, in Detroit but in South Carolina and Alabama, respectively – out of range of the United Auto Workers and an example of the use

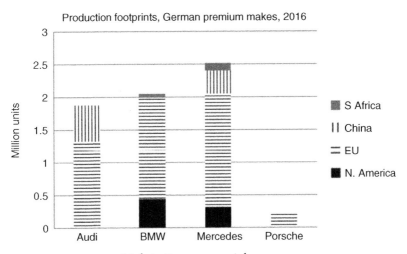

FIGURE 3.12 Made in Germany – mainly
Data sources: OICA, Autopolis

of lower-cost satellite locations around core automotive regions, in this case within a country. They also have plants in South Africa, building for the right-hand drive markets. More about all of this in Chapter 5.

## THE ONCE-DOMINANT AMERICANS HAVE RETREATED TOWARDS ISOLATIONISM

In contrast, the Americans have been going backwards. Their 2016 manufacturing footprints are shown in Figure 3.13. Both GM and Ford remained heavily dependent on their home market of North America, together with light trucks, etc. Moreover, since then, GM has surrendered its position in Europe by selling it out to PSA. Not that this was the first attempt, as it gave serious consideration to selling it to a combination of Magna (the large Canadian components group) and Sbrbank of Russia after the GFC. Both GM and Ford have struggled to make adequate profits in Europe for years. It remains to be seen whether Ford will persevere there, given its announced North American strategy of concentrating on the light truck family. This is a real come down for Ford also, which used to dominate the British market, had a respectable and long-standing

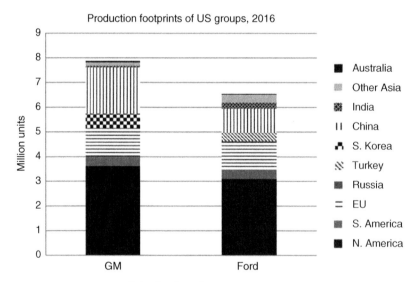

FIGURE 3.13 Going backwards
Data sources: OICA, Autopolis

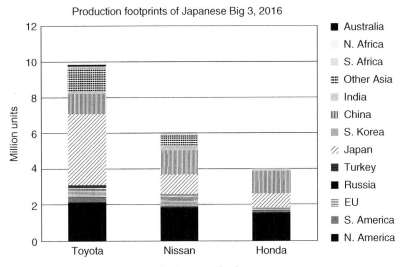

FIGURE 3.14  Toyota the Japanese leader
Data sources: OICA, Autopolis

position in Germany, had a successful operation in Valencia in Spain, and had led the way by replacing national entities by creating Ford of Europe early on.

## TOYOTA STANDS OUT AS THE GLOBAL LEADER
### AMONG THE JAPANESE MANUFACTURERS

Figure 3.14 shows the manufacturing footprints of the Japanese Big Three. Toyota, while still building half of its vehicles in Japan – and totally dominating the scene there – is well spread out geographically, as are Nissan and Honda. All three are underweight in Europe, because of the resistance of the European makes, but also because many European buyers mainly see Japanese cars as worthy and reliable but neither fun to drive nor stylish.

## HYUNDAI-KIA HAS BEEN THE ONLY RECENT NEWCOMER
### TO THE CLUB OF GLOBAL GIANTS

We have seen Japan as the major new entrant into the world of automobile manufacturing, particularly exploiting its mastery of

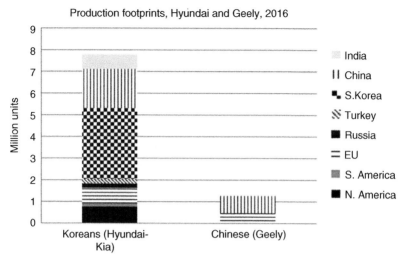

FIGURE 3.15  Only one other challenger
Data sources: OICA, Autopolis

manufacturing to compensate for an initial lack of scale. The only other new major new entrant has been Korea, or Hyundai-Kia, to be precise, whereas there continues to be a conspicuous absence of a major Chinese challenger, despite China's huge overall production volumes. Figure 3.15 shows the manufacturing footprints of Hyundai-Kia and Geely, the only Chinese manufacturer to have established any sort of presence outside China. Hyundai-Kia has become a true global super major, by its own efforts – just as the Japanese did. Geely is only in the list by virtue of its acquisition of Volvo Cars and is a relatively small player even then.

Figure 3.16 shows the overall result by 2016. What we have is a global semi-oligopoly, led by VW for the Europeans and by Toyota for the Japanese, with the Americans falling behind, and one Korean manufacturer, Hyundai-Kia. Whether to include the Renault-Nissan Alliance in the small club of global super majors is perhaps a moot point, depending on how well integrated together one thinks they are. The 2018 arrest of Carlos Ghosn in Japan may hint at some underlying tensions with respect to plans for closer integration.

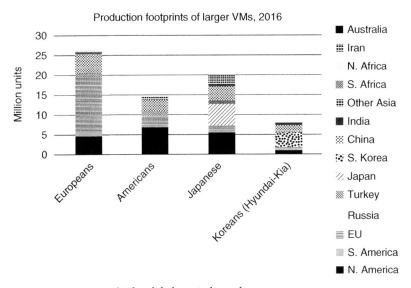

FIGURE 3.16 The global semi-oligopoly
Data sources: OICA, Autopolis

Today, we are simply part of the way along a long path to a global oligopoly. The fact that we have not yet achieved it is to a large part attributable to government interference, in the form of tariff and non-tariff trade barriers, and financial support provided to national champions to protect them from global competition.

## IS CHINA PLAYING A DIFFERENT GAME?

The puzzle, of course, is the absence from this exclusive club of one or more Chinese-owned giants, given that the country accounts for almost a third of world production of light vehicles. The answer, of course, is that China has chosen to put the development of much of its light vehicle industry in the hands of joint ventures with foreign partners, who bring the necessary technology and know-how – and much of the investment funds – lured by the huge market. The central government also historically delegated a surprising level of authority and responsibility for the development of the automotive industry to the provinces. Again, this seems surprising, given China's determination to lead in key sectors. The answer may be more threatening to the established semi-oligopoly than appears at first sight. China seems to have concluded that conventional automotive technologies are just that – conventional – and that this is a sector that is heading into the sunset and therefore not a high priority for Chinese investment of money and human capital. Let the foreigners make the investments and carry the risks. The Party may simply have decided to allow the population enough cars to keep it politically quiet – but not to allow full-scale Western-style mass motorisation, with all its environmental consequences. China has a huge environmental problem, including GHG emissions. There is simply not room in large Chinese cities for that many cars. China is not a democracy or an open market and the Party decides. China has attracted seven times as much electric vehicle (EV) investment from carmakers (Euro 21.7 billion) as the whole of the EU (Euro 3.2 billion).[4] The front runners, the Volkswagen Group, Daimler AG and Nissan, have provided the bulk of the investment in China, driven by its aggressive electric vehicle policy. This policy requires carmakers to obtain credits for the production of EVs that are equivalent to 10 per cent of the overall passenger car market in 2019 and 12 per cent in 2020. BEV (battery electric vehicles) sales in China were 50 per cent higher in 2016 than in the United States and Europe combined.[5] And this may be but a stepping stone to a Chinese-led real revolution in personal people transport systems. China is already applying restrictions to the use of ICE-powered vehicles in its cities. It could well be preparing an end run around the whole of the conventional automotive industry. The position of the Europeans could be seriously undermined by their problems with their preferred prime mover, the direct-injection diesel engine, as revealed by the Dieselgate scandal.

[4]    Transport & Environment, June 2018.
[5]    *Global Automotive Supplier Study 2018*, Lazard-Roland Berger, December 2017.

### THE VEHICLE MANUFACTURERS' DISTRIBUTION
### AND RETAILING STRUCTURES GIVE THEM CONTROL
### OVER MARKETS

Government interference is not the only constraint upon rationalisation of the industry. The upstream sectors of the industry – the development and production of sub-systems, components and materials – have undergone massive changes over the last fifty years, with greatly increased technology content, the pursuit of minimum cost through maximum scale and a redefinition of how responsibilities are shared out. This is explored in Chapter 4. In sharp contrast, the whole downstream sector, after the finished vehicle leaves the assembly plant, has changed little in over fifty years. This is true right across all the developed automotive markets, with only minor local variations.

The vehicle manufacturers' distribution and retailing networks and practices constitute a major anomaly, compared to other sectors of the economy. They are their Peculiar Institution. The manufacturers control the wholesale distribution of new cars in the significant markets themselves, either directly through a subsidiary or through independent importers, who are often exclusive to a brand or a group. There are officially no independent wholesale distributors of new cars, although some small actors live by redistributing misallocated vehicles across or between national distribution networks. Sales to retail customers (individual purchasers) almost always take place through networks of dealers, franchised by the manufacturers and exclusively representing their brands. These are independent retailers in name only. In reality, they are more akin to factory outlets, whose prime role is to push the output of the assembly plants into the markets. Unlike true independent retailers (in food, for example), they cannot pick and choose which products they sell. They must 'shift the iron', whatever their manufacturer franchisors tell them to push. They are allowed only narrow gross margins and further remunerated by ex-post factor bonuses, based on achievement of sales targets 'negotiated' with the manufacturers. There are no volume-based discounts in this relationship. This is, in fact, indirect control by the vehicle manufacturers over their sales strategies and transaction prices. Most dealers are fairly small businesses, powerless against their huge manufacturer 'partners'. While an increasing proportion are part of dealer groups, the dealer contracts are still with individual dealerships. All this reinforces the manufacturers' control over their retail networks.

## THE DISTRIBUTION SYSTEM IS INEFFICIENT, COSTLY AND ENCOURAGES OVER-PRODUCTION

This is a hugely inefficient system, with vast capacity redundancies caused by the multiplicity of brand-exclusive networks. Spend time in any showroom and see how little traffic there is. The assets, physical and human, are grossly underutilised. The manufacturers force their dealers to invest hugely in showy palaces, in the hope that this will attract more customers – who basically hate the dealership experience and the pushy selling. They feel the dealers are not on their side, as indeed they are not. Adding up the cost of physically moving cars from the assembly plant to the dealerships, the cost of dealer stocks of new cars, the showrooms, the staff costs, the huge advertising campaigns, the provisions for warranty costs, and you have 30–40 per cent of the pre-tax cost of a new car generated after it leaves the assembly plant. This is accompanied by vast over-competition in new car sales. Consumers have learned to expect and receive discounts from list prices. Margins for both dealers and manufacturers are too low. Fixed costs are high and break-even points too high, which creates a further incentive to go for volume, regardless of the effect on margins. In Europe, both dealers and manufacturers get rid of new cars that won't sell by pre-registering them, i.e., registering them in their own names. This instantly transforms them into zero- or low-mileage used cars, which can be dumped into the market without worrying about trying to respect the manufacturers' official list prices. Retail sales are pumped up by offering consumers personal leasing packages that remove the need for them to put up the money. This practice leads

to dangerously many sales to insolvent customers, potentially replicating the US sub-prime mortgage disaster.

In many countries, personal and business tax incentives have
stimulated the emergence of a large fleet sector, i.e., sales to corporate
and public bodies, large and small. The larger ones, such as short-term
rental companies, can and do obtain huge discounts on their purchases
of new vehicles. The manufacturers trade directly with these, by-
passing their own dealers, at least in Europe. This is very difficult for
them in the United States, where dealership rights are enshrined in
state laws and almost impossible to circumvent. The cars coming out
of fleets flood into the use car market, with the help of auction houses.
Smart dealers have learned that they can make much better margins
on used cars, a market not controlled by the manufacturers, providing
they actively profile their stock to match local demand. Three out of
four sales transactions in a mature market are of used cars. Retail
customers have also got smart and increasingly buy used rather than
new cars, leaving the latter to the fleets.

## IT ALSO ENCOURAGES EXCESSIVE PRODUCT PROLIFERATION, UNDERMINES PROFITABILITY AND INHIBITS REAL COMPETITION

The manufacturers try to stimulate the new car market by proliferat-
ing the number of models they offer. This bloats their fixed costs and
contributes to further raising their already too high break-even points.
Customers love this, as they don't perceive the cost penalties, hidden
behind the discounts and deals. The manufacturers have all shortened
their product life cycles to try to maintain market interest in frequently replacing one's car. This leads to an accelerated flow of de-
fleeted and traded-in cars, which puts downward pressure on used car
prices and thus on new car pricing. A further vicious circle. This is
where the most pernicious effect of the brand-tied retail channels is
felt: there is no countervailing force, there are no large independent
distribution and retailing groups that would normally push back by
de-listing the products that don't move. This is the price of obsession

with control. Huge sums – as large as the manufacturers' R&D expenditure – are spent on brand advertising, in a vain attempt to create product differentiation, which simply isn't there in volume cars. Watch the TV commercials, almost none of them addresses actual product features, they are all about life style and macho driving fantasies. Pity the poor stylists, who have to come up with something new enough to attract yet conventional enough not to offend. 'We no longer design products, we design experiences', in the words of a leading stylist. Really? It is in fact very rare that someone comes up with a genuinely new product concept, such as the MPV. Most of this is fantasy talk, meaningless to the average motorist looking for practical transportation at an affordable price, principally second hand. And how about the desperate search for names for new products, which have to work in multiple languages?

All this not only costs a fortune, it inhibits the necessary shake-out of excessive products, brands – and manufacturers. It also erects huge entry barriers against would-be new entrants. One can only sell new cars with the by-your-leave of the established oligarchy, which controls market access. A country cannot on its own export cars, only its manufacturers can – assuming they have access to overseas distribution networks that belong to their affiliates or parent groups.

## QUASI-MONOPOLY RENTS IN THE DEALER AFTERMARKET MAKE UP FOR INADEQUATE PROFITS ON NEW CARS

Everyone knows that computer printers are cheap but you pay for it when you want to buy a 'genuine' replacement cartridge, unless you get one from a re-filler. New cars are arguably underpriced, such that neither volume car manufacturers nor their franchised dealers can survive financially in this business. It's different in premium cars, for which a real oligopoly functions, market discipline is observed, product cycles are less hectic and new car margins are healthier. Once the manufacturer and dealer have almost competed their margins away to sell a new car to you, they try their utmost to make you a captive customer for service and repair. There's a certain convenience factor in this, although it's severely diluted by the single-brand dealer networks, further thinned out to reduce intra-brand competition on new car discounts. There are simply too few dealer workshops of most brands for them to be within a convenient distance of home or work. The thinning out is defeated by the Internet, which abolishes physical distance in shopping around for a car. But that doesn't work when you have to take your car somewhere for service or repair. There's some comfort in the notion that the organisation that sold you the car remains responsible for keeping it in good operating condition. But then there are the coercions: the implication – it can't legally be said in most jurisdictions – that going to an independent repairer during the warranty period will invalidate your warranty, that not having a dealer stamp in the service booklet will reduce the resale value of the car. This isn't done out of gratuitous nastiness but rather out of financial necessity: dealerships make most of their profits on workshop hours, which are usually priced at 40–50 per cent higher than at independent repairers. Scare tactics keep the owners of new cars loyal to them but that doesn't last into subsequent ownership cycles.

Independent repairers are numerous. They are mainly small and gain from greater proximity to the residences and places of work of customers, reinforced by the fact that they support all makes and models. They are more accessible – you get to talk to the owner and often the technician, not to a service receptionist. But their very independence is their weakness. Their competence generally depends on the skills and experience of an owner or small team. It is difficult to verify a priori. Attempts to organise them into branded and disciplined chains have met with very mixed results. Yet a great majority of car owners have recourse to them, increasingly so as cars get older and into successive ownership cycles. Their collective share of the service and repair aftermarket reaches 75–80 per cent in the more open countries, such as the United States, United Kingdom and Australia, as low as 40–45 per cent in more tradition-bound countries, such as Germany. In general, the owners and operators of light vehicles flee the franchised dealer workshops from the second ownership cycle on.

The manufacturers do their utmost to restrain this, by the means cited above but also by trying to limit the independents' access to the technical information they need to carry out servicing and repairs. These obvious restraints on trade are fought by the independents and regulators but are reborn with every new development in vehicle technologies, notably electronics and the associated diagnostics. One of the latest versions is the proposal to suppress diagnostic plugs, so that on-board systems are only accessible through the manufacturer's proprietary intranet. This is a long and on-going struggle.

Nor do dealers make much margin on spare parts. They are strongly encouraged to source them from their manufacturer, who takes the lion's share of the gross margin on parts, most of which come from independent parts suppliers. Of course, spare parts are inherently high priced. It costs a great deal of money to organise the procurement of them, including the manufacturers' obligation to support their models up to ten years after the end of production; to build, stock and operate their warehouses; to run the distribution systems that make them readily available in a short space of time to every dealer workshop. These systems are generally taut and efficient, with the workshops encouraged to pre-plan their work and pre-order the parts. They do, however, suffer an estimated 20–25 per cent cost penalty through their brand-exclusivity, a horizontal or lateral fragmentation. For their part, the independent repairers are supplied by networks of independent parts distributors, who source the parts from producers who may be suppliers to the manufacturers or not. The distributors often live under the price umbrella set up by the manufacturers with their list prices. As they support all makes and models of cars (as do the independent repairers), they do not suffer from the lateral brand-specific fragmentation. However, there has historically not been much incentive for them to tauten supply chains and reduce intermediate inventory levels. They push the responsibility for range assembly (to ensure coverage of all applications) back onto the suppliers. This causes redundancy in references between different suppliers of a given category of parts. Their attempts at getting their workshop customers into organised networks have generally not been very spirited or effective. The large self-styled trade groups are in effect but purchasing cooperatives, living by obtaining lower prices from the suppliers. All this may, however, break down, as aggressive players make acquisitions in the independent parts sector and consolidate it. There are signs that the long-standing tacit alignment of list prices between the franchised and independent aftermarkets may be breaking down. Ultimately, this constitutes a massive threat to the volume vehicle manufacturers, who derive some 40 per cent of their operating profits from spare parts sales, which form only 10 per cent of their total turnover – and that in a good year for new car sales.

Crash repair parts are an especially juicy set of manufacturer-dealer mini-monopolies. The category most consumed is of course sheet metal parts, notably front wings. Making these involves multiple massive tool steel die pairs and streets of large presses – one cannot form deep pressings in one stroke, as the sheet metal tends to tear. The tooling investment required is huge, creating natural manufacturer monopolies. Crash repairers are mainly independent small businesses, dealing with all makes and models of vehicles. They don't have the time to shop around and it's convenient for them to source all the parts they need for a given job from a dealer of the relevant make. Thus a double monopoly. The dominant sheet-metal parts pull the others through this channel with them, as crash repairers usually want parts from a single source. It's an immensely lucrative trade for the manufacturers. Copy parts are made by independent suppliers, using dies in softer materials, which will do for shorter production runs. There are independent quality certifiers. But the repairers are risk averse, as an ill-fitting part is a time and cost nightmare for them. There are also problems of range coverage with independent suppliers. In France, visible body parts come under artistic copyright laws, so that copy parts cannot even legally be distributed. Probably the most logical solution is for insurers, who represent one of the few pools of concentrated buying power, to negotiate prices with the manufacturers. Once again, the manufacturers try to persuade the motoring public of the evils of copy parts, even claiming that they can make a vehicle unsafe in the event of a crash. Given that the visible parts that are so protected are not part of the safety structure, this is not very plausible. The most lurid claim was that a female driver in Spain had been decapitated in a crash by a copy engine compartment hood. It was, of course, a myth. Neither the accident nor the person involved could be identified.

## THE DOWNSTREAM SECTOR OF THE INDUSTRY IS MARKED BY IMMOBILITY AND AUTHORITARIANISM THAT CREATE CONFLICTS WITH REGULATORS

What is so striking in all this is the immobility in the downstream sector of the industry. The franchised dealership system was pioneered by Ford in the United States, in order to ensure adequate service and repair support in the very early years of motorisation. It has been with us ever since. In theory it should go. But there is no one to challenge it. As mentioned earlier, it is embedded in state dealer laws in the United States. In Europe, such exclusive vertical agreements are in violation of Article 83 of the Treaty of Rome, so the European Commission grants a Block (sectoral) Exemption for a number of years at a time. At the 2002 renewal, they pursued two objectives. The first was somewhat to redress the imbalance of power between manufacturers and dealers by granting the latter certain rights, such as representing multiple makes, selling their businesses without needing their manufacturer's approval and being allowed to source parts from the independent aftermarket. The reaction of the aftersales director of a large automobile manufacturer to this last proposition was brutal: 'We put them in business, we are entitled to expect their loyalty in parts sourcing'. In the event, so few dealers even attempted to exercise their new rights that at the next renewal the Commission no longer put new car sales under an automotive-specific block exemption but under the general regime on vertical agreements, which is not constraining upon it at all. Its second objective, which it has continued to pursue, was to ensure the survival of the independent aftermarket, so that vehicle owners would have an alternative to the franchised dealer workshops. Maintaining this is an on-going fight, with Right to Repair (principally meaning equitable access to technical information) campaigns run by the independent aftermarket sector on both sides of the Atlantic.

All this is in stark contrast to the huge changes that have taken place over the last fifty years in the upstream sector of the industry, that of the systems, components and materials suppliers. Why all this defensiveness? In large measure, of course, because the manufacturers and dealers fear the loss of quasi-monopoly rents, upon which they critically depend for their financial survival. But there is also a pattern in the whole automotive sector of authoritarianism. This is not because of some evil disposition or original sin but the result of the very nature of automobiles and the very tough disciplines required to managed their lengthy and complicated development and production chains. We explore these aspects in Chapter 4.

## IN SUMMARY, THE INDUSTRY IS OLIGARCHIC AND NOT FULLY OPEN TO COMPETITION

World light vehicle production went through distinct phases of rapid growth, competitive consolidation and resumed growth. Consolidation among manufacturers led first to national then to global oligarchies. Globalisation has enabled huge gains in effective scale and therefore in unit costs. The industry has moved from exporting cars to transplanting factories, under both economic and political pressures. The outcome has been surprising: the Japanese and European manufacturers have stayed on top. The industry is splitting between Asian-European passenger cars and American light trucks. The American manufacturers were the first to globalise production, while VW led the Europeans in globalising its operations. The German oligopoly in premium cars remains unshakeable. The once-globally-dominant Americans are retreating into light trucks and towards isolationism. Toyota stands out as the global leader among the Japanese manufacturers. Hyundai-Kia has been the only recent newcomer to the club of global giants. There are no major Chinese global players and China may be playing a wholly different game. The vehicle manufacturers' peculiar proprietary distribution and retailing structures give them control over markets. This system is inefficient, costly and encourages over-production. It also encourages excessive product proliferation, undermines profitability and inhibits real competition. Quasi-monopoly rents in the dealer aftermarket make up for inadequate profits on new cars. The downstream sector of the industry is marked by immobility and authoritarianism that create conflicts with regulators.

# 4 A Highly Disciplined Global Partnership: the Components Suppliers

Modern cars are extremely complex and sophisticated. To the traditional and themselves-greatly-improved body structures and mechanical, hydraulic and electrical systems have been added a profusion of electronic controls. Almost no function is left untouched. Hundreds of sensors, logic circuits and actuators ensure comfortable, safe and efficient performance. Increasingly sophisticated materials are used. Up to 6,000 components are assembled together. The whole design has to work together perfectly and be able to be manufactured in huge volumes. Complete vehicles have to be produced within the most demanding constraints of quality, reliability and – last but not least – unit cost. The results are indeed remarkable: automobiles today are convenient, good to drive, safe and reliable as never before. At equivalent functional content, they have come down in real cost and price. They represent outstanding value for money. The product choice is vast – we would argue unnecessarily so.

The effort is unceasing. Every vehicle manufacturer is ruled by a product plan that stretches years into the future, with regularly planned updates to or replacement of existing models, and fresh additions to the range. The industry has imposed upon itself accelerated product development and introduction cycles that are often extraordinarily short. Eighteen months is now a common timespan for developing and launching a new model. Materials, parts and systems come together in a fascinating ballet, choreographed across countries and regions. The planning effort is unique and constantly repeated, from the initial ideas for a product all the way through to ensuring that it is properly supported in operation. The automotive industry has been *the* greatest triumph of organisation of the twentieth century and retains that character today. And, as it has grown so hugely in volume, in value and in global dispersion, the task has become ever-more challenging.

All this requires an astonishing degree or coordination and discipline, akin to that required by a major military operation – again and again. Is it any wonder, then, that the automotive industry displays an authoritarian, not to say military management culture? It has always been led by very strong personalities. This is no sector for the reticent or faint-hearted. Individual manufacturers have strong and distinct cultures, which often render mergers and acquisitions in the sector difficult to implement. The industry is justly proud of its products and its achievements. It is consequently a difficult one to challenge, as we shall see in Chapter 5.

## MASSIVE INVESTMENT REQUIREMENTS FORCED A HUGE INCREASE IN DELEGATION OF RESPONSIBILITY TO SUPPLIERS, WHO REMAIN LARGELY INVISIBLE

At the very beginning of the automotive industry, the pioneers themselves had to design and make almost every part of the car, except for a few already available items, such as pneumatic tyres (previously developed for bicycles), wheels, lamps, seating and glass. They had to be polymaths and strong organisers – or they failed. The great majority did fail, with very few surviving the transition from craft shop to industrial enterprise. The initial level of vehicle manufacturer integration – the share in the value of the finished vehicle made by them – was perforce very high. It remained so for a long time, essentially through the era of mass-producing a single model, with only slight and infrequent changes made to it. Henry Ford even invested in his own steel mill to get adequate supplies, backed by his own iron mines and a railroad to transport the ore. GM set up its own component divisions, which grew to be very large. Two generations later, in

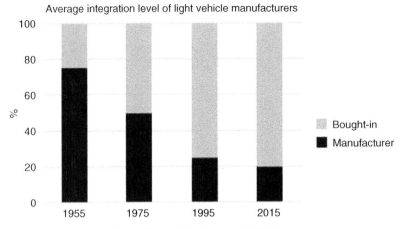

FIGURE 4.1  A steady transfer of responsibilities
Source: Autopolis

the heyday of its own era of single-product mass production, Renault still made 50 per cent of the content of its cars.

However, as the industry grew phenomenally after World War II and vehicles, their sub-systems, and the components and materials used in them became ever more sophisticated, complex and diverse, the manufacturers increasingly delegated responsibility for these to specialised suppliers. They simply could not afford to take on so much of the design and production responsibilities and required investments by themselves. The inevitable result was that, over a period of forty years from the 1950s, the supply sector grew prodigiously, not only riding on the growth of vehicle production but tripling its share in their value, from 25 per cent to 75 per cent, as shown in Figure 4.1. That share has now stabilised at around 80 per cent on average, with individual variations by manufacturer and model. Suppliers have become highly specialised by function and are expected by their vehicle manufacturer customers to invest heavily in new technologies, in design capability for applying them to their vehicles, in the required means of production and in following them wherever they set up in the world. Even though the suppliers' share in the total value of vehicles had stabilised by the year 2015, with the increasing sophistication of virtually every element that goes to make up a modern car – for example, software-driven systems, IT systems, materials design – their sales continued to grow enormously. The suppliers developed highly specialised suites of products aimed solely at the automotive industry. Due to the special nature of the automotive industry – characterised by high volumes, complex manufacturing and tightly run development and supply chains – there is generally little overlap with other industries or customers. The sector is also relatively invisible. With very rare exceptions, consumers have no idea that so much of their vehicle is the creation of suppliers, or of who these suppliers are. Suppliers' brand names appear on their products, where legislation has forced manufacturers to accept this. Dealers sell replacement parts made by them but in boxes bearing the brand of their franchisors, the vehicle manufacturers. Only independent parts distributors and garage technicians are really aware of their identities.

## THE SUPPLY SECTOR HAS GROWN ENORMOUSLY – EVEN MORE THAN THE VEHICLE MANUFACTURERS THEMSELVES

The inevitable result has been colossal growth in the supply sector. It is very difficult to put a value on the sales of all suppliers but from 1955 to 2015 global light vehicle output was multiplied by 6.3, the content of the average vehicle by value probably doubled and the suppliers' share of it leapt from 25 per cent to 80 per cent. This suggests that they collectively grew fortyfold in sales, which is almost 10 per cent per year, compound. There are annual statistics published for the top 100. These are not small local companies. Figure 4.2 shows the 2016 sales breakdown by world region for the ten largest. They range from $18 billion to $45 billion per year. The largest are bigger than many smaller vehicle manufacturers. They are far from limited to sales in their regions of origin. Note that all of these numbers exclude sales to the independent aftermarket, which are significant in those product lines subject to wear and tear and thus to replacement.

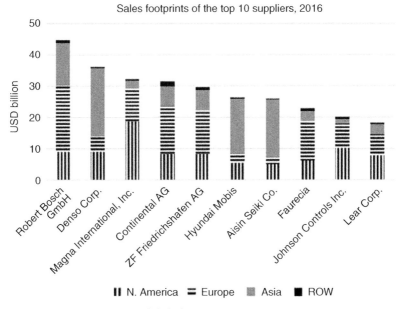

FIGURE 4.2  Large global players
Data source: Automotive News

## THESE ARE THE TRUE TECHNICAL SPECIALISTS
## OF THE AUTOMOTIVE INDUSTRY

Despite their size, the suppliers remain based on one or a limited number of technologically specialised sub-sectors:

- Robert Bosch GmbH (German owned), the largest and oldest, started in ignition systems. The company's symbol is an image of a rotor from a magneto, the original Bosch invention that enabled the spark ignition system in the very first internal combustion engines. Its main areas of business are gasoline engine systems (it pioneered fuel injection, starting with aircraft engines), diesel engine systems, chassis system controls, electrical drives, starter motors and generators, car multimedia, electronics, steering systems and battery technology. Although it is now out of braking systems, it pioneered ABS (anti-lock systems).
- Denso Corporation (Japanese) is specialised in heat exchangers, power train control, electronic and electric systems, small motors and telecommunications.

- Magna International, Inc. (Canadian) is in body, chassis, exterior, power train, electronic, vision, closure and roof systems and modules.
- Continental AG (German) is in advanced driver assistance systems, electronic brakes controls, foundation brakes, stability management, tyres, chassis systems, safety system electronics, power train electronics, interior modules, instrumentation and technical elastomers.
- ZF Friedrichshafen AG (German) is in transmissions (for both light and heavy vehicles), chassis components and systems, steering systems, clutches, dampers, and active and passive safety systems.
- Hyundai Mobis (South Korean) is in chassis systems, cockpit and front-end modules, stability control, steering, airbags, LED lamps, sensors, electronic control systems, hybrid power trains and power control units.
- Aisin Seiki Co. (Japanese) is in body, brake and chassis systems, electronics, and drive train and engine components.
- Faurecia (French) is in seating, emissions control technologies, interior systems, exterior components, modules and structural parts.
- Johnson Controls, Inc. (American) is one of the largest specialists in complete automotive seats and seat components.
- Lear Corporation (American) is in seating and electrical distribution systems.

The supply sector also spends more on R&D, as a percentage of sales, than do the vehicle manufacturers.

## THE SUPPLY SECTOR HAS GLOBALISED AT LEAST AS MUCH AS HAVE THE VEHICLE MANUFACTURERS

The international diversity of the ownership of suppliers is notable, a witness to how much the supply sector has globalised. One factor is that the supply sector is so much less visible than vehicle manufacturing, and so somewhat less exposed to protectionist tendencies on the part of governments. The growth of sales of the supply sector has of course varied by world region, in proportion to the sales volumes of the vehicle manufacturers in each. Figure 4.3 shows how the sales in each region of the top 100 suppliers have grown between 2002 and 2015. Their overall sales increased by 95 per cent, from current USD367 billion to 717 billion over the period, representing 5.3 per cent a year of compound growth. Probably

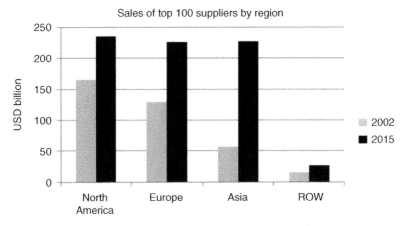

FIGURE 4.3 Global sales growth of the top 100 suppliers
Data source: Automotive News

80 per cent of this growth is attributable to the growth in volume and value of systems and components production but another 20 per cent is the result of concentration in the sector. There has been a steady drum-beat of takeovers and mergers for decades, which has increased the share and dominance of the larger suppliers. The greatest source of recent growth has of course been China within the Asian region, which has multiplied sales in the region by a factor of four. But sales in Europe grew by 74 per cent, whereas those in North American did so by only 43 per cent, reflecting the general weakening of the US industry.

## MARKET SHARES HAVE SHIFTED BUT AN UNSHAKEN OLIGOPOLISTIC ESTABLISHMENT REMAINS IN PLACE

There has been a dramatic shift in market shares, as shown in Figure 4.4. The North American-owned suppliers, who dominated the sector fifty years ago, have all but stagnated, growing by a mere 7 per cent from 2002 to 2015. The Europeans, despite the relatively slow growth of vehicle production in their region, nevertheless grew their sales by 130 per cent. The big winners were the Asian-owned suppliers, who collectively grew by 240 per cent.

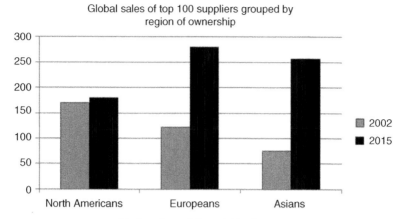

FIGURE 4.4 Market share shifts within the top 100
Data source: Automotive News

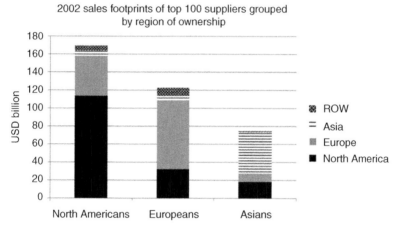

FIGURE 4.5 Sales footprints by regional ownership in 2002
Data source: Automotive News

## THE SUPPLY SECTOR HAS STEADILY GLOBALISED

In 2002 (see Figure 4.5), those suppliers in the top 100 on average achieved 65 per cent of their sales within their region of origin, with the Americans the most geographically diversified, thanks to their having taken positions in Europe early on. This had fallen to 55 per cent by 2015 (Figure 4.6). Again, the huge growth in vehicle production in China accounts for

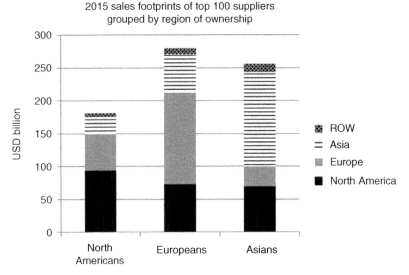

FIGURE 4.6 Sales footprints by regional ownership in 2015
Data source: Automotive News

much of this shift, as European-owned suppliers have tapped into it, as well as the Asian-owned ones. Noticeable is how the North American-owned suppliers have lagged, as Asian and European vehicle manufacturers have taken the lion's share of this growth in China.

## GERMAN SUPPLIERS ARE INCREASINGLY DOMINANT AMONG THE EUROPEANS

German-owned suppliers have consolidated their positions within the European group – see Figure 4.7. Their share of sales has increased from 58 per cent to 67 per cent. The French-owned suppliers have seen their share fall from 25 per cent to 17 per cent. Only Spain has gained share, with the emergence of three Spanish suppliers in the top 100. Of the total of thirty-two European-owned suppliers, eighteen are German and four French. Germany generated 52 per cent of all European automotive patents in 2017, distantly followed by France, many of them from the supplier sector. This is both a reflection and a driver of the dominance of Germany within the European automotive industry.

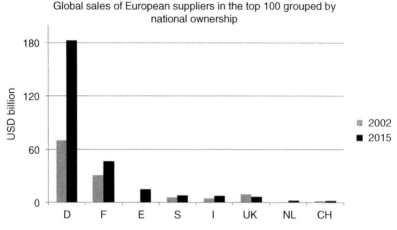

FIGURE 4.7  The growing power of German suppliers
Data source: Automotive News

## THE GLOBAL SUPPLIER OLIGOPOLY IS STABLE AND HARD FOR NEWCOMERS TO PENETRATE

There have been few new entrants from other regions. Of the thirty-nine Asian-owned top 100 groups, no fewer than thirty remain Japanese. There has, however, been a significant incursion of South Korean suppliers, five in number by 2015, the fruit of the huge development of vehicle production by Hyundai-Kia in particular, but also of its efforts to reform and restructure the previously weak national components sector. Only three Chinese suppliers, one Indian and one Singaporean have joined the top table so far. The traditional Western + Japanese oligarchy remains very much in control. These are big companies. Bosch, the largest in 2015, reported sales to automotive OEM (original equipment manufacturers, i.e., vehicle manufacturers) sales of USD44.8 billion.

The heavy investment requirements, coupled with the price pressures that are exerted along all the supply chains, starting from the vehicle manufacturers, have driven a search for global scale and considerable merger and acquisitions activity. The result is now close to a global oligopoly in almost all the specialised supply sectors. Some local sub-contractors remain, providing capacity reserves or

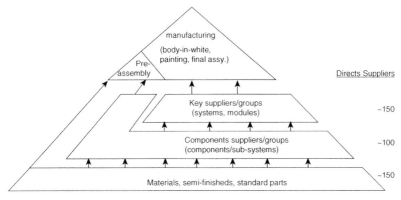

FIGURE 4.8 Tiering in the automotive supply chains
Source: Time for a Model Change

performing assembly tasks, but they are very vulnerable to price pressures and lower-cost competition. Suppliers in general achieve returns on sales (ROS) 1–2 per cent better than those of the vehicle manufacturers, especially if they have their own strong intellectual property, in products or processes.

## THE GROWING COMPLEXITY OF VEHICLES AND PROGRAMMES, AND THE ASSOCIATED TRANSACTION COSTS HAVE DRIVEN A TIERING OF THE SUPPLIER SECTOR

The transactional burden of dealing directly with a huge number of suppliers has already been noted. This has been very greatly reduced by the introduction of a system of progressive delegation. The supplier sector is divided into 'Tiers', denoting the roles and capabilities of the various players (depicted in Figure 4.8).

There is a clear hierarchy, closely matching the physical and virtual (control) structure of the complete vehicle:

- Tier 0: Overall systems integration services, supplied directly to the vehicle manufacturers, when not exercised by them internally
- Tier 1: Systems design and integration, supplied directly to the vehicle manufacturers

- Tier 2: Sub-systems and parts, generally supplied to a Tier 1/Tier 0 supplier
- Tier 3: Standard parts and materials, usually supplied to Tier 1 or 2 suppliers, although sometimes directly to the vehicle manufacturers
- Tier 4: Commodity parts, supplied to all levels

Whereas forty years ago a national vehicle manufacturer would have high integration levels and deal with hundreds if not thousands of primarily national suppliers directly, a global manufacturer now deals mainly with Tier 0 and Tier 1 suppliers, with a few exceptions for materials (e.g. steel coil) and consumables (e.g. adhesives and fasteners). Manufacturers have typically held on to the design and production of these key domains themselves:

- The body shell, with its energy-dissipating crash safety structures, plus doors and hatches.
- The engine, transmission and final drive in most cases. The 'minority' transmissions (automatics in Europe, manuals in the United States) often come from independent suppliers.
- The overall physical design and systems integration of the vehicle as a whole. Much software comes from outside vendors, although Tesla is a notable exception in this respect, having mainly developed its own.

This situation remains stable and is likely to do so in the future, with a structure based on interlocking oligopolies, until there is a revolution in transportation

These arrangements have been stable for a number of years, with little changes in the frontiers between areas of responsibility, indicating that they are effective. Moving to electric drivetrains is likely to increase delegation, with the vehicle manufacturers outsourcing the prime mover. But the biggest shift has been caused by the rapid and large increase in electronic control systems in virtually every function within the vehicle, plus communications and interfacing with the vehicle's environment. Road vehicles have evolved a true nervous system, with intense levels of communication between its parts and, increasingly, with the world beyond the vehicle itself. Concerns about one or more powerful suppliers effectively capturing this heart of the product were already being aired thirty years ago. A complete upset and loss of control by the vehicle manufacturers is probably unlikely as long as automobiles and trucks remain primarily autonomous, under the control of their drivers. All this changes in a world of vehicles automatically driven under central control. In such a scenario, the bodyshell plays a much-reduced role; the dynamic driving performance of the vehicle is greatly reduced and driveline much simplified; the control functions are mainly transferred to an outside central agency. Leadership will pass to providers of transportation services. Uber's attempts to integrate information about public transport facilities into its offering in London is a pointer in this direction. Today's vehicle manufacturers could lose their lead roles.

Within each tier and in each technically specialised domain within the tier, we now have a more or less complete oligarchy of suppliers. Ironically, the least complete oligarchy is that of the vehicle manufacturers themselves. The whole automotive sector in fact consists of a set of interrelated oligopolies, with the notable exception of the downstream sales and service sector, in which the manufacturers have almost universally managed to resist the emergence of large independent retailers, common in sectors such as food.

## THE CLOSED NATURE OF THE SUPPLY CHAINS IS A STRONG BARRIER AGAINST INCURSIONS

In reality, there are no open, fully competitive markets within the industry, as understood by classical microeconomics. There are not, in fact, true market interfaces. These are what we see in a sector such as petroleum and petroleum-based chemicals. If you own an oil well, you can simply sell its output on the Rotterdam spot market, or contract with major customers. And/or build yourself a refinery. You can again sell the motor fuels and naphtha it produces on the open market. You may decide to feed your naphtha into your own catalytic cracker and make ethylene, the basic building block of petrochemistry. You could sell that and/or invest in making polyethylene. And so on, right down to the most complex and expensive chemical entities. Apart from those patented as pharmaceutical products, these are commodities, with usually no more differentiation than by their degree of purity. It all functions like a tree, in which the sap flows from the trunk to the limbs, branches and twigs. Crucially, there is normally a marketplace interface between each of the different levels, in an arborescent set of markets. These are open chains.

The automotive industry functions in reverse. It is like a great river system. Streams flow into rivulets, rivulets into rivers, all converging down to the final estuary. Everything is driven by the end purpose, as in teleological philosophy. In vehicle production at least (the aftermarket is a bit different) intermediate products have no independent value of their own. A brake pad, for example, is only useful once mounted on the vehicle for which it is intended. Otherwise it is of no more use than as a very ugly paperweight. There is no market trading. Volumes and prices are negotiated and contractually set in advance. Because of the natural poly-oligarchical structure of the sector, each producer has rather few customers, who are mainly powerful and able to dictate commercial terms. These are usually negotiated in order to leave enough margin for the supplier to survive and develop their activities – which are essential to their customers. There is commercial conflict but considerable technical mutual dependence. This is not the result of some evil conspiracy or cartel but of the very nature of the end products and the resources deployed to design and manufacture them on a huge scale.

## SUPPLIERS HAVE ALMOST NO INDEPENDENT MARKET POWER BUT A POWERFUL INFLUENCE ON THE TECHNOLOGICAL BASES OF THE INDUSTRY – AND ITS UNIT COSTS

As a result of the concentrated customer structures and contractual relationships, suppliers in general have very little market power. Their brands are largely invisible to the general or motoring public. No one but a participant in the industry, some financiers and enthusiasts know what make of a given component is built into a given model of vehicle. The only clearly visible exceptions are tyres, which have a large aftermarket and strong consumer brands, and which are mainly sold through independent tyre merchants and tyre chains – some of the latter owned by tyre manufacturers. Garage mechanics know their product brands and their customers usually delegate the choice to them. It is also influenced, in the independent aftermarket, by which suppliers the local parts distributors choose to represent. In the franchised dealer aftermarket, almost everything carries the brand of the franchisor, i.e., the vehicle manufacturer. Dealer parts are, in fact, massive private label programmes.

Relationships are not, however, as one-sided as the previous discussion might seem to imply. What the suppliers do have is technological power, as there are so few in any specific sector – which does not preclude them from being in more than one specialised area. As with Bruce Henderson's example of the pre-downsizing American car industry, each oligarchy is in effect self-regulating: if a supplier overprices, they won't secure new contracts; if they underprice, they drive themselves out of business financially. Manufacturers will often single-source for a given model or platform but will not normally do so across their whole model range. They abhor monopolies. They will tolerate these for a while when someone introduces a major technical innovation, such as Bosch with fuel injection or ABS. But they will eventually encourage the emergence of one or more new competitors. The whole system functions more like a feudal society, with its social strata and reciprocal obligations, rather than a market economy. Again, this is not the result of some evil conspiracy but of the very nature of the end products and of the scale of the resources that have to be deployed to design and manufacture them.

## THE WHOLE INDUSTRY IMPERIUM IS HIGHLY DISCIPLINED AND STABLE

The whole set up is in fact remarkably stable and, like a feudal economy, is really only vulnerable to internal acts of outright folly or invasion from outside – which is very difficult to achieve. Each sub-sectoral oligopoly is protected by strong barriers to entry, based on large investments in specific technologies, designs and production facilities. Direct competitive incursions are rare but some family-style relationships have been broken up, notably the traditional Japanese *keiretsu*, in which each manufacturer had its own distinct set of suppliers, who were treated very much like family members, more or less junior. Major technical disruption is a much more serious threat. The industry can no doubt cope with electrification. It won't be sudden, because of the sheer inertial mass of the vehicle parc and consumers' investments in it, plus the obvious challenge of providing recharging points. It can take many forms, from total – BEVs (battery electric vehicles), through PHEVs (plug-in hybrid electric vehicles, with an ICE and generator as range extender), mild hybrid and down to mere stop-and-start with some electrical energy storage. Plain BEVs will be simpler but hybrids are inherently more complex. Some suppliers may disappear, there may be fewer brake pads consumed, thanks to regenerative braking. There already are new suppliers, of batteries, motors, power electronics and control systems. But the structure can cope with all of this, provided the changes are not too sudden. Much more threatening is autonomous driving, which could ultimately change the whole nature of transportation systems and vehicles, and of the industry's technical hierarchies.

The long, complex and hugely invested supply chains all function to the tempo of the product cycle and the production programme. Again, this is no classical market place, in which supply adjusts to demand, with price as the intermediating function. All is planned in advance, more or less accurately, particularly the investments in product development and production capacities. It arguably comes closer to the Soviet Gosplan system than any other sector. The disciplines are quasi-military in nature. And there is no ambiguity about who are the commanders, at least for the present. The vehicle manufacturers rule the system with a rod of iron. They have to. And it is all an enormous and unequalled achievement of industrial planning, investment and discipline.

## COMPLEX SUPPLY TRADE-OFFS ARE MADE BETWEEN PROXIMITY AND PRODUCTION COST

Just as water finds the lowest level it can, so any business sector will tend to seek out the lowest possible cost position. As we have seen, there is a relentless drive to achieve lower cost through maximising the scale of production, of which globalisation, and platform and module strategies, are the most obvious manifestations. It's not all perfect: there is a permanent conflict between trying to have a product for each market mini-segment and standardisation. The latter drive is not helped by the increasing 'tightness' of vehicle designs, intended to minimise aerodynamic resistance and weight while maximising interior space versus exterior size and crash protection. But the overall pressure to contain and reduce costs remains extremely strong. Which is in itself a reason why a given components sector cannot casually or easily be entered into.

Besides scale, the other evident focus is on factor cost, which primarily means labour rates. There are therefore trade-offs constantly made between finding a lower-cost production location and the additional logistical costs thus incurred – and this at all levels of the supply chains. And here the industry often comes into collision with the interests and policies of national and regional governments, as we shall see in the next chapter. All this is very much a function of what systems or parts we are discussing, and of which activities.

## COMPLETELY BUILT-UP LIGHT VEHICLES ARE NOT EXPENSIVE TO SHIP, PARTICULARLY ON MAJOR OCEAN ROUTES

As far as cars and other light vehicles are concerned, transport costs are not a major inhibiting factor to distant sourcing, at least within a continental land mass. Rail, using specialised two- or three-decker carriers, is very effective, where there is a good railway infrastructure, as in Europe or the United States. The normal procedure is to

FIGURE 4.9  Cost-effective shipping of CBUs
Picture credit: Wallenius Wilhelmsen

ship by rail to local distribution centres within a continental region, or to a port for export to another region. Trainloads of cars, or part trainloads incorporated into a freight train, are to be seen everywhere. This has helped enable a steady drift of assembly capacity within Europe from West to East, notably to the Czech Republic, Slovakia, Poland and Rumania, in search of lower wage costs and easier availability of sites for new assembly plants and their surrounding supplier parks. Although the trend, in volume cars at least, has been towards local production, as soon as a distant market becomes significant, a good deal of trans-oceanic shipping of cars and light vehicles still goes on. Unit costs are remarkably low because of the use of huge ro-ro (roll on, roll off) ferries. This is known in the shipping trade as specialised bulk, as the cargo is homogeneous. It also has the unusual and helpful property of loading and unloading itself. The largest such ships can carry up to 6,000 cars at one time. Wallenius Wilhelmsen, one of whose ships is pictured in Figure 4.9, is one of a number of shipping companies that specialise in transporting vehicles of all kinds worldwide. Despite the distance, the costs of shipping CBUs (completely built-up units) have never been much of a protective factor for a local vehicle industry. Nor would they have inhibited its ability to export – large specialised car carrier ships were first built to carry VW Beetles to North America. There is even a shipper that specialises in transporting used cars from Japan to New Zealand. Incidentally, short-sea shipping is also important within Europe and its immediate periphery, as it is in effect a peninsula, with few places far from the sea – as demonstrated by the Vikings centuries ago.

## THE EFFECTIVE SOURCING RADIUS DEPENDS ON WHAT IS BEING SHIPPED

The effective supply radius for systems and components is determined by size, weight, cost and variability (number of different variants used). Seat assemblies, which are bulky, delicate to ship and specific to the individual vehicle, will normally be put together very close to the vehicle assembly line, in the sequence of vehicles moving down that line, and at very short notice. It is now common for suppliers of such items to have their own final operations conducted at a supplier park, within the periphery of the vehicle manufacturer's assembly plant or very close to it. At the other extreme, integrated circuits can come from anywhere in the world. Figure 4.10 illustrates the potential supply radius for some categories of product. It should be emphasised that this is a supply radius within a continental region with a developed transport infrastructure, such as North American or Europe or, increasingly, China. As previously noted, the industry has almost totally adopted just-in-time supply. This gets significantly more difficult if there is an ocean barrier along the way. But within a land region, materials, sub-assemblies and parts move around extensively, sometimes several times over. This is what has made Brexit a major source of uncertainty and concern for the industry in the United Kingdom.

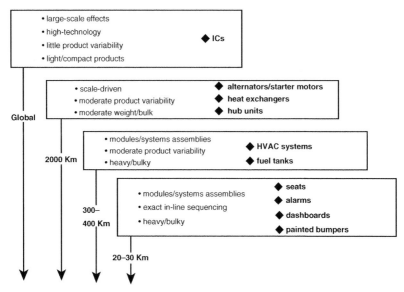

FIGURE 4.10  From how far can I source?
Source: Autopolis

## SUPPLIERS ARE OBLIGED TO FOLLOW THEIR CUSTOMERS
## IN TRANSPLANTING PRODUCTION FACILITIES
## ACROSS THE WORLD

Sub-systems, components and materials suppliers are called upon to support their customers world-wide. This may require co-location with the customers' facilities or location somewhere else within the same country. The latter is often not a matter of cost optimisation but of restrictions to imports in closed markets, a matter to which we return in the next chapter. Even within an open-market region, suppliers build up concentric networks: research and product development will stay in the country of origin of the supplier, as may highly automated operations not sensitive to direct labour costs but requiring very skilled support; applications engineering may be partly decentralised; labour intensive processes, notably assembly, can be decentralised to lower-cost, more distant locations and countries, as long as the products are fairly standardised and do not have to be matched one-for-one to the individual vehicle.

Setting up a CKD (completely-knocked-down) assembly operation in a protected foreign market is not usually a practical problem, although it is an inherently expensive way to do things. A full kit of parts for each car to be built is imported, minus what can be procured locally at lower cost. SKD (semi-knocked-down) is a variant on this, with some parts brought in on a flow basis. One can step up from there to importing parts in bulk and running a full assembly operation. The problems come when the host government insists on a minimum level of local content, in order to ease the burden on the country's balance of payments, to encourage the development of local industries and to create manufacturing jobs. Local enterprises have to be found that can take on the tasks, which essentially involve replicating parts designs from the original suppliers in the vehicle manufacturer's home market. This usually works up to a point. There are often quality and cost problems. The transplanted Japanese manufacturers in the United States encountered them when they at first tried to source from the local supplier community. They were appalled at the performance of the American suppliers they tried to work with. They were forced to persuade their accustomed Japanese suppliers, part of their *keiretsu*, or supplier families, to transplant as well. Committed to achieving 80 per cent European content, these same manufacturers first of all sourced from local UK suppliers for their UK transplant assembly lines. This worked for a while, as long as those suppliers merely had to replicate existing Japanese designs. It ceased to work once they were expected to innovate and seek out lower-cost sources for certain operations and items. The businesses were simply too weak in terms of their engineering and management resources. There can also be problems with what constitutes local content. Some measure it by value, some by weight. Some consider it achieved when the last manufacturing operation is conducted in the host country. We encountered a particularly egregious example of this, with an assembly made in Asia, delivered to an Eastern European country, adorned with a label that read 'Made in xxx' – and therefore considered to be of national origin. The opportunities for creative interpretation and cheating are almost endless – and usually driven by the need to tap into greater economies of scale and lower costs sources via imports, in the face of government restrictions on free trade.

## THERE IS AN IDEAL SEQUENCE OF LOCAL SCALE-BUILDING AND OPENING UP THE MARKET, WHICH IS ONLY VERY RARELY ACHIEVED

It can ultimately work. The historical idealised sequence of development of a local supply sector is outlined in Figure 4.11. In the initial Stage 1, CKD assembly replaces CBU imports; limited local purchases of materials and components are made. In Stage 2, local production of vehicles changes over to normal line assembly, although on a small scale. Local content rules force the creation of a local supply base, much of which will not be internationally competitive, such that vehicle

| Stage | Type | Characteristics |
|---|---|---|
| | Initial | • CKD assembly |
| | | • Limited local purchases |
| 2 | Localisation | • Line assembly |
| | | • Imposed local content |
| | | • Local supply base |
| 3 | Sealing up | • Volume assembly |
| | | • Export facilitation |
| | | • Build-up of scale, specialisation |
| | | • First exports |
| 4 | Integration | • Specialisation |
| | | • Built into regional supply chains |

FIGURE 4.11 Supply industry historical development sequence

exports are only possible through heavy subsidies. In Stage 3, vehicle assembly, focused on a strictly limited number of products, passes the volume threshold at which they can be exported. The foreign currency gained can be applied to importing other vehicles and those systems and components that cannot be competitively sourced from within the country. This is typically helped by getting global suppliers to set up locally, providing technological and engineering support from their home bases, and taking the exports into their own commercial relationship networks. In Stage 4, the tariff and quota barriers are removed. Competitive local suppliers supply into the parent region.

Reaching Stage 4 – establishing a viable, internationally competitive local supply sector – assumes certain critical conditions, particularly great-enough scale. There must be enough local vehicle production volume for some local components manufacturing to reach critical scale. This does not have to be true of all categories of parts. Local factor costs and business conditions must be favourable, including enlightened support from local government agencies. Internal and international logistic infrastructure and operations must be efficient with respect to cost and time. Foreign parent companies must be willing and able to incorporate their local operations into their global networks. Under these circumstances, the comparative advantages of different locations can be brought into mutually reinforcing play. A component best made in a highly automated facility will be produced in an advanced economy, best able to support that kind of operation. It will be shipped to a lower-cost country for labour-intensive assembly into a system, which can then be used in a local assembly plant and also exported, the whole network operating on a just-in-time basis. This typically happens in countries or regions clustered around a major automotive region. This concept is developed further in Chapter 5. It is much more problematic where distant territories are concerned. Note that the supply chains, extended though they may be physically, are still essentially closed ones. It is simply not possible for a small local supplier independently to approach foreign customers in the industry and hope to obtain business in this industry. Booths at trade fairs alone won't do it.

IN SUMMARY, THE SUPPLY SECTOR IS CENTRAL
TO THE AUTOMOTIVE INDUSTRY BUT DIFFICULT
FOR LOCAL SUPPLIERS TO BREAK INTO

Designing and mass-producing increasingly complex automobiles is a daunting task. The pioneers, operating on a tiny scale, often had to make most of the vehicle themselves. High levels of vertical integration on the part of the vehicle manufacturers persisted into the era of mass-production of single models, infrequently and little modified. As production volumes exploded and products proliferated after World War II, it became impossible for manufacturers to carry so much of the burden of design and production themselves. The changes were gradual but, over forty years, the share of suppliers in the value of vehicles tripled, from 25 per cent to 75 or even 80 per cent. Combined with the growth of vehicle production, this gain share of value propelled a huge growth in the supply sector, far outpacing that of the manufacturers. Out of this have emerged very large global players – the sales of the largest ones exceed those of many vehicle manufacturers. The suppliers are true technological specialists of the industry, required to make their own massive investments in technology development, product design and production facilities. The suppliers have gone even further than the vehicle manufacturers in globalising their businesses, driven to it by both their customers and their insatiable hunger for scale, under heavy pricing pressure. The move of vehicle production towards Asia and China in particular has been matched in the supply sector, with most growth in Asia/China and least in North America. While market shares have shifted, an unshaken oligopoly remains in place. German suppliers have become increasingly dominant among the Europeans. The global supplier oligopoly is stable and very difficult for a newcomer to penetrate. Thus Asian-owned suppliers are still dominated by Japanese companies. There are very few South Koreans in the club and even fewer Chinese or Indians. The growing complexity of vehicles and programmes, and the associated transaction costs have driven a tiering of the supply sector, which has radically reduced the number of suppliers that each customer has to deal with. This situation remains stable and is likely to remain so in the future, with a structure based on inter-locking oligopolies, until there is a revolution in transportation. The closed nature of the supply chains makes new incursions very difficult. Suppliers have almost no independent market power but a powerful control over the technological bases of the industry – and its unit costs. The whole industry imperium is highly disciplined and stable. Complex supply trade-offs are made between proximity and production cost. Completely built-up light vehicles are not expensive to ship, particularly on major ocean routes. The effective sourcing radius depends on what is being shipped. Suppliers are obliged to follow their customers in transplanting production facil-ities across the world. There is an ideal sequence of local scale-building and opening up the market, which is only very rarely achieved, with a country's automotive industry truly founded on comparative advantage.

# 5    Tense Relationships: the Automotive Industry and Government

### THE AUTOMOTIVE INDUSTRY HAS ALWAYS BEEN UNDER PUBLIC SURVEILLANCE

While they have brought us enormous benefits, automobiles are obviously potentially dangerous if badly used. This has caused them to be subject to safety-related regulation from their earliest days – the legendary man with a red flag who was required to precede them in the United Kingdom, to warn other road users of the approaching juggernaut. The UK's Driver and Vehicle Standards Agency publishes a rather charming historical account of the progressive introduction and tightening of safety requirements since the Motor Car Act of 1903 first required driving licences.[1] The results are quite striking: the number of vehicles on the road in Britain was multiplied by more than tenfold from 1937 to the present day, whereas the number of road deaths per year halved.

All this has been achieved at the cost of considerable effort, sometimes against stiff resistance. Even today, there has been vocal opposition in France to the reduction from 1 July 2018 of the national speed limit on undivided roads outside urban areas from 90 to 80 km/hour. Yet the results have been impressive across the developed world. But the 80:20 observation prevails: the developing world generates 20 per cent of the vehicle-km but 80 per cent of the casualties. It is a matter of inexperienced and often irresponsible driving; poor road infrastructure, without segregation of pedestrians, cyclists, animals and motor vehicles; and vehicles in poor

---

[1]    www.gov.uk/government/publications/history-of-road-safety-and-the-driving-test/
history-of-road-safety-the-highway-code-and-the-driving-test.

condition and frequently overloaded. Progress in road safety comes under these three main chapters: behaviour, infrastructure, vehicles.

The idea of motor vehicles travelling at high speeds in opposite directions along undivided roads with no grade separation at intersections and often poor lines of sight is a frightening one. The miracle is that there are not more accidents, at least in the long-motorised societies. Only a small proportion of roads were originally built with the motorcar in mind. Most country roads and city streets correspond more to the age of the horse and mule. It is a tribute to the self-discipline of the great majority of drivers that motor vehicles collide with each other, with other road users, or with static objects so infrequently. Great strides have been made in driver education and training, and in enforcement of traffic laws. But there remain many lapses in attention, judgement and behaviour, which still need to be worked upon, most especially in the newly motorised countries. Road signage and signalling have also made dramatic progress, and not only reduce the likelihood and severity of impacts but also traffic congestion. The ethos is still mainly libertarian: that the motor car is a great instrument of freedom, and that access to the road infrastructure should be mainly unrestricted and free. But we shall most likely see further and further restrictions until we perhaps have to file journey plans and book slots, as has long been the case with flying, whether commercial or private. Tolling on specific highways, tunnels and crossings is broadly accepted, although to a different degree in different countries. The mere idea of universal tolling, i.e., charging for all use of the public infrastructure, as a function of time and journey, remains politically challenging, although technically feasible already. But there is broad social acceptance, at least in the well-motorised countries, of checks on speeding and driving under the influence of alcohol or drugs. It is all part of the age-old tension between individual irresponsibility and societal norms.

## VEHICLE SAFETY STANDARDS WERE THE FIRST AREA
## OF CONFLICT

The first area of conflict between the industry and governments is of course that of vehicle safety standards. Speedometers and safety glass in windscreens became compulsory in the United Kingdom in 1937. Since then, safety standards have proliferated. In Europe, they are now mainly set by UNECE, the United Nations Economic Conference for Europe, based in Geneva; in the United States, by the National Highway Transportation Safety Agency (NHTSA). They now cover virtually every aspect of the vehicle and its use, and must be adhered to by both domestically produced and imported ones, under a system of type approval. The aspect most visible to the public is the protection of the occupants of vehicles in the event of a collision, with another vehicle or a stationary object. The costs of this are high in terms of both the price of new cars and of added weight, which conflicts with the reduction of fuel consumption and $CO_2$ emissions. A whole complex engineering science has developed around the absorption of the energy of impact by means of crumple zones, while safely channelling it around a rigid cell that protects the occupants. In parallel, much effort has gone into restraining occupants from being hurled around inside the safety cell or even ejected from it, and limiting injuries to them when they do hit an interior surface. Seat belts started to come in during the 1960s and have become universal, with fastening them a legal requirement. Pre-tensioners have enhanced their effectiveness. Airbags, steadily increasing in number, provide even more effective protection. The automotive industry can be proud of the improvement in passive safety, i.e., the reduction of the risk of death or injury once a collision is happening that has been achieved over the last 50 years.

Again, this has not been without conflict. It took time for attitudes to change – particularly on the side of the industry. The initial trigger point in the United States was arguably the 1965 publication of Ralph Nader's classic, *Unsafe at Any Speed: The Designed-In Dangers of the American Automobile,* which particularly criticised GM's innovative (for the United States) Corvair, with its rear-mounted air-cooled engine, and generally accused Detroit of ignoring safety. The National Traffic and Motor Vehicle Safety Act of 1966 mandated the authority of the NHTSA to develop and enforce safety requirements. Its first notable action was to impose the mounting of seat belts in new road vehicles. Even this modest measure was controversial, with some claiming that forcing occupants to wear them was an infringement on personal liberty. The statistics on lives saved were irrefutable, however. A long succession of other measures followed. But the industry continued to drag its feet. In 1972, Lee Iacocca, president of Ford Motor Company, famously said that safety didn't sell cars. General Motors tried offering airbags in the early 1970s and gave up, in the face of minimal customer interest. Perhaps they were not adequately promoted. Chrysler opposed them for a number of years. The only manufacturer to actively promote safety in the United States was Volvo, which acquired the culture through its Swedish home. This only appealed to a minority audience.

## THE AUTOMOTIVE INDUSTRY LONG TRIED TO IGNORE THE RESULTS OF INDEPENDENT CRASH SAFETY TESTING BUT EVENTUALLY HAD TO YIELD

As an example of the resistance, the US automotive industry long tried to ignore the results of independent crash testing of its products, the New Car Assessment Program (NCAP), introduced 1979 by the NHTSA. The same attitude initially prevailed in Europe. Euro NCAP is a voluntary vehicle safety rating system created by Vägverket (the Swedish National Road Administration), FIA (the Fédération Internationale de l'Automobile) and International Consumer Research & Testing, and backed by the European Commission, seven European governments, as well as motoring and consumer organisations in every EU country. Note the Swedish origins of the programme and the fact that it was supported by government and consumer agencies. In the early 1990s, independent crash testing was viewed by the European industry as an infringement upon their prerogatives, a quite undue interference into the way in which they conducted their business. The tide started to change, however, on both sides of the Atlantic in the early 1990s, with consumers taking notice of safety features and beginning to demand them. The attitudes of vehicle manufacturers changed and crash safety began to be treated as a marketable characteristic. Obtaining five stars in NCAP or EuroNCAP ratings has become a matter of advertiseable pride. And NCAP testing has spread to Australasia (ANCAP), Latin America (Latin NCAP) and China (C-NCAP). The NCAP family's safety reports are based on the performance of the vehicles in a variety of crash tests, including front, side and pole impacts, and impacts with pedestrians.

A long list of vehicle design standards has been developed, from lighting to outside rearview mirrors to fuel tanks. The regulations seek to protect not only the occupants of a vehicle but others, such as pedestrians, who may come into accidental violent contact with it. Consumers have generally accepted the extra costs involved. But it is clear that the initiative has come not from the industry, which has to bear the extra product costs, nor from consumers who lack the information to press for such measures, but from public and semi-public bodies. There is no progress without this continuing creative tension. The results have been wholly positive. Once the tide turned, vehicle manufacturers co-operated actively and vigorously. A considerable body of knowledge has grown up in the field of secondary crash safety, i.e., protecting vehicle occupants and others from the consequences of an impact that is happening. This involves very sophisticated design of safety cells and energy-dissipating structures and pathways, greatly improved restraints for occupants within the safety cell and pedestrian impact protection. The chances of death or serious injury resulting from most impacts have been very substantially reduced. They can, of course, never be wholly eliminated.

Of note is the increasing emphasis in recent years on active safety, i.e., trying to avoid a crash or make it less severe. ABS (anti-lock braking system) was an early innovation in this respect, followed by stability control, cruise control and proximity detection, lane wandering detection and driver drowsiness alerts. All these features, which to a degree substitute an automatic system for the driver, have been made technically possible and economically accessible through control electronics. The ultimate goal, of course, is autonomous driving, which promises to take the fallible driver out of the control loops entirely. If and when it comes, it will completely change the nature of driving, of the automobile – and of the industry. Again, the pressure for it comes from outside agencies – safety agencies but also, most notably, the IT giants. This is the ultimate threat and sunset scenario for the conventional automotive industry and much more profound one than simply putting in all- or part-electric drivetrains.

## ENVIRONMENTAL PROTECTION AND FUEL CONSUMPTION HAVE BECOME THE MAJOR SOURCES OF CONFLICT IN MORE RECENT TIMES

Time was when the tobacco industry actually claimed that smoking was beneficial for health, in the face of all the medical and epidemiological evidence. How that has changed! In the good old days in the United States, from 1945 to the mid-1970s, no one cared too much about automotive emissions or fuel consumption. There seemed to be an endless availability of fresh air and $1 would buy you five gallons or more of gasoline at the gas station. Happy days! 'Tomorrow's roads today', proclaimed a Maryland state government poster of 1962. Motoring was good for America and for Americans. The more the better.

But soon the sunny picture darkened. By the early 1960s, it became clear that the Los Angeles Basin, prone to atmospheric temperature inversions, was suffering from an increasingly serious problem with photochemical smog, traced back to tailpipe emissions from its huge and growing automobile population. The freeway culture had collided with the environment. CARB, the California Air Resources Board, was signed into existence by the then governor, Ronald Reagan – a Republican. There was a clear mandate to do something and CARB acquired considerable powers, including that of setting auto emissions standards for California, by delegation from Washington, something that no other state of the Union could do. It conducted and contracted much research into atmospheric photochemistry and set demanding standards for future vehicles that would be permitted to operate on California roads. Other jurisdictions, in Washington and in Europe, followed its lead. It formulated requirements for decreasingly polluting vehicles using conventional drivelines and fought many battles with Detroit, which insisted that these were technically impossible or at least impossibly expensive. CARB largely won these arguments, for example, demonstrating that a conventionally powered ULEV (ultra-low emissions vehicle) car would incur an additional factory cost of only $70. It did less well in trying to force the manufacturers to achieve 10 per cent of their sales in the form of ZEVs (zero-emissions vehicle), i.e., BEVs (pure battery electrics). Recharging from the electricity mains merely shifted the emissions from Los Angeles to the hugely polluting Four Corners coal-fired power station in New Mexico. GM made a valiant attempt to produce a marketable ZEV but the EV1, massively heavy thanks to its large lead-acid battery pack and with a distinct preference for travelling in straight lines, found barely any takers because of the vast inconvenience that resulted from its limited range and long charging time. This was idea well ahead of its time and of the technology of that time.

## THERE HAS BEEN A CONTINUOUS CLASH BETWEEN ENVIRONMENTAL GOOD INTENTIONS AND REALITY, AS PERCEIVED BY THE INDUSTRY

Here was a classic clash between what was often portrayed as environmental virtue and the industry's resistance and scheming. The problem being, of course, that the industry has always been very heavily invested in its existing technologies, perfected over decades, and which have given very good service – except with respect to emissions. More progress was achieved by sensible innovation, notably the fitting of three-way exhaust catalysts, to deal with NOx, CO and unburnt fuel – and by the influx into California of smaller, lighter and more fuel-efficient Japanese cars. But Detroit's image was tarnished and its competitive position in its home market weakened. Nevertheless, the exhaust emissions control technologies, involving both catalysts and the ultimately near-universal adoption of fuel injection in the place of carburettors and of electronic engine management systems did the trick with noxious emissions – or seemed to have done.

Reducing fuel consumption had never been a major objective in the United States, until its domestic oil reserves and production started to run down, and its vulnerable dependence on oil imported from unfriendly or potentially unstable sources became evident. As related earlier, higher taxes on motor fuels have been and remain a political non-starter there. European countries, in contrast, taxed these fuels heavily from early on, in part to protect the balance of payments, as there were very few domestic oil fields until the North Sea discoveries, and as a very convenient source of tax revenues, along with alcohol and tobacco. Forced downsizing through the CAFE regulations were not a great success in the United States, driving many consumers away from passenger cars. Other countries, such as Canada and Australia, taxed at a level between the United States and Europe. Oil-producing countries and even China until recently taxed negligibly or even subsidised motor fuels. The invention of fracking and the consequent access to massive new oil reserves within the continental United States, which have restored its lost position as the world's #1 oil producer, seem for a while to justify the American way.

## GREENHOUSE GAS EMISSIONS HAVE NOW TAKEN OVER AS THE MAJOR AREA OF CONCERN – AND CONFLICT

Now global warming has emerged as a real planetary issue to spoil the party once again. This is, of course, a hugely contentious issue, philosophically and politically. Suffice it to say that the great majority of governments did become concerned with reducing GHG (greenhouse gas) emissions, and notably that of $CO_2$ from road vehicles, particularly cars. Road transport is not the largest global contributor but it is the fastest growing, apart from aviation. The three main automotive regions followed different paths: downsizing of cars in the United States, with smaller engines; mild hybrids, pioneered with great courage in a small car by Toyota with the Prius, in Japan; and the diesel engine in Europe. Diesel engines had already taken over in heavy trucks and buses, in railway locomotives and in ship propulsion from the 1930s. Mercedes built diesel cars as early as 1936 but these remained very unattractive, although fuel-efficient, for a long time – under-powered, noisy and unpleasant to drive. GM tried dieselising some its larger cars in response to CAFE. The results were so unattractive that they put the American public off diesel cars for a generation. Japan never accepted them. But, for the European manufacturers, they became the magic solution to reconciling fuel efficiency with driveability, once the common rail injection system had been developed, which enabled very precise and even multiple bursts of fuel supply straight into the cylinders of small engines, as in large truck, railway and marine engines. And this was especially true for larger, faster premium European cars, particularly when a larger diesel engine, of two-litre cubic capacity and upwards is paired with a modern multi-ratio automatic transmission. Diesel penetration of the new car market reached 80 per cent for these and over 50 per cent for all new cars. There were wide variations between countries, much influenced by government fuel taxation policies. In Southern Europe, diesel fuel was taxed significantly less than gasoline, so it could cost 30 per cent less at the pump. This, together with the better fuel economy of diesel cars, was a powerful incentive for consumers to buy them. These were further reinforced when governments introduced first registration fees and annual vehicle taxes that were strongly slanted in favour of vehicles that had low $CO_2$ emission. All in a good cause and the European industry enthusiastically played along. It had found its silver bullet. Or so it was thought.

## DIESELGATE IN EUROPE IS A SYMBOL OF WHAT HAPPENS WHEN CONFLICTING OBJECTIVES ARE NOT CLEARLY AND TRANSPARENTLY DEALT WITH

Unfortunately, there was a worm in the beautiful shiny diesel car apple. Diesel engines are more fuel efficient than gasoline engines because they operate at higher temperatures and pressures. They therefore generate more nitrogen oxides ($NO_x$), which are dangerous lung irritants. They also require the injection of the fuel as a fine mist of tiny droplets at the top of the compression stroke. The droplets do not burn completely, causing the engine to emit very fine sooty particles under ten microns in diameter, which are carcinogenic. Particulate emissions can be reduced by decreasing the fuel/air ratio but this exacerbates the $NO_x$ problem. That can be reduced by increasing the fuel/air ratio but that increases the particulate emissions and increases fuel consumption. The solution is to find the best balance and then remove the pollutants from the exhaust gases. Particulate filters can handle the particulates and are periodically cleaned by an extra injection of fuel causing them to be burnt off the filter surfaces. $NO_x$ can be dealt with by injecting a urea solution into the exhaust. This reacts with the $NO_x$ to produce water and $CO_2$ in small quantities. This is the AdBlue system. It means, of course, an extra tank for the urea, a dosing pump, pipe work and a control system, which is all additional cost. Many European manufacturers decided they could forgo this by simply better tuning the injection system. It didn't work on the road, with $NO_x$ emissions many times greater than the legal limit. So they decided to cheat by burying a routine in the control system that applied a different injection regime when the vehicle is on the test stand than when it is being driven on the road. Almost inevitably, they were found out, by American academics as it happens. And that was the beginnings of Dieselgate, which has led to massive fines, lawsuits, dismissals and resignations, and even arrests.

Claims that this was the work of engineers somewhere down the management chain who did it because they couldn't meet their objectives won't wash. Everything is meticulously documented in this industry, notably in order to trace origins and attribute blame (preferably to a supplier) if something does go wrong. These were conscious decisions on the part of senior management. But why take such a lunatic risk? Why did no one challenge the decisions? One reason is cultural: as was explained earlier, the industry is very hierarchical and authoritarian, to an almost military degree. These are giant corporations, with long histories and strong individual traditions that think highly of themselves. To admit to a major mistake is very difficult for them. And consider what happens to the competitor who takes the initiative in this, if the others don't then follow their lead. There is a certain herd instinct. This is, in fact, a very conservative industry where technical risk is concerned.

## THE CONSTANT UNDERLYING FACTOR IS INADEQUATE UNDERSTANDING OF EACH OTHER'S PURPOSES AND CONSTRAINTS

The other factor, which is central to the argument of this book, is the nature and quality of the industry's relationships with governments. The CEO of a large supplier commented to us many years ago that the industry wasn't very good at them. The industry fundamentally believes that it should set its own rules – witness the initial hostility to independent crash testing – and tends to oppose the tightening of regulations. The numerous cases of industry foot dragging and claims that something is impossible, followed by surrender and the thing becoming possible have made legislators and regulators suspicious. They therefore up the ante to put more pressure on the industry. There were prolonged confrontations between the industry and the European Commission over the mandatory fitting of three-way catalysts and then, critically, over progressively tougher $CO_2$ emissions limits. Negotiations over the latter were particularly tough but the European industry thought it had successfully achieved a four-dimensional optimisation, similar to squaring the circle or cubing the sphere, in reconciling emissions standards, driveability $CO_2$ limits and unit costs, to give itself a unique competitive advantage.

## THESE PROBLEMS ALSO DANGEROUSLY COMPROMISE THE INDUSTRY'S REPUTATION AND IMAGE

The resulting political and media scandal also shone the spotlight on a parallel problem: misleading fuel economy figures. It has long been known in the industry that the rolling road test cycles that were in use until very recently were not representative of real driving conditions. Also, the vehicles were prepared such that they did not correspond to the ones users actually drive. Tyres were pumped up to reduce rolling resistance, to a point which could make the vehicles unsafe in road usage. Gaps and apertures were taped over to smooth airflow. Outside protuberances were removed. Accessory drives were disconnected. Real consumption figures are as much as 20 per cent higher than those given by the tests. Governments did not challenge this. There was a kind of tacit agreement over it. Although much has been made in the media of late that this is defrauding consumers, they are in fact used to treating this kind of information relatively, i.e., to make comparisons between different offerings. No one believes they will get the broadband speed advertised by their provider but the data are still useful in choosing between them, as long as it's not wildly distorted. But that doesn't work with government $CO_2$ emissions standards, which are absolute numbers to be respected. And especially not when the results put individual models into lower tax classes than they should. Nothing offends governments more than businesses cheating on taxes. Competition authorities also greatly dislike collusive behaviour and the abuse of dominant positions. The European industry did not endear itself with the Commission though its attempts to prevent EU citizens from buying cars across borders and by its actions in the service and parts aftermarket.

All these things have contributed to an atmosphere of mistrust. A very successful, important and powerful industry quite naturally feels that it is entitled to sympathetic regulation. In the case of Europe, a procedurally strong but politically weak Union (it is not a federal state) is vulnerable to lobbying pressure from a sector that is extremely important for some Member States. The US government has the power to influence and guide the industry but has been politically forced to exercise it in sometimes distorted ways, as we saw over fuel economy standards.

## THE INDUSTRY REMAINS A POWERFUL WORLD OLIGARCHY AND LOBBY, ABLE TO PLAY GOVERNMENTS ON SECTORAL DEVELOPMENT POLICY

The primary subject of this book is sectoral development policy. This is a further and very important dimension of the relationship between the automotive industry and the government of nations or regions that play host to it. Governments – national or supra-national, as in the case of the EU – are conflicted over the industry. On the one hand, they want to enforce competition rules and technical standards. On the other, they want their automotive industry to prosper, if they have one. The industry is very large and a mainstay of the economy in some countries, and has considerable lobbying power, which it does not hesitate to use. It is ever ready to dangle the carrot of economic development and employment, or to wave the stick of plant closures and job losses. In the countries where it is strongest, it places itself in the 'too big to fail' category. The industry is often portrayed – or portrays itself – as 'strategic', principally because of its undoubted contribution in the United States and Britain to victory in World War II. But also, perhaps less obviously, to that of the USSR, which was able to out-produce Germany in tanks, thanks to its previous huge investment in building tractors and combine harvesters, plus diesel engines to power them, as part of the collectivisation of agriculture in the 1930s. Countries that have an automotive industry seek to keep it. Many that do not would like to have one. It is, in many cases, an affair of state – but of a state that is in effect running to catch up with the industry.

In a purely free trade world, based on comparative advantage alone, the industry would remain centred in its major markets, with most production based there. New markets would be served by means of exports of built-up vehicles, especially given the low cost of transporting them by sea. Of course, the world is not so simple and is to a large degree founded upon trading blocs, with many tariff and non-tariff barriers to trade remaining, particularly for motor vehicles. The industry can largely make its own locational decisions, based on the economic rational of sourcing radii, within those blocs and as a function of the tariff and non-tariff barriers that separate them. The automotive industry development cycle is by now well established, as was briefly discussed in Chapter 4:

- As a national economy reaches the take-off point, demand for automobiles explodes – there is a powerful threshold effect in operation, situated somewhere around USD5,000 in personal disposable income per capita. This soon causes the national government to close off the market to imports, both to ease the drain on the balance of payments (unless it is an oil producer) and to protect a fledgling national industry, where there is one.
- The first step is to ban imports of CBUs (completely built-up units). The industry's first response to this is to import CKD (completely knocked-down) kits, each containing the parts for an individual car.
- Then pressure comes on to source locally, initially for the easiest items. Local content requirements then grow, forcing the progressive establishment of a full local supply base. This is often flanked by incentives to export, which can be rewarded by the right to import non-local models and components.
- Attempting complete autarchy rarely works, especially as the technological base of road vehicles has both broadened and deepened, driven by market and regulatory pressures, unless a country has a sufficiently large internal market.
- Other countries can stay in the game as linked-in players, deploying a limited set of functions – with the links established within the global empires of the largest manufacturers. Others may continue as pure manufacturing satellites, generally offering lower wage rates at the periphery of the major automotive regions. But this is a precarious position, always vulnerable to displacement by a yet-lower-cost country.

## COUNTRIES CAN BE CLASSIFIED BY THEIR ROLES
## WITHIN THE GLOBAL AUTOMOTIVE INDUSTRY

In Figure 5.1, we show 2017 world production by region. Within each region we have loosely categorised the different vehicle-building countries of the world into three categories, in decreasing order of national control over the industry:

- **Core:** those countries with a full set of automotive capabilities under their ownership and control. This includes full vehicle engineering and production but also a substantially complete set of systems and components suppliers.
- **Major Satellite:** those countries which produce substantial volumes of vehicles but which do so largely under the control of foreign companies. In some cases these are countries that used to be core but have lapsed from it as the automotive industry has globalised.
- **Peripheral:** smaller producers, under the control of foreign companies.

The categories are not wholly 'clean', in that core countries also are hosts to other countries' satellites, often from more than one country; and companies' product development, production and sourcing networks do not always coincide. R&D and major product development are usually centred upon the home country but applications engineering is often decentralised. This is true of both vehicle manufacturers and suppliers.

The results may seem surprising, particularly the high proportion of non-core, and especially the categorisation of China as a satellite country. This is the direct result of the globalisation of the industry that has taken place under the continued control of the established oligarchy of vehicle manufacturers, discussed in Chapter 3. With varying degrees of success, national governments have tried to lure vehicle manufacturing to their shores but any success in that respect has typically complied with the rules of that oligarchy.

There is only a handful of what can be described as core automotive countries within Europe:

|  | Million units 2017 |
| --- | --- |
| Germany | 5.6 |
| France | 2.2 |
| Italy | 1.1 |
| Sweden | 0.2 |
| European Core | 9.2 |
| European Major Satellites | 10.2 |
| European Periphery | 3.2 |
| CIS | 1.6 |
| USA | 11.2 |
| North America Satellites | 6.3 |
| South America | 3.3 |
| Japan | 9.7 |
| South Korea | 4.1 |
| Malaysia | 0.5 |
| Asia Satellites | 37.0 |
| Asia-Oceania Periphery | 1.0 |

FIGURE 5.1 National vehicle production in million units in 2017 by degree of control
Data source: OICA statistics

- Germany is a clear one, with a full set of technological, engineering and production capabilities, home to VW as one of the three global mega-groups in volume cars, as well as Ford of Europe and Opel (now owned by PSA). It is also home to the three leading premium car producers – Audi, BMW and Mercedes – and to the specialist Porsche. It builds over 5 million vehicles a year. It increasingly dominates the automotive sector in Europe. It is by far the greatest generator of automotive patents within Europe (Figure 5.2), ahead of Japan and well ahead of the United States in this respect. It is home to 18 of the top 100 suppliers, on a par with the United States but behind Japan. All these firms have worldwide plant networks. As described earlier, successive German governments have consistently supported their national automotive industry for the past eighty years and more, with a considerable degree of success. The industry, led in this respect by the VW group, has re-established German influence over the country's historical Central European hinterland and further afield into Latin America, Spain and – most significantly – China.

| | | |
|---|---|---|
| Germany | 2,556 | 52% |
| France | 803 | 16% |
| Sweden | 343 | 7% |
| Italy | 309 | 6% |
| United Kingdom | 200 | 4% |
| Switzerland | 128 | 3% |
| Austria | 113 | 2% |
| Peripheral states | 183 | 10% |
| Total European region | 1,935 | 100% |

FIGURE 5.2 Automotive patents granted in
Europe in 2017
Data source: ACEA automobile industry
pocket guide, 2018–2019

- France still hosts two major manufacturers, Renault and PSA. The former is global but really only through its control of Nissan. PSA is still mainly European and has reinforced this regional focus through its acquisition of Opel/Vauxhall from GM. Light vehicle production in France has halved from its historical maximum of over 3.5 million and the French components sector has only a few global players. State intervention in industry has always been strong in France, following the mercantilist policy pioneered by Louis XIV's great finance minister, Colbert. Renault was nationalised in 1945, ostensibly because its founder Louis Renault was deemed to have been a collaborator under the Occupation. State influence has persisted, with a minority shareholding, even after Renault was privatised. The automotive industry has been a national development priority but with less effect than in Germany. There is a permanent conflict between allowing it to develop internationally and prioritising job creation in France.
- Italy is almost out of the race, with very much diminished national production and a national champion, Fiat, that leans heavily on its acquisition of Chrysler for any semblance of global presence. Gone are the days when it was difficult to determine whether Italy was Fiat or Fiat was Italy. Fiat had considerable international influence in the past, investing heavily in Brazil and in the Soviet bloc. The components industry is very much thinned out, with Magneti-Marelli its most consequent member.

There is a long tradition of government influence over industry in Italy, symbolised by the creation of IRI (the Istituto Ricostruzione Industriale) in the early 1920s, in fact pre-dating the Fascist state. Post–World War II governments strongly supported Fiat and Alfa Romeo in the past but at the price of distorting investment decisions, notably through the creation of major assembly plants in the underdeveloped Mezzogiorno. This is another example of conflict of priorities between industry and government.

- Sweden is an interesting case of a small country that is home to a disproportionate number of large players: Volvo Cars (now owned by Geely, which provides scale gains for both), with a semi-premium positioning, a reputation for safety engineering and a unique image; and Volvo Trucks and Scania (owned by VW); plus SKF and Autoliv, both global component suppliers.

There is a substantial contribution by satellite countries in the European automotive region, some of which are large producers:

- Spain out-produces France with 2.8 million units per year but is not an industry leader, with all its assembly plants in foreign ownership and only a limited Spanish-owned supplier sector. The Spanish government pragmatically facilitated the transformation from a closed and autarchic automotive economy to one integrated into the European region, putting activity and employment ahead of national pride. Spain under General Franco was a closed automotive market, surrounded by high tariff walls, with a dominant and highly protected national manufacturer, SEAT, building products licenced from Fiat. This was part of General Franco's fiercely mercantilist economic policy. Anyone entering the Spanish automotive industry was required to achieve 90 per cent local content, off a low-volume and uncompetitive set of national suppliers, and to fulfil export quotas in return for tax exemptions and other financial support. Renault and later PSA attacked this near-monopoly, establishing major plants in Spain, operating under the existing local-content regime. The required vehicle exports were absorbed into their European distribution networks, as their plants in Spain built vehicles identical to those made in France, except for one curiosity, the Renault 7, a four-door saloon version of the Renault 5. Ford, anticipating the death of Franco and Spain's eventual entry into the EEC, acted completely differently. Needing an extra assembly plant for the then new Fiesta, it made a deal with Spain whereby it could source parts from wherever it wanted, against a commitment to export twice the value of its imports. By our calculations at the time, this gave it a 15–20 per cent unit cost advantage against SEAT in particular. The so-called Ford Law therefore put a 10 per cent ceiling on Ford's market share in Spain, to prevent it from doing too much damage to the established domestic competitors. Its new plant in Valencia (opened in 1976) exported two-thirds of the 250,000 cars it produced per year, which Ford could easily absorb into the rest of Europe, as the Fiesta was its first B-class car. GM Europe eventually followed suit with a large plant in Zarragoza, which also exports most of its output. This is a classic example of the breakdown of national tariff and non-tariff barriers and of the merging of a national industry into a larger whole, Europe in this instance. It also illustrates the power that a major world vehicle manufacturer can exert over a national government.

- The United Kingdom, building 1.8 million units in 2017, follows, again as a result of a pragmatic revolution. Having failed to support its national industry effectively, with the result that it virtually died, the British government invited in the Japanese transplants and did not seek to oppose Tata's later acquisition of Jaguar-Land Rover. But ideology is now trumping business reality and Brexit is a mortal threat to the transplants, which rely on complete logistical integration with the rest of Europe. There were no white knights for the British-owned supply sector, which almost disappeared. The patent statistics in Figure 5.2 underline how much of a satellite Britain is within the European automotive industry.

- Turkey (1.7 million units) is another case of a country that has moved from attempted autarchy to regional integration, with a number of foreign-owned assembly plants, some suppliers and mainly exporting into the European Union. Renault faced a somewhat similar situation in Turkey as in Spain in the late 1970s. A closed market, 90 per cent local content required of manufacturers, with pressure to export. Both Renault and Fiat had plants in Turkey at Bursa, the former in a joint venture with the Turkish army NCOs' retirement fund, Oyak. It built the Renault 12, identical with that built in France, but at 60,000 units per year, compared with the 500,000 units capacity of Renault's giant assembly plant in Flins outside Paris. Bursa achieved excellent quality and the low cost of Turkish labour compared to French more than compensated for the lesser scale in the labour-intensive assembly operations. Engine and transmission production was with individual machine tools instead of transfer lines, imposing a cost penalty of about 10 per cent on the complete car. The disaster was in component procurement. Most had to be sourced in Turkey, to achieve the 90 per cent local content. Local sources were in the main hopelessly uncompetitive on cost and quality (the lack of which creates additional cost because of rejects), with some parts costing 1,000 per cent of what they did in France. Aluminium from the state monopoly supplier was at twice the world market price. The net result was a car with a manufacturing cost of 170 per cent of its French equivalent. The option of 'doing a Ford' was considered, involving a full-scale 250,000 unit/year assembly plant, exporting two-thirds of its volume. The economics worked, the politics could not: 'which of our French plants would you care to close to make room for the inflow of cars from Turkey?' Unimaginable for a state-owned company given an explicit mission to generate exports and French jobs, with a strong communist union presence. Forty years on, Turkey has its place in the Renault European production network, as in the European industry as a whole, as we shall see later. The lesson is the same: the need to achieve economic scale, and for exports to support it, through the ability to absorb those exports somewhere else.

- Iran (1.5 million) is largely autarchic, through political circumstances, but would otherwise be a mainly French-controlled satellite.
- The Czech Republic (1.4 million) is a clear case of pragmatism before pride, which has led to the very successful revival of its national brand, Škoda, by full integration into the VW group. A number of global component suppliers also use the country as a manufacturing base.
- Slovakia (1 million units) is a purely opportunistic creation, with its government vigorously encouraging foreign investment in the automotive sector, on the basis of low labour costs. The country did have a certain previous industrial base, through being made into a weapons producer within the Soviet bloc.
- Romania (0.4 million units) is a smaller Czech Republic, with its national brand, Dacia, revived by Renault, and which has attracted investments from a number of component suppliers as a low-cost production location.

Then there is a long 'tail' of other, more peripheral contributors, ranging from Poland (0.7 million) right down to Tunisia (2,000 units). Some of these countries, such as Poland, Belgium, Slovenia or the Netherlands, previously had vehicle assembly plants; others are more recent entrants. Morocco (0.4 million) is another Slovakia. A characteristic common to all the satellites and peripherals is that they are within logistical reach of the West European automotive heartland, with the possible exception of Iran.

The CIS (Commonwealth of Independent States) is the rump USSR, dominated by Russia in automotive terms. Nikita Krushchev's shoe banging at the UN was the highlight of his one visit to North America. He was said to have been horrified at the mass motorisation he saw in the United States. At any rate, this was never a priority for the Soviet Union, although the more industrialised East European members of the Soviet Bloc motorised to a significant extent by their own means with some foreign help, notably from Fiat. Deeply resistant to foreign investment, the USSR pursued automotive autarchy, producing largely dismal products. This policy was completely reversed in Russia after the collapse of the USSR. Almost everything has been handed over to foreign interests, a process culminating in the sale of Avtovaz to Renault. Light automotive vehicles are simply not a national priority. Scarce technical and economic resources are diverted into the oversized armaments sector. This is a policy of complete surrender.

The North American region is in part dominated by the US-owned manufacturers, although itself a satellite for Japanese, Korean and German premium manufacturers. Canada and Mexico are assembly and supply satellites. After World War II, the attitude of Detroit was very much that government should not interfere with it. 'What's good for GM is good for America.' This changed radically with interventions on safety, emissions and the CAFE-forced downsizing. This last opened the door to the Japanese invasion and led to the two successive bailouts of Chrysler, and to its bankruptcy and that of GM, following the GFC. In this latest episode, Uncle Sam turned distinctly demanding, forcing rationalisations of products, plant closures and limitations on the prerogatives of the UAW. In effect, the US government has aided and abetted the progressive withdrawal of Detroit from the world scene. But the United States is by no means an automotive monolith. The Big Three always had assembly plants distributed across the country, to be close to the centres of demand. Individual states provided strong incentives for the establishment of satellite assembly plants, starting with the three leading Japanese but later adding others, plus Hyundai, Mercedes and BMW. The Canadian and Mexican governments also played their parts, to their countries' considerable advantage.

South America is dominated by Brazil, which contributes 83 per cent of its output, with Argentina a long way behind, although linked to it via the Mercosur trade pact. The other countries are insignificant. The whole is to a large extent a satellite, operating behind tariff and quota barriers to imports. It remains largely isolated, with relatively few out-of-region exports. Brazil has been described as 'the country built behind tariff walls' (BBC New Files, 3 August 2018). The results have not been wholly happy, including for its automotive sector. Very few Brazilian-owned automotive enterprises have made their mark on the world. Autarchy does not work very well in a globalised industry.

The Asian region has two core countries, Japan and South Korea. As well as having established global production networks over the years, both countries remain huge manufacturers and exporters – almost 10 million units per year of all kinds are built in Japan and 4 million in South Korea. The creation of their automotive industries was a massive bootstrap effort, which received heavy and consistent government support. They were in effect priority national projects, which enabled each country in turn to break into the previously Western automotive club. Japanese manufacturers and Hyundai have established strong presences in North America, although much less so in Europe, and more lately in China. South-East Asia is virtually a Japanese automotive empire. Even highly nationalistic Malaysia – an isolated semi-autarchic hold-out – has been penetrated by Daihatsu (Toyota). Clarity of purpose and forceful persistence have paid off, although at an unquantifiable cost. India is in effect a large satellite and China is a huge one, with almost every major foreign automotive manufacturer involved. This may be quite a perceptive policy, foregoing any attempt at breaking into the global automotive oligarchy and prioritising sectors (including the military) in which China has a real chance of becoming a serious if not dominant contender. It appears to have played ju-jitsu with the automotive giants, rather than Japanese- or Korean-style frontal assault. All the other countries in Asia-Oceania are minor players, with the exception of Thailand, which has played purely opportunistic satellite – and with considerable success. Contract assembly of foreign models at low levels of integration persists in a few countries, such as Taiwan and Malaysia. This is only justified by the existence of tariffs and quotas that penalise imported vehicles. It makes very little economic sense and does not generate exports or create any particular body of local competence.

In effect, governments have little effective control over the industry, unless they choose to close off their national market or that market is actually or potentially very large. The global automotive industry is, for the most part, an oligarchic tight ship, powerful and used to playing national governments for support.

### IN SUMMARY, MANY COUNTRIES THINK THEY ARE CALLED TO BE LEADERS IN THE INDUSTRY BUT VERY FEW ARE CHOSEN

The automotive industry has always been under public surveillance. Vehicle safety standards were the first area of conflict. The automotive industry long tried to ignore the results of independent crash safety testing but eventually had to yield. Environmental protection and fuel consumption have become the major sources of conflict in more recent times. There has been a continuous clash between environmental good intentions and reality as perceived by the industry, starting with air pollution in California, moving on to CAFE in the United States and similar strong concerns in Europe and Japan. Greenhouse gas emissions have now taken over as the major area of concern – and conflict. Dieselgate in Europe is a symbol of what happens when conflicting objectives are not clearly and transparently dealt with. The constant underlying factor is inadequate understanding of each other's purposes and constraints, which is the central theme of this book. These problems also dangerously compromise the industry's reputation and image with consumers. Yet the industry remains a powerful world oligarchy and lobby, able to play governments on sectoral development policy. Countries can be classified by their roles within the global automotive industry – core (full set of capabilities, at both manufacturer and supplier level), major satellite and peripheral. Germany is the core country in Europe, followed at some distance by France, with Italy almost out. There are number of satellites – Spain, the United Kingdom, Turkey, the Czech Republic and Slovenia, and some smaller peripherals. The United States is core in North America, but increasingly isolated in product terms. Brazil is an isolated satellite. Japan and South Korea are core in Asia, with Malaysia as a tiny autarchic would-be, and a huge satellite group, over twice the size of the cores, thanks to China's peculiar position. Governments really have very little power to influence the development of the industry on their territory, unless this has a huge market potential – or they choose to cut it off from the world.

*****************

This, then, is the background against which we reflect upon the birth, life and death of the automotive industry in Australia:

- An almost miraculous innovation, which transformed personal transport and much of the world but whose perceived social utility, once so very positive, has begun to wane.
- A market that is reaching the limits of growth and very likely faces future decline.
- Products whose technologies, brilliantly deployed for over a century, are becoming unfit to match the tightening environmental problems of the planet.
- An industry that has undergone a spectacular globalisation and consolidation, based on a powerful interlocking set of oligarchies, leaving little room for national players.
- Governments often have difficulty in dealing with the very powerful players and attractions of this industry.

# 6 Enthusiastic Adopters: Growth and Change in the Australian Car Market

Like most of the colonies of the British Empire, those in Australia underwent a railway-building boom that lasted until well after Federation. Whereas the transcontinental lines were only finally completed with the opening of Alice Springs to Darwin in 2004, each of the future states built substantial rail networks within their populated areas, for both passenger and freight transport, notably agricultural products. Individual mineral lines were added later, principally in Queensland and West Australia. The large cities (Sydney, Melbourne, Brisbane, Adelaide and Perth) all built suburban passenger networks. Victoria and New South Wales in particular had extensive main-line and rural networks, which reached their peak in the 1930s. The rail industry in Australia differed from those in the United Kingdom and the United States in that it was mainly state-owned from early on, but it went through the same life cycle.

The growth and modal breakdown of freight traffic have some similarities to those in the United States. Figure 6.1 shows the development of bulk freight traffic. Road (the shaded part of the chart) has only ever played a minor role. Rail (the grey part) has always dominated this, with a spectacular expansion in recent years caused by the minerals boom, with rail linking inland mines with the export ports. The importance of coastal shipping (the black part; no statistics available before 1994) has diminished.

Conversely, non-bulk freight (Figure 6.2) has long been dominated by road transport (the shaded area of the chart), although rail (the

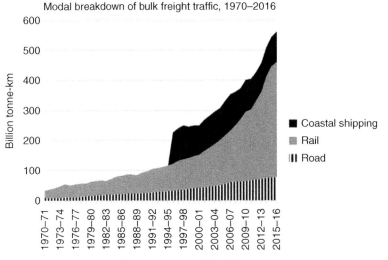

FIGURE 6.1 Rail dominates bulk freight
Data source: bitre statistical yearbooks. No data for coastal shipping before 1994

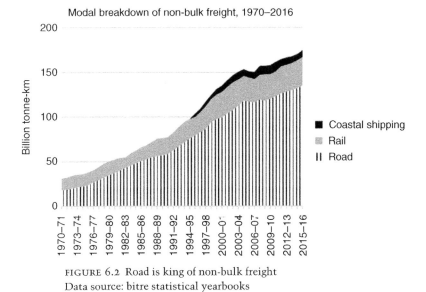

FIGURE 6.2 Road is king of non-bulk freight
Data source: bitre statistical yearbooks

grey part) has shown new growth since the late 1980s, thanks to container trains, with significant traffic on the standard gauge

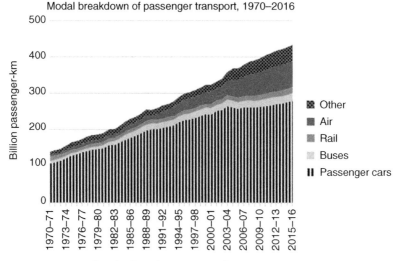

FIGURE 6.3  An American pattern of passenger transport
Data source: bitre statistical yearbooks. "Other" is motorcycles plus non-freight use of LCVs, HCVs and ferries

inter-state network. Coastal shipping (in black) grew a little at the end of the twentieth century but no longer now.

## PASSENGER TRANSPORT: THE CAR TAKES OVER

As in the United States, road has absolutely dominated passenger transport for decades (Figure 6.3), with a fast-growing share for air travel (dark grey, second from top in the diagram). Passenger cars (the shaded part) are responsible for two-thirds of the passenger-km. 'Passenger cars' here includes MPVs and SUVs. Buses (light grey) and rail (medium grey) are minor actors. Apart from a few inter-city lines, primarily radiating from Sydney and Melbourne, most long-distance rail travel is generated by tourist trains. The growth in rail passenger-km has come largely from the busy suburban networks.

## FILLING UP WITH CARS: ONE OF THE MOST MOTORISED
##    COUNTRIES IN THE WORLD

Australia was one of the earliest countries to motorise. As was the case in the United States, the great distances between population

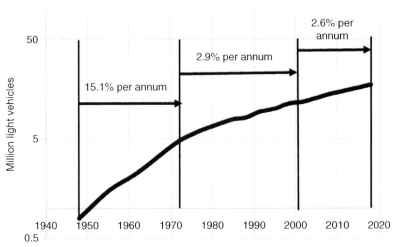

FIGURE 6.4 Filling up with cars
Data source: ABS surveys

centres, combined with relatively under-developed public transport (rail, etc.) systems, made the automobile an unavoidable proposition for the great majority of people. Figure 6.4 shows the growth of the parc (number in use) of light vehicles, using a log scale to show the changes in rates of growth rather than in absolute numbers. It grew at 14.2 per cent per year compounded from 1948 to 1973, from 800,000 to 5 million. This was truly the heroic era of motorisation. Part of this early very fast growth was achieved by keeping vehicles in service longer and longer (made possible by their improving quality and durability – plus a dry climate), with their average age increasing year by year, until it topped out at eleven years in 1996: thereafter, it gradually fell again, as new sales caught up. The year 1973 saw the First Oil Shock and was a turning point in most automotive economies. The growth of the parc slowed dramatically: 2.9 per cent a year from 1973 to 2001 and 2.6 per cent from 2001 to 2018. Within this last figure, passenger motor vehicles (PMVs, passenger cars + SUVs) grew at 2.3 per cent but light commercial vehicles (LCVs) at 3.5 per cent, reflecting the growth of the service economy and couriers (including Internet shopping deliveries).

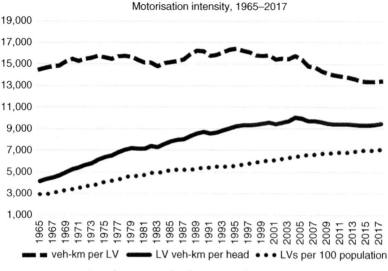

FIGURE 6.5  Almost completely motorised
Data source: bitre statistical yearbooks

The motorisation of Australia is about complete. Figure 6.5 shows how the trends have virtually stabilised. The number of light vehicles per 100 population (the dotted line) is now climbing only very slowly. The actual level in 2017 was 707 per 1,000, which is exceeded by only the United States and Canada. The vehicle-km driven per light vehicle per year (the dashed line) has been gradually declining in recent years. This is typically the result of more vehicles per family unit, each being driven less. Consequently, the vehicle-km travelled per head (the solid line) is now virtually stable. We can therefore expect the parc of light vehicles to grow only very slightly more than the population. We have reached maturity and saturation.

## THE AUSTRALIAN MOTOR VEHICLES MARKET REALLY TOOK OFF AFTER WORLD WAR II – AND HAS CONTINUED TO GROW

Once the reduction in prices brought cars within the reach of the majority, and the functionality and durability of the products made them truly viable for everyday use, demand for them increased hugely. Figure 6.6

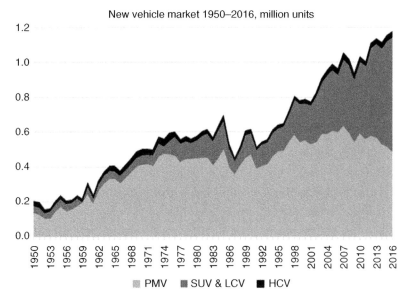

New vehicle market 1950–2016, million units

PMV   SUV & LCV   HCV

FIGURE 6.6  After much growth, a saturated market?
Data sources: AAI yearbooks, OICA

shows the growth of the market since 1950. The light grey area of the
chart is passenger motor vehicles (PMVs), i.e., cars and other vehicles
used as cars. The medium grey is SUVs and LCVs (light commercial
vehicles). The black area is HCVs (heavy commercial vehicles, i.e.,
trucks and buses). By 1955, Australia boasted 153 registered cars per
1,000 head of population, a remarkably high figure for the immediate
post-war period. The market grew almost explosively until the First Oil
Shock in 1973, then slowed, taking off again even more vigorously from
the 1990s and gradually slowing since, with only a minimal dip associated with the GFC, which barely touched Australia. Sales per head of
the adult population have in fact stayed level since 2006, at around
65 per 1,000. Sales growth is therefore roughly equal to that of the
population. Saturation is clearly upon us. Whether something else
will take over from the automobile as we know it today is unclear.
What is very noticeable within the overall sales envelope is the stalling
in the growth of demand for conventional passenger motor vehicles

(PMVs) and the corresponding expansion in SUVs, driven by a change in consumer preferences, and in light commercial (LCVs)s, driven by the growth in the services sector.

## BUT A SEA CHANGE HAS TAKEN PLACE WITHIN THIS GROWING MARKET

This quantitative growth has been matched by a very important qualitative change in the new vehicle market, a major shift in product mix. Markets for personal vehicles reflect society, incomes, wealth, lifestyles and cultural and social preferences, but with a certain inertia. Australia started into its phase of intensive motorisation with cars derived from US practice and these stayed around longer than in the United States itself. By 2000, the United States had forcibly downsized its new car market, as described earlier. Australia had not, as Figure 6.7 shows. The shading in the columns corresponds to the per cent share of the new car market in each country, starting with the smallest cars at the bottom and ending with the largest at the top. A, B, C, D and E refer to European size classes, from very small to very large. A typical modern 'A' car would be a Fiat 500. A 'B' car, a Ford Focus, etc., up to an 'E' car, which would be

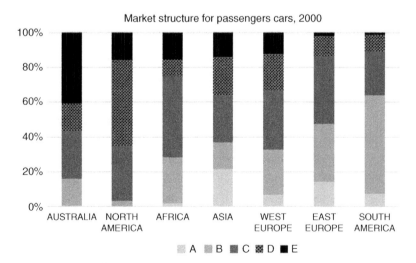

FIGURE 6.7 In a time warp
Source: Time for a Model Change

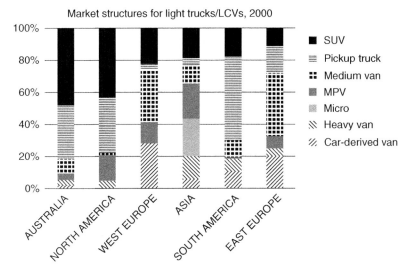

FIGURE 6.8  A love of SUVs
Source: Time for a Model Change

large, big-engined RWD (rear wheel drive) sedan. US customers, fleeing
the CAFE-imposed forced downsizing of cars, extensively turned to
SUVs and other light trucks as substitutes, as related earlier.

Australians also went for SUVs but for more genuine reasons:
a national passion for the outdoors, travel on the many dirt roads and
camping. By 2000, they already sold more than the different categories
of light commercial vehicles (LCVs) taken together – see Figure 6.8.
This is characteristic of developed large-area countries, with long distances to drive, many dirt roads, opportunities for off-roading and (in the
case of much of North America) harsh winter conditions. Western and
Eastern Europe, Asia and urban South America are too crowded for
these vehicles to be very popular. Pseudo-SUVs ('soft-roaders' and
'cross-overs') – in effect passenger cars in new dresses – came later. Pickup trucks were and are disproportionately popular in Australia and
North America, partly for agricultural reasons, which also applies
across rural South America.

All this may seem trivial and irrelevant but it is not: knowing
about consumers, how they live, how they drive, which vehicles they

therefore buy and which they might want to buy, are absolutely
critical to a proper understanding of this sector. Without this, sound
policy for it cannot be formulated. This is a product-driven business,
in the most literal sense. But the markets for these products are deeply
rooted in the character of individual societies.

## FEW COUNTRIES HAVE CHANGED AS MUCH
## AS AUSTRALIA HAS IN THE LAST THIRTY YEARS

What we have seen is a delayed reaction to profound changes described in
almost all aspects of Australian society over the last thirty years. This is
well summed up in the text below, from mccrindle.com.au:

> Australia is a nation in transition. In the span of a generation,
> Australia's population has increased by more than half.
> Demographically we are ageing, with an average age 7 years older
> than it was 3 decades ago, but with a life expectancy 7 years greater
> than it was in 1984.
>
> Our growing population is being achieved not only through this
> increased longevity, but also through record births – more than
> 300,000 per year. This is more than 25% higher than the peak of the
> original post-war baby boom. Yet as significant as this natural
> increase is, the largest source of our population has been growth
> through immigration, with significant shifts in the Top 5 countries
> of birth. In 1984, the Top 5 countries of arrival were all European
> (and New Zealand) while today both China and India are in the Top
> 5 with Vietnam and the Philippines not far behind.
>
> While the population has increased by 51% since 1984, the
> workforce has increased by 81%. Three decades ago the average full
> time worker took home just under $19,000 per year in a time when
> the average house price was less than $150,000. Today annual
> earnings exceed $73,000 with the average house price in most
> capital cities exceeding $520,000. From an employment
> perspective, the Australian workforce has transitioned from
> industrial in 1984 to professional today. The largest industries by

workforce were all industrial in 1984 while today professional, scientific, technical, IT and the financial sectors make up the biggest employers along with mining and utilities.

In 1984 almost 2 in 3 Australians were married while today less than half are. And the 'never married' proportion has increased from 1 in 4 to 1 in 3. From a religious perspective, Christianity is still the religion of more than 3 in 5 Australians, down from 3 in 4 in 1984. Meanwhile the 'no religion' proportion has doubled and the 'religion other than Christianity' numbers have increased from 265,600 to 1.68 million today.

In addition to these demographic changes, the shifts in our national identity are significant. However deep the old affections run, there is now a recognition of Australia as a cultural hub, a technology exporter, a fashion destination, a small business nation and a nation hosting iconic events.

It seems that Australians are comfortable in their own skin – embracing of this sunburnt country with all its iconic landmarks, yet proud of the cultural achievements and our diverse cities. There's an understated confidence that welcomes the world to this unique landscape, yet has the posture to proudly list off our cultural achievements.

There is a depth to our reflections on 21st Century Australia. The iconic language and Australiana are retained and reinterpreted with a new sophistication, and without the cringe. Our cultural identity is also being interpreted beyond the beach or sport. Multiculturalism has come of age in Australia. You can tell because there is little self-consciousness and even less tokenism expressed. Rather the cultural mix is in our national DNA, it's part of our lifestyle – it's who we are. The fact that more than 1 in 4 of us weren't born here seems unremarkable – as though it has always been thus. Many comments celebrated the richness of our lifestyle that comes through the input of so many cultures.

Amidst massive national and global change, the Aussie spirit is alive and growing in the 21st Century. What it means to be

Australian has morphed to meet the challenges and diversity of our changing times. Australians hold strongly to an identity and 'Aussie values' yet these are more sophisticated and mature, and represent our place in a world of global interactions.

In 2017, no less than 26 per cent of Australia's population of 24.6 million were foreign-born, the highest percentage in the developed world. Another 11 per cent came from the traditional sources – Oceania (mainly New Zealand), the British Isles and the rest of Europe, a further 11 per cent from Asia and 4 per cent from the rest of the world.

## A SLIGHTLY BELATED BUT FUNDAMENTAL SHIFT IN PRODUCT MIX

The really striking phenomenon in the Australian market for personal passenger vehicles is a radical change in product mix, which happened slightly late and quite violently. From 2005 on, the traditional large rear-wheel-drive Australian car suffered a precipitous loss of market share, as Figure 6.9 shows. From the early 2000s, the sales of conventional passenger cars ceased to grow and started to decline from around 2010. Within that envelope, large car sales volumes shrank dramatically, caught between a strong downsizing movement within cars and the explosion in sales of SUVs. All the recent growth has been captured by SUVs and light trucks, particularly since 1990. A minority of these are used for commercial and farm purposes but the great majority are bought as substitutes for passenger cars, as in the United States. This is not surprising, given Australia's topography, large number of unsealed roads and passion for outdoor activities. Today's Australian new vehicle market resembles that of the United States but with the shift having been more natural than the American one, which was triggered by the forced downsizing of passenger cars from 1980, aimed at cutting fuel consumption without politically impossible increases in motor fuels taxation. Note that few SUVs or light trucks were Australian-built, with the Ford Territory, the

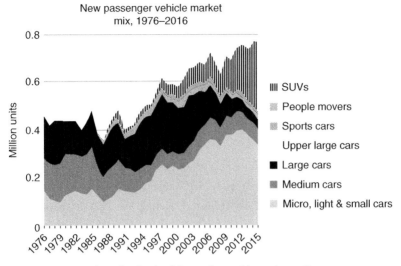

FIGURE 6.9 The death of the traditional large Australian car
Data source: AAI yearbook 2017

Holden Adventra SUV and passenger-car-derived Utes as the only exceptions and these, of course, only until local manufacturing finally ceased in 2017. The market for traditional large RWD Australian-designed and Australian-built cars went into steep decline. They were squeezed between the growing sectors of SUVs and smaller cars, with overall market growth not enough to compensate. The trend was only gradual at first but sharply accelerated from 2005. Intention-to-buy surveys of retail customers show a collapse for large cars from nearly 30 per cent of intentions in 2000 to around 5 per cent today, with SUV buying intentions rising from 15 per cent to 35 per cent. Leading up to 2017, traditional large Australian RWD cars were mainly bought by fleets, notably those in the public sector, where one would expect to see the strongest remaining manifestation of preference for buying Australian cars.

At the peak, some 80 per cent of locally produced RWD sedans were purchased by fleets, often because of choice restrictions imposed by the fleet managers for Australian-made vehicles. Once the novated lease option – which usually incorporated a 'user-chooser' option –

became more ubiquitous within fleets in the mid-1990s, the local vehicle producers' share of the market started to decay. The loyalty held up reasonably well across the fleet sector and was still around 40 per cent by 2017, but had little effect on the actual purchasing choices of retail customers for new cars.

## THE TRADITIONAL LARGE AUSTRALIAN CAR SEGMENT WAS TORN APART

The traditional large RWD car segment has been torn apart in three directions, as depicted in Figure 6.10, which is based on an actual analysis of models in the Australian passenger car market conducted in 2015. Size – measured in simple form by overall length – is the horizontal axis. Price is on the vertical axis. The diagram has been simplified, as the price bands for each model would not come out

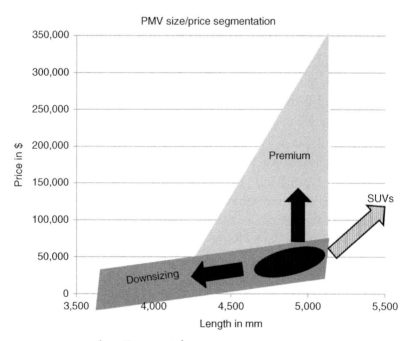

FIGURE 6.10 Torn apart three ways
Source: Autopolis

clearly in print. Traditionally, passenger car models in the volume sector were spread across a price/size band (the medium-grey area across the bottom of the chart); poor people bought small cars, better-off people bought bigger cars. The depth of the band deepened over time, as manufacturers offered more derivatives, variants and options. But price ranges remained relatively small within a model. The light grey triangle represents the premium car sector. This has a completely different price-size relationship, including huge differences between variants and options – up to 100 per cent in some cases. Whereas consumers in the volume sector basically buy a means of transport, those in the premium sector are demonstrating their enthusiasm for the product, or their wealth or both. The traditional large cars sat within the black oval, at the right-hand end of the volume car continuum. The Toyota Camry is at the left end of the oval, the Ford Falcon and the Holden Commodore are across the middle of it, the Holden Caprice and the imported Chrysler 300 on the right.

The Australian car segment in the market was effectively reshaped in three directions:

- Downsizing, driven by the Asian car invasion.
- The out-of-diagram trend towards SUVs, essentially an American-type influence, but with a consumer preference for Asian and European brands and products.
- And the growth of the premium segment, primarily propelled by European brands. These brands have clearly opted to exercise their collective strength to secure premium prices (far higher relative to volume cars in Australia than in Europe or the United States), rather than volume.

The causes were multiple but deeply rooted in the changing nature of Australia: increased traffic congestion in the large metropolitan areas, which took a lot of the fun out of driving – not much point in a buying a fine big car for two hours of commuting. The pressure of escalating housing prices put pressure on households' motoring budgets. Increasing multiple-vehicle ownership encouraged the specialisation of vehicles – smaller cars for commuting, SUVs for the weekend. Increases in the prices of domestically produced and decreases for imports, with smaller cars and almost all SUVs imported, contributed to the shift. There was less emotional attachment to owning an Australian car. There was a growing realisation on the part of the Australian consumer that the traditional Australian sedan offered no functional benefits over the smaller, front-wheel drive models such as Toyota Corolla, Mazda 3 and Hyundai I30 for city and suburban use, and, sadly, could not match the prestige or emotional benefits provided by Asian and European up-line sedans and SUVs. The share of the 'fleet' sector in new sales increased by almost 40 per cent from 1983 (33 per cent sales to businesses and 5 per cent to government) to 2016 (48 per cent and 4 per cent, respectively). While government purchasing still continued to favour domestically built vehicles, novated leasing gave business users more of a free choice. Having half of new sales go to business buyers creates a stream of often high-specification low-mileage de-fleeted cars into the used car market two to three years later. Many private buyers no longer bother to look for new cars. All this puts a downward pressure on new car prices, especially as cars sold to fleets often attract significant discounts from the list price in the first place.

All these trends described for Australia were discernible in some form in overseas markets years, if not decades, ago: in the United States, forced downsizing and the Japanese invasion; and in Europe, the huge growth of the German premium brand manufacturers. Europe additionally used to have a semi-utilitarian market segment, served by cars that were cheap in relation to their size, typified in its time by the Renault 4, the Citroën 2CV and the original VW Beetle. It withered away with rising incomes and stiffening crash safety requirements. Crowded urban Asia has a large urban market segment for mini-cars and car-LCV hybrids, starting with the Thai tuk-tuk, but also found in crowded urban Italy with the ubiquitous Ape (bee). This segment in turn borders on vast markets for light two-wheelers – scooters and mopeds.

## TROUBLE IN STORE: THE FLEET MARKET

If you want a sure sign of impending trouble for a vehicle manufacturer, look at its dependence on sales to fleets, whether public sector (government departments and agencies, armed forces, etc.) or private (companies operating their own fleets, leasing companies/long-term rental, or short-term rental car hire). Retail purchasers, i.e., private individuals and small businesses, do have some power to extract discounts – and they exercise it, with the manufacturers and their franchised dealers foolishly encouraging this by means of premature obsolescence and pre-registrations. Corporate buyers can exert much more pressure, as a function of their size. Short-term rental companies have great flexibility in deciding when to retire and sell on part of their existing fleets of vehicles. They can and do exert huge pressures for discounts on new vehicles – up to 40 per cent has been reported – buying directly from the manufacturers. Manufacturers and dealers, desperate to sustain production and sales volumes, charge enthusiastically into the fleet market gin palace, to emerge with a nasty profit hangover, repent and pursue retail sales, then go through the cycle again. The manufacturers' infatuation with the fleet market is very much akin to a dance with the devil. Although possibly successful in increasing volumes and revenues (but less so, profits) in the short term, it will almost inevitably damage the brand by removing any pretentions of prestige – anyone who has been driven around town in a scruffy cab with the almost inevitable differential whine drowning out normal conversation is going to be hard to convince that even the 'dressed up' version of the same car is going to cut the mustard at the school drop-off or the golf club. Conversely, Mercedes's reputation for durability is reinforced by its presence in cabs in Europe. It all depends on the product thus showcased.

Figure 6.11 shows what should have been a dire warning. The numbers are not exact, as there were changes in the categorisation scheme for classes of vehicles in the statistics. But the trend is all too clear. The bottom two sections of each column show sales of small

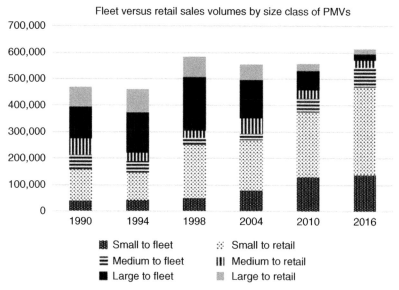

FIGURE 6.11  Over-dependence and collapse
Data source: AAI yearbooks

cars to fleets (lighter shading) and to retail customers (darker). The fleet/retail split changes over time, with retail remaining dominant but fleet sales of small PMVs increasing dramatically between 1998 and 2016. No dangerous reliance on the fleet sector here. The next two sections up are for medium cars. The sector stagnated in size but fleets moved from 50 per cent of it in 1990 to 75 per cent in 2016. The dramatic impact was in large cars. The market for them boomed from 194,000 units in 1990 to 292,000 in 1998 – with the fleet share of those volumes increasing from 61 per cent to 72 per cent – a dangerous and growing dependency, as it turned out. Then it crashed back down to 42,000 in 2016, with fleets now taking 54 per cent and much of their buying switching to smaller cars.

## THERE ARE AS YET ONLY WEAK SIGNALS OF DISENCHANTMENT WITH THE AUTOMOBILE

And what of the future for the Australian car market? It continues to grow steadily, with a now-established product mix. After the initial

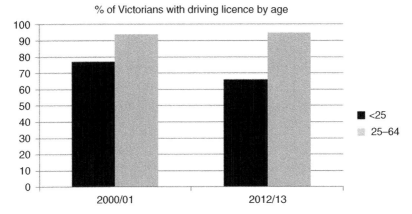

FIGURE 6.12  A flagging enthusiasm for driving among the young?
Data sources: The Conversation, VIC Roads, ABS

distress over the shutdown of Australian light vehicle production, no one seems to be shedding too many tears for the traditional large cars of the past. As in other developed countries, there is in Australia a decreased enthusiasm for driving among the younger members of the population, reflected in fewer of them holding driving licences than in earlier years – Figure 6.12, which may bode ill for the future, not just in terms of the number of cars sold but of interest in new and sophisticated cars. As yet, this is a weak signal as many of the under-25s may change their attitude, once they have families and suburban houses.

## TOO LITTLE, TOO LATE AGAINST THE FLOOD
##     OF IMPORTS

In 1979, Holden adopted a European (Opel)-inspired design for its mainstream Commodore product line to replace the American-inspired Kingswood, albeit retaining much of the drive-train engineering that had been in use since 1963. Ford, too, adopted a style heavily influenced by its German and English product lines (Granada) for its 1979 XD Falcon. As was the case with the Commodore, Ford retained the drive train and basic architecture from its previous models (dating back to the 1960 XK Falcon in many respects) for the XD. But it was too little, too late for the domestic products in the Australian market. The underlying platforms and the packages were hopelessly dated and out of tune with the new Australia.

Commencing in the early 1960s already, with Toyota (Land Cruiser, Toyopet, Tiara, Corona, Crown), Nissan (Bluebird, Cedric), Mazda (360, 800) and Hino (Contessa) Isuzu (Bellet), the Japanese imports, although originally ridiculed by the local press, soon achieved a high level of acceptance by the Australian public. Although generally technically unsophisticated, the products achieved this penetration by way of competitive pricing (despite the high import tariffs at the time) and relatively high equipment levels. By the close of the decade, Toyota and Nissan were both involved in local assembly of their high-volume products to circumvent those tariffs and the import quotas. The steady rise of the Japanese brands, in particular Toyota, Nissan, Mazda, Honda and Mitsubishi, continued throughout the 1970s. During this period, Leyland Australia failed in its attempts (the Kimberley/Tasman and P76) to compete directly with Holden, Ford and Chrysler and withdrew from local manufacturing. Chrysler, too, faltered and proceeded to downgrade its local involvement and hand its Tonsley Park manufacturing facilities to its local alliance partner, Mitsubishi.

As Figure 6.13 shows, Japanese imports continued to hold the position they had achieved, while new sources appeared. South Korean imports made a significant impact. But not as much as those from Thailand, which have surged following its Free Trade Agreement (FTA) with Australia, which proved very one-sided – almost no Australian-made cars were sold in Thailand after the FTA was executed. The thin trickle from China and India has almost dried up – Great Wall, for example, tried in Australia but soon failed. A few tens of thousands of vehicles now come from the Americas, essentially Jeeps and some Mercedes and BMW SUVs from the United States. There ought to be a much greater opportunity for American manufacturers in an SUV-mad market but their light truck products are generally too large and crude and too thirsty for local tastes. Sales of vehicles from

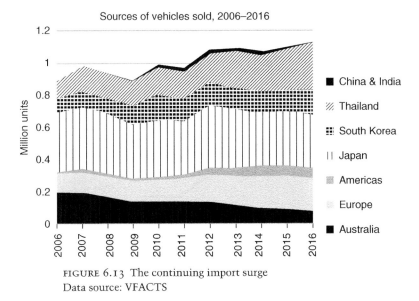

FIGURE 6.13  The continuing import surge
Data source: VFACTS

European countries have grown significantly. In 2016, 45 per cent of these came from Germany but this understates the role of German manufacturers, as they also export from their operations in other countries within Europe. The data for this exhibit is based on countries of origin, not manufacturer brands. Light vehicles made in Australia took 73 per cent of the national market at their peak in 1987 – the share for passenger motor vehicles was 86 per cent. By 1997, this was down to 38 per cent, to 20 per cent in 2007 and 8 per cent in 2016.

## TARIFF AND TAX CHANGES HAD A SIGNIFICANT IMPACT AFTER 2000

Australia deliberately reduced its tariffs on imported cars (more about this in Chapter 7). As these reductions stripped away protection from imports, the market share of Australian-made passenger motor vehicles (PMVs) fell rapidly (see Figure 6.14). The tipping point at which imports exceeded locally produced vehicles was reached in 1998.

The Goods and Services Tax (GST) was introduced in 2000. It replaced a number of other taxes, including the Wholesale Sales Tax.

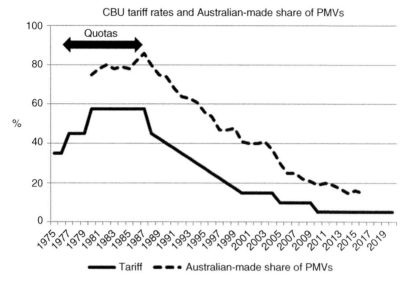

FIGURE 6.14 The protection stripped away
Data source: AAI yearbook 2017

One effect of this was to reduce the prices of new cars in Australia. From a high point of 57.5 per cent in the late 1980s, the tariff on imported vehicles was reduced to 15 per cent in 2000 and subsequently to 5 per cent in 2010. Thus, market protection was virtually eliminated. At the same time, the financing arrangements applying to company-supplied vehicles changed with the introduction by the financing sector of novated 'user-chooser' leases. Rather than being locked into a restrictive Holden-Ford choice, employees were able to select other brands and models. As we have discussed, European cars were becoming more affordable for Australian consumers at the time so many drivers took advantage of the new flexibility in leasing schemes. A typical situation was that a driver might have selected, say, a mid-spec Audi A4 in place of a Holden Calais, which was around the same price. Many drivers were willing to sacrifice more overt aspects such as vehicle size, outright performance and equipment levels for the perceived added prestige that came with the European marques.

In terms of the national ownership of the marques sold in it, today's Australian light vehicle market is dominated by Asian vehicle manufacturers, as can be seen in Figure 6.15, followed by Europeans and Americans. The American share includes Australian-made Holdens and Fords but principally consists of imports, many from Asia. The Japanese share includes Toyota's sales of Australian-built cars. German marques dominate in the European categories: the VW brand achieves 63 per cent of all European volume marque sales; Mercedes, BMW, Audi and Porsche 83 per cent of all European premium marque sales. The Australian market today is a 'modern' one, dominated by the European–Japanese vehicle design cultures. The old Australian–American influence is virtually dead. The best-selling passenger car model line in Australia in 2016 was the imported Toyota Corolla, although Toyota's best-selling line by a small margin was in fact the HiLux LCV.

Australia changed hugely as a society in the seventy years between 1945 and 2015, from a culturally fairly isolated country still with strong links to Britain, to a far more open and diverse society, in touch with the whole world. Its tastes in vehicles changed with it, while remaining adapted to local motoring needs – which had themselves changed considerably, becoming more similar to those of other developed countries. This might have presented huge opportunities for the local industry but also created challenges which were ultimately to prove fatal.

## CURRENCY MOVEMENTS HAVE OFTEN BEEN BLAMED FOR UNDERMINING THE LOCAL MANUFACTURERS

Blame has been placed on currency movements for the flood of imports. But this charge needs to be examined more closely. The discussion is often framed in terms of the exchange rate between the Australian Dollar (AUD) and the US Dollar (USD) but Australia has other important automotive trading partners. Figure 6.16 tracks the value of four major currencies – the USD, the Euro (with the pre-Euro Deutsche Mark converted into Euros), the Yen and the South Korean

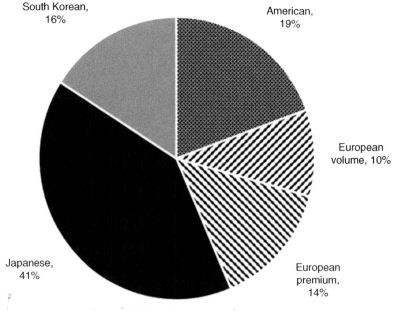

FIGURE 6.15  An Asian–European market
Data source: AAI yearbook 2017

Won – over a period of almost fifty years. In broad terms, each of these currencies (with the exception of the Won) steadily bought more and more AUD from 1970 to 2000. Then the trend reversed, as the rise in world commodity prices provoked the Australian mining and mineral exports boom. There has been a reversal of that since 2013, following the end of that boom.

The movement of the AUD against the Yen was the most relevant, in the light of the continuous penetration of the Australian car market by Japanese imports in the 1970s and 1980s. It should have slowed it down. But the Japanese manufacturers were able to overcome this obstacle, thanks to their greater production scale, more efficient production methods, consequently falling costs (in Yen) – and by offering products that Australian consumers wanted. Sharp rises in fuel prices following the two oil shocks in the 1970s also

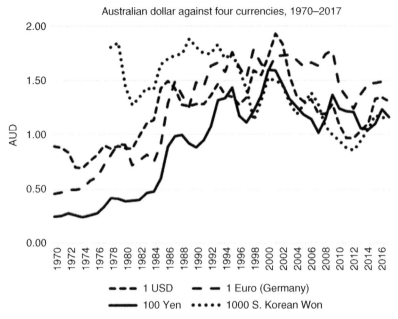

FIGURE 6.16 How many Australian dollars could one buy?
Data source: OECD

contributed to an increased interest in smaller, lighter, more fuel-efficient cars than the traditional Australian offerings, which had become larger, heavier and less fuel-efficient. South Korea followed suit, followed again by Thailand, thanks to the Australia–Thailand Free Trade Agreement, which was hopelessly one-sided in automotive industry terms (more about this in Chapter 10).

## BUT THE MORE FUNDAMENTAL PROBLEM WAS THEIR COST POSITION

Holden and Ford Australia were producing their Australian models on specifically Australian platforms with uniquely Australian parts, the whole at very low volumes, compared to increasing volumes per platform and part for the leading global manufacturers and suppliers. They had a growing competitive cost problem. They were forced into raising the prices of the Falcon and Commodore by $10,000 over the 1990s,

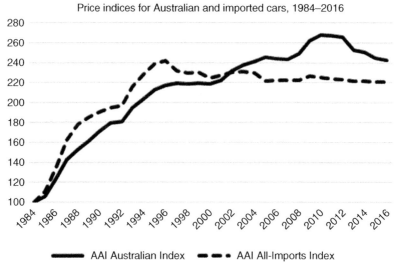

FIGURE 6.17  Breaking ranks
Data source: AAI yearbook 2017

relying too much on their traditional brand strength with Australian
consumers. This created a dangerous exposure in the face of foreign
competitors, particularly Asian ones. But brands that had been priced
at a premium over the local product also became more competitive on
price. Mainline and semi-up-line European brands such as VW/Audi,
Peugeot/Citroën, Renault and Volvo elected to pass on some of their
currency gains, which brought their products into consideration for
consumers who would have previously only considered a locally produced vehicle. Consumers were suddenly able to obtain the 'imported'
cachet at a more affordable price.

Figure 6.17 tracks price indices for Australian and imported cars
from 1984 to 2016. Until 1995, the prices of imported cars rose faster
than those of Australian-made cars. Then the latter stabilised for a few
years. But at that point the imports broke ranks and their prices started to
fall. They held steady when Australian-made prices started to rise again
around 2001–2, and the gap steadily widened, only to narrow again from
2013, by which time the Australian manufacturers were in a near-
desperate situation and frantically trying to regain domestic volume.

## NOT ALL THE CURRENCY GAINS WERE PASSED
## ON TO CONSUMERS

But not all is quite as it seems. The currency and productivity gains of the imported marques and models may not have been fully passed on to Australian consumers. Figure 6.19 compares how many AUD one could buy with Yen to the price index trend for imported Japanese cars. The exchange rate fluctuated quite violently but the general trend from around 2000 was for a weakening of the Yen against the AUD. The Japanese price index remained relatively stable. One could not reasonably expect local car prices in Australia to be adjusted to every short-term currency movement. There are new car stocks in the distribution and retail channels. Leasing and finance companies have made price commitments based on expected future residual values and have a very major interest in these remaining stable. But the chart does convey an impression that these prices might have come down

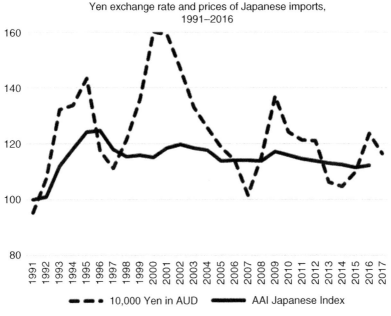

FIGURE 6.18 Not all the currency gains passed on?
Data sources: OECD, AAI

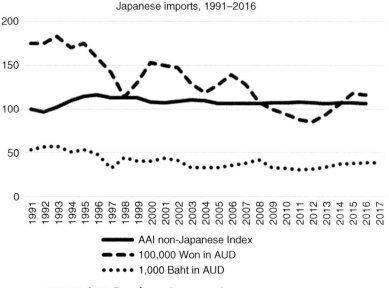

FIGURE 6.19 Even less price aggression
Data sources: OECD. AAi yearbook 2017

more than they did. The marques that built cars in Australia were also large importers. They had to avoid their imported models undercutting their Australian-built ones by too much.

A similar but perhaps slightly clearer picture emerges for the non-Japanese imports, as shown in Figure 6.19. The South Korean Won lost value against the AUD, with some fluctuations until 2012 and the end of the mining boom. The Thai Baht also depreciated against the AUD, although not quite as steeply. But the prices of these imports barely budged. The importers were making hay under the price umbrella held up by Australian-built cars.

## THE INDUSTRY'S CONTROL OVER ITS END MARKETS
## MADE PRICES STICKY IN THE UNITED KINGDOM

How could this be, in a supposedly open and competitive market place? Is the industry able to exercise collective control over market prices? The answer is Yes, and there is a historical precedent that demonstrates it. At the end of World War II, the Bretton Woods system of fixed exchange rates was instituted. This collapsed in 1971 but most of the EEC countries agreed in 1972 to maintain stable exchange rates, keeping them within a 2.25 per cent band of fluctuations – the so-called European currency snake. This was replaced in March 1979 by the European Monetary System (EMS) and a European Currency Unit (ECU) was defined as a reference, with an Exchange Rate Mechanism (ERM). The United Kingdom was part of these arrangements but got into increasing financial difficulties. Facing enormous pressure of speculation against the Pound Sterling (£), it left the system on 'Black Friday', 16 September 1992. The exchange rate of the £ against the ECU collapsed.

As the United Kingdom imported 80 per cent of the new cars that it bought, car prices in the British market had to rise, and duly did so, in line with the devaluation of the £. The UK economy eventually recovered from the shock and humiliation and arguably benefitted from a now floating £, which then strengthened again on the foreign exchanges. Therefore, the £ prices of imported cars in the United Kingdom should have come down again, and with it the overall level of car prices. But they did not. Figure 6.20 shows what happened. The dotted line tracks the

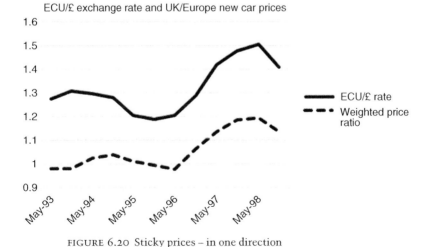

FIGURE 6.20 Sticky prices – in one direction
Data source: European Commission

trend in the ratio between UK and continental European prices, weighted for model mixes in the different markets, calculated in ECUs at the prevailing rates of exchange. They held steady around 1, i.e., price equality, until mid 1996. Then the £ started to strengthen – the black trend line. UK new car prices ought to have come down but they did not and the UK/continent price ratio increased for no valid reason. UK new car prices, which had adjusted upwards when the £ fell, failed to adjust down again when it rose on the exchanges. They were sticky – in one direction.

In extreme cases, the same car sold in the United Kingdom for 50 per cent more than in Europe. The importers made exceptional profits. The pressure on the then-beleaguered British manufacturers, Rover in particular, eased. The industry referred to the United Kingdom as Treasure Island. The inevitable public backlash followed. The Consumers Association launched a vigorous campaign, backed by the media. The House of Commons Trade and Industry Committee held a hearing and roundly condemned the manufacturers. The Monopolies and Mergers Commission (MMC) held a thorough full-scale investigation, which confirmed the pricing abnormality, labelling it the result of a Complex Monopoly, in which no two parties overtly colluded but all parties tacitly behaved in a parallel fashion.[1] It thereby confirmed the fact that vehicle manufacturers controlled end market prices by fixing list prices for their franchised dealers and controlling the latter's ability to discount from them by limiting their gross margins and paying retroactive bonuses.[2] Which means that the presence of multiple brands and manufacturers with their tied dealers had not of itself ensured a competitive market place. So much for the Herfindahl Index, which purports to measure competitive intensity by the number of competitors. But it stopped short of condemning the mechanism which enabled that control – the franchised dealership system itself.

[1]   *New Cars: A Report on the Supply of New Motor Cars within the United Kingdom*, 2000.

[2]   Known as Recommended Retails Prices in the United Kingdom. There was an attempt in 1998 to abolish these for electrical goods, ended by the Monopolies and Mergers Commission in 2012.

The MMC's report fed directly into the 2001 review of the European Automotive Block Exemption Regulation (BER) by the Directorate General for Competition of the European Commission. As noted in Chapter 3, the Commission also stopped short of attacking the franchised dealership system itself. The subsequent 2010 BER put this system of vertical agreements under the general BER for all sectors, which relies on market share thresholds to detect possible violations. As virtually no vehicle marque or manufacturer exceeds these thresholds in any individual European market, there are in effect no restrictions. The Commission didn't deny the anti-competitive nature of the franchised dealership system, it simply chose not to fight that particular battle with Europe's powerful automotive industry, with its formidable lobbying power in Brussels.

## THERE ARE SOME ANALOGIES IN AUSTRALIA

The analogy with the Australian situation is not total. Yet there is enough similarity to raise the suspicion that Australian consumers paid a price for keeping Australian car plants in business. The same brand-exclusive franchised dealer retailing systems operates in Australia as virtually everywhere else. The importer-distributors are either subsidiaries of the manufacturers or in an exclusive relationship with them. The same indirect control over end prices can therefore be exercised. The Australian Competition and Consumer Commission (ACCC) undertook a review of new car retailing in Australia and identified three areas of concern[3]:

- Customers being hindered in their exercise of their rights under Australian consumer law during the process of buying new cars;
- Concerns remaining about the effect of limited access to information and data required to repair and service new cars;
- Consumers not receiving accurate information about the fuel consumption or emissions performance of new cars.

---

[3]    *New Car Retailing Industry: A Market Study by the ACCC*, December 2017.

More bluntly put:

- Manufacturers and their dealers deliberately coerce customers. This includes not only making them sign non-disclosure agreements in the case of disagreements over warranty claims, but also putting pressure on them to stick to over-priced dealer workshops and 'genuine' parts, on which they critically depend for their own profitability (the cross subsidy of insufficiently profitable new car sales by service and parts was explicitly identified in the ACCC's report).
- The manufacturers and importers reneged on their voluntary agreement with the Australian Automotive Aftermarket Association to make technical information available to the independent aftermarket on reasonable terms.
- Inaccurate information about products amounts to deceptive advertising.

In their December 2018 bulletin on automotive law, HWL Ebbsworth Lawyers reported that there was still no update as to the timeline and scope of the changes being implemented. However they noted the key proposed legislative changes:

- The Australian Consumer Law to provide additional clarity to consumers about when they are entitled to a refund or replacement under consumer guarantees.
- A mandatory scheme for car manufacturers to share technical information with independent repairers.
- Changes to the Franchising Code of Conduct to correct the imbalance of power between dealers and distributors (i.e. importers, in the absence of manufacturers producing in Australia).

The ACCC appears to consider that a good degree of competition obtains in the selling of new cars, precisely because no actor has a dominant market share, and there are many of them. This is the theory of the competitive economics of the corner shop. Our analysis is that this simplistic happy state does not apply in this particular industry. The overall contention of this book is that it is imperative to understand the real functioning of a sector before attempting to regulate it or legislate for it.

Our conclusion therefore is not the conventional one that under-priced imports invaded the Australian market and unfairly displaced perfectly good native products. It is that these native products had become old-fashioned and too expensive, and that they no longer matched the needs, expectations and tastes of a very much changed society and car-buying public. If anything, the penetration of the imports was slowed by the anti-competitive distribution and retailing networks. Prices were kept above what they might have been, in an attempt to protect the domestic manufacturers. Whether this fundamental shift in the make-up of the Australian new car market should have been made more rapidly, more slowly or not at all should have been a matter for informed policy making. Our contention is that there was not enough analysis done about what was happening to the automotive industry in Australia and in the wider world to inform these choices properly. It does not mean that there was no information available or debate about the direction to take, for there certainly was much of it, including plenty of early signs of trouble. But insufficiently well informed.

## IN SUMMARY, THE AUSTRALIAN CAR MARKET BOOMED BUT CHANGED, LEAVING THE LOCAL MANUFACTURERS FIGHTING AN UNSUCCESSFUL REAR-GUARD ACTION

Australia had its own railway boom but, as elsewhere, the car took over and the country has become one of the most motorised in the world. The Australian motor vehicles market really took off after World War II and has continued to grow. But a sea change has taken place within this growing market, reflecting the fact that few countries have changed as much as Australia has in the last thirty years. There has been a slightly belated but nevertheless fundamental shift in product mix. The traditional large Australian car segment was torn apart between Asian smaller cars, European premium cars and SUVs. Over-dependence on the fleet market on the part of the domestic manufacturers spelt trouble in store for them. They reacted too little, too late against the flood of imports. There are as yet only weak signals of disenchantment with the automobile. Tariff and tax changes had a significant impact on the market after 2000. Currency movements have often been blamed for undermining the local manufacturers but the more fundamental problem was their cost position. Not all the currency gains were passed on to consumers. The industry's control over its end markets made prices sticky in the United Kingdom. There are some analogies in Australia.

# 7 The End of a Life cycle the Rise and Fall of the Australian Light Vehicle Industry

AUSTRALIAN VEHICLE ASSEMBLY BEGAN PRIOR
TO WORLD WAR I ON A VERY SMALL SCALE

At the beginning of the twentieth century, the Australian economy was heavily reliant on primary industries, notably wool, and, to a lesser extent, wheat and dairy. There was no large-scale industrial production. What little manufacturing did exist was focused at the artisan level – building materials manufacture (bricks and tiles), furniture making, farm machine repairs, etc. There was some nascent bicycle manufacturing, albeit still at very low-scale levels. The participation of the (not yet federated) Australian States in the Boer War of 1901 critically demonstrated the degree to which Australia depended upon British-made arms and armaments. In 1907, the Lithgow Small Arms Factory was established in an effort to reduce that dependence and consequent vulnerability.

Australians were quick to notice the work that was progressing at that time in France, Britain, Germany and the United States to design and manufacture road-going automobiles. In 1900, the first petrol-driven car was imported to Sydney. During the first decade of the century there was a steadily increasing flow of vehicles imported from those countries from manufacturers such as Darracq, De Dion, Wolseley, Argyll, Rolls Royce, Benz and Oldsmobile. These cars were invariably expensive and, by today's standards at least, often fragile and unreliable.

There were efforts being undertaken in Australia during that decade, too. In 1896, Herbert Thompson designed and released the 'Phaeton' steam-powered car. In 1901, Harley Tarrant built Australia's first petrol-powered car. The last remaining example of a Tarrant is on

FIGURE 7.1 Early days – a 1906 Tarrant
Source: Museums Victoria

display in the RACV building, in Melbourne. A Tarrant is shown in Figure 7.1. Between 1901 and 1907, Harley Tarrant built a total of twelve cars, initially using a Benz engine but eventually rising to an estimated 90 per cent local content. In 1903, Tarrant formed the Melbourne Motor Works. The very low volume of the Tarrant operations made it difficult to remain competitive: in 1908 the price of a Tarrant two-cylinder car was 375 Pounds while a four-cylinder Model T Ford was around 200 Pounds. This was a harbinger of many things to come.

Tarrant continued the development of the car until 1907, after which he concentrated on importing Benz and Ford vehicles. In 1909, the Adelaide coachbuilding firm Duncan and Fraser, which had been importing Oldsmobile vehicles from the United States, took on the agency to import and sell Model T Fords, which proved to be an outstanding success in the Australian marketplace. They were simple, rugged and low-priced by the standards of the time. By means of its advanced manufacturing and assembly techniques, Ford's Highland Park, Michigan, plant was able to mass-produce these vehicles in high volumes, which resulted in a dramatic reduction in price over the decades of its manufacture, as we saw earlier. On its release in 1908, the price of a Model T was around USD900 – by 1925, the price had been reduced to less than USD300.

## GOVERNMENT REGULATIONS DURING WORLD WAR I SET THE SCENE FOR A NASCENT COACH- AND BODY-BUILDING INDUSTRY

In 1914, the Australian Parliament passed the War Precautions Act, which placed an embargo on importation of car bodies in an effort to save foreign currency reserves and shipping capacity. Local coach-builders, particularly Holden & Frost and T. J. Richards, were quick to see and capitalise on the opportunity provided by this change. Additionally, many body parts manufacturers took advantage of the situation, gearing up to manufacture body components to be installed on imported chassis.

In 1917, the Australian government placed an embargo on the importing of CBU (completely built-up) vehicles. This was brought about as a result of restrictions caused by World War I, notably the drain on foreign exchange. It had the effect of encouraging local firms to become involved in the production of motor vehicles. Here we see the characteristic response of a national government to the swelling tide of vehicle imports. A number of local plants were established, operating on a CKD (completely-knocked-down) or SKD (semi-knocked-down) basis, with credit against import duties given for a company's total national content level.

In the 1920s, an Adelaide-based coachbuilding and wheelwright firm, T. J. Richards, which had been established in 1885, commenced the assembly of Dodge and Chrysler vehicles (Figure 7.2). This business was eventually bought by Chrysler to form Chrysler Australia.

The manufacturing activities were eventually relocated to Clovelly Park (Tonsley Park), south of Adelaide where Chrysler

FIGURE 7.2  Production at T. J. Richards, Adelaide, 1925
Source: State Library of South Australia

(Royal and Valiant) and eventually Mitsubishi (Sigma, Magna and 380) vehicles were manufactured. In 1925, Ford Australia was formed as a subsidiary of the Ford Company of Canada. It established its manufacturing facility at Geelong (see Figure 7.3) where Model Ts, Model As and later V8s, Pilots, Customlines, Prefects, Zephyrs and Zodiacs were assembled.

The Ford Company of Canada ownership allowed Ford to import vehicles at the 'British Preferred' tariff rate, which was significantly lower than the general 'MFN' (Most Favoured Nation) rate. Ford subsequently established assembly and manufacturing plants at Broadmeadows, Victoria; and Homebush, New South Wales. It also had local assembly plants in Adelaide, Perth and Brisbane, reflecting the continuing strong role of individual states within the Federation. Note Ford's consistent policy of investing in its own plants, rather than acquiring existing ones. Individual manufacturers have and have always had significantly different management philosophies.

Another Adelaide coachbuilder and saddlery, Holden and Frost, which was established in 1859, began trimming motor bodies in 1910 at

FIGURE 7.3 Ford Geelong plant under construction, 1926
Source: State Library of Victoria

its facility in King William Street, Adelaide (Figure 7.4 and 7.5) and completed their first one-off body for an imported Lancia chassis is 1914. In 1923, Holden Motor Body Builders Pty Ltd opened a twenty-two-acre facility in Woodville, South Australia, which was at that time the largest motor body works in the British Empire (Figure 7.6). At that site, Holden built bodies for Dodge, Overland, Durant, Hupmobile, Ford and General Motors. In 1924, Holden built 22,060 bodies, approximately half of which were for General Motors.

In 1926, General Motors Australia (GMA) was formed. Holden was severely affected by the downturn in business activity resulting from the Great Depression and in 1931, GMA acquired Holden to form General Motors-Holden. This was part of GM's early overseas investment phase, during which it also acquired Opel in Germany and Vauxhall in the United Kingdom. The US industry was a generation ahead in its development and scale-building compared to that in Europe.

FIGURE 7.4  Production at Holden Motor Body Builders, King William St, Adelaide, 1925
Source: Neil Pogson, Holden Retirees Club

FIGURE 7.5  Production at Holden Motor Body Builders, 1925
Source: Neil Pogson, Holden Retirees Club

FIGURE 7.6  GM-Holden production at Woodville, South Australia, 1930s
Source: State Library of South Australia

Holden subsequently established assembly and manufacturing
plants at Fisherman's Bend, Victoria; Elizabeth, South Australia;
Pagewood, New South Wales; and Acacia Ridge, Queensland. Prior
to World War II it built bodies for General Motors (Vauxhall,
Chevrolet, Pontiac, Oldsmobile and Buick) on chassis imported to
Australia. The Holden story up to the mid-1980s is vividly presented
in two Quantum TV programmes.[1]

There were other attempts at car building during the interwar
years. Brands included the 'Australian Six' (Figure 7.7), the 'Southern
Six', the 'Summit', the 'Flying Kangaroo' and the 'Southern Cross', none
of which achieved meaningful market success. They were playing
pioneer in the age of the assembly plant.

---

[1]   https://www.youtube.com/watch?v=IR8BhiiAWTo#action=share, https://www
.youtube.com/watch?v=EvU13TvzQ_M

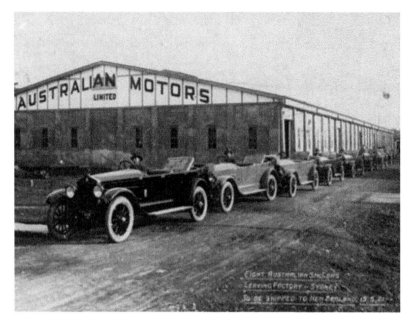

FIGURE 7.7  Australian Six vehicles leaving the factory
Source: State Library of Victoria

## IN THE LATE 1930S, THE AUSTRALIAN GOVERNMENT COMMITTED TO FULL AUSTRALIAN CAR MANUFACTURING

By the 1930s, the Australian government already saw the need to develop the country's secondary industries. An increased manufacturing capability was seen as necessary to (a) increase the country's security and defence capability, (b) provide employment opportunities for returning defence personnel and (c) serve as a nation-building mechanism. The industry was indeed strategic at the time, given its vital role in the mass production of armaments, notably armoured fighting vehicles.

In a statement to the House of Representatives on 17 May 1939, Prime Minister Robert Menzies stated:

> The Commonwealth Government has definitely decided that motor vehicle engines and chassis are to be manufactured in

Australia and that there should be no undue delay in establishing the industry.

1. Defence preparedness, industrial expansion, conservation of overseas funds, immigration, employment and utilisation of Australian raw materials are among the principal reasons underlying this decision.
2. The Commonwealth Government is not able to grant a manufacturing monopoly to any single company.
3. The Commonwealth Government desires that any company formed to undertake manufacture should be Australian in character and policy.
4. The Commonwealth Government considers it essential that the prices of motor vehicles to be manufactured in Australia must be reasonable and the public interest in this respect will be protected.

The Commonwealth Government has not made any decision as to what its desires would be on the subject of the proportion of the capital of any company formed which should be Australian prescribed. Proposals which are under consideration embrace the following:

1. A company with all-Australian capital
2. A company with Australian capital in combination with capital subscribed by an overseas motor vehicle manufacturing organisation – the respective proportions to be determined at a later date.

The Motor Vehicles Agreement Act of 1940 awarded Australia Consolidated Industries the right to manufacture a car in Australia. This plan was shelved as a result of World War II and the Act was repealed in 1945. Still, the general intent of the Australian government was obvious – there would be full manufacture of cars in Australia within a short period of time. There was also a clear need for component suppliers to establish or upgrade their Australian operations.

In 1939 also, the government passed the Motor Vehicle Engine Bounty Act, which promised a bounty of £30 per engine produced in

Australia. Along with the Motor Vehicle Agreement Act, the Bounty Act was repealed in 1945.

As World War II neared its end, interest in building Australia's industrial infrastructure – and in particular, a fully functional automotive industry – revived. The government saw this as a key step in transitioning Australia from being a predominantly primary to a secondary industry country. In 1944, citing reasons similar to those expressed previously, the Labor Government, under Ben Chifley, requested proposals from interested parties in respect of the establishment of full automotive manufacturing in Australia. This was a bold step.

The establishment of a complete manufacturing industry was remarkable, in the circumstances. In 1939, when Prime Minister Robert Menzies first announced the government's intention to foster the industry, Australia's population was 6.97 million. By 1948, when the first Holden was released, it had risen significantly, but was still only 7.7 million. At the time, Australia had not developed a sophisticated secondary industry: by far the greater proportion of Australia's GDP was derived from primary industry – agriculture, grazing and mining. It was a testament to the foresight and deft management of the industry on the part of all governments up to the 1970s that what was essentially a bootstrapping exercise, succeeded and the industry became largely self-sustaining.

At the end of World War II, it was only the US-based vehicle manufacturers (rather than those in Germany or France, or even Britain) that were in a position to even consider expansion into a country like Australia. Given their respective pre-war involvement in the Australian market, it was to be expected that General Motors and Ford would submit proposals to the Government for the establishment of full-scale automotive manufacturing in Australia. Whereas prior to the war, both General Motors and Ford had expressed quite negative – dismissive, in fact – views in respect of their setting up full manufacturing in Australia, both provided proposals in response to the Chifley government's requests.

The Ford proposal sought to involve the Australian government by way of equity and liability. As a result of the combined effects of the

Great Depression (which hit Australia particularly severely) and World War II, Australia's finances were not in a robust state. The notion of having to contribute public funds to the automotive manufacturing venture was not attractive to the Australian government, so the Ford proposal was declined.

On the other hand, General Motors proposed what appeared at the time to be a cleaner, more acceptable offering to the government. Although the proposal did require finance to be provided by Australian banks, General Motors did not require – allow, in fact – any equity stake to be taken by the Australian government. The General Motors proposal effectively shielded the government from risk or ongoing liability. It also excluded the government from having any meaningful control over the venture.

## THE FULLY INTEGRATED MANUFACTURERS CONTINUED
## TO BE FLANKED BY A NUMBER OF ASSEMBLERS

Such was the level of unsatisfied demand for new cars in the post-war years that it remained a sellers' market. Initially, the industry became more dispersed, rather than more concentrated. Rationalisation of the industry came much later. At the same time as the Australian government encouraged and supported the establishment of fully integrated manufacturers, it also allowed the creation of a number of what we would call assemblers – operations that built existing overseas designs, in small volumes and at low levels of national content, sometimes on an SKD (semi-knocked-down) or even CKD (completely knocked-down, i.e., from imported kits) basis. The list is quite long:

- The British Motor Corporation (Australia) was formed in 1954 as a merger of the Austin Company of Australia and Nuffield Australia, reflecting the 1952 merger of the respective parent companies in Britain. During the 1950s, 1960s and 1970s, the BMC plant in Zetland, NSW, performed full manufacture of a number of Austin and Morris vehicles, as well as CKD assembly of others. Models manufactured at Zetland boasted a high local content (up to 98 per cent, depending on model) and included the Morris Major/Austin Lancer, Morris 850/Mini Deluxe/

Mini K/Mini Cooper, Mini Moke, Morris 1100, Austin Freeway/
Wolseley 24/80, Morris 1500, Morris Marina, Austin 1800, Austin
Tasman/Kimberley and Leyland P76.

- Standard Triumph formed Australian Motor Industries (AMI) in 1958,
  assembling CKD Standard Vanguards and Triumph Heralds as well as low-
  volume models from Rambler (from American Motors – AMC) and
  Mercedes Benz. This plant went on to assemble Toyota cars and was later
  taken over by Toyota in its first industrial investment in Australia

- In 1946, Rootes Group commenced Australian assembly at its Port
  Melbourne plant. Among the models assembled there were the Hillman
  Minx/Super Minx, Hillman Imp, Hillman Arrow/Hunter, Singer Gazelle,
  Sunbeam Rapier and Alpine and the Humber Super Snipe, Hawk and Vogue.
  After Chrysler took over Rootes Group in 1965, the plant assembled Dodge
  Phoenix and Mitsubishi Galant vehicles until it was closed in 1972 and
  production was transferred to the Tonsley Park plant in South Australia.

- Continental and General Industries built a new assembly plant at
  Heidelberg, Victoria, in 1955 to assemble Renault (10, 12, 16 and 18),
  Peugeot (404 and 504), Citroën (ID and DS) and Studebaker models. The
  plant was acquired by Renault Australia in 1966, and ceased operations in
  1981.

- Martin and King, a long-established body builder and assembler, began
  Volkswagen assembly in 1955 at Clayton in Melbourne; by the mid-1960s
  this plant was manufacturing sheet metal body panels and engines. After
  1968, the plant reverted to assembly of Volkswagen, Datsun and Volvo
  models. It was subsequently acquired by Nissan.

- Pressed Metal Corporation was originally established in the 1930s to
  assemble Austin vehicles in its Enfield, NSW plant. Models subsequently
  assembled there included the Austin A40/A50/A55, Austin-Healy Sprite,
  Austin Gypsy, MGA, MGB, MG Midget, the Leyland Mini, Moke and Land
  Rovers.

This wide array of manufacturing and assembly activity exemplifies
the combination of the burgeoning market for cars in the post-war
decades and the effects of the government's industry protection policies. However, given the size of the Australian market, none of these
efforts was likely to generate the sort of scale required to make for
a sustainable industry.

## AFTER A RAPID START, AUSTRALIAN AUTOMOTIVE MANUFACTURING STARTED TO FALL BEHIND THE WORLD TREND FROM QUITE EARLY ON

Figure 7.8 tracks Australian production of light passenger motor vehicles (PMVs) from 1950 to 2017 in million units per year. The shaded area corresponds to annual production volumes. The grey shading is volume that ended up sold in the domestic Australian market. The black shading is that generated by export sales. The black line (right hand scale in per cent) tracks Australia's share of total world production of these vehicles. The results are quite striking. Australian production grew at a heady pace of 10 per cent per year from 1950 to 1971. Then it stalled abruptly, as market growth ceased and oscillated around a slow declining trend until the mid-1980s, when the import surge began. Thereafter it went into accelerated decline, where volumes destined for the home market were concerned, with only an upward blip in 2003. The growth of exports temporarily restored overall production volume, reaching a new peak in

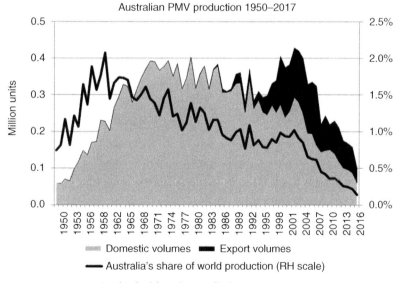

FIGURE 7.8 Climbed fast then stalled
Data sources: AAI, Australian Automotive Statistics

2003. But then the fall accelerated. In relative terms, Australian output growth initially outpaced the rest of the world. Until 1961, essentially because the Australian economy, undamaged by war, grew quickly and there was that great pent-up demand for cars to fulfil. But even in 1961 it barely exceeded 2 per cent of world production. Then the rest of the world speeded up, Australia slowed down, and it was a steady slide all the way to the end of the industry in 2017, apart from that brief surge in the early 2000s. A gradual but inexorable slide towards extinction.

## THERE WAS A YAWNING GULF IN THE SCALE OF OPERATIONS

This inexorable trend casts a great deal of light on what took place in the Australia. The competitive structures of the global automotive industry today are absolutely not those of 1945. It is particularly important to understand the globally networked nature of the industry. The vehicle manufacturers operate interlinked networks of sites, for engineering and product development; for vehicle assembly and their own systems and components production; and for sourcing from independent parts suppliers. The lengthy and complex development and supply chains are tightly managed. This means that local vehicle operations have to establish their own survivable roles within these global empires, unless they are totally protected by tariff and other trade barriers. A competitor that does not enjoy sufficient national scale in a volume-driven industry has to specialise in a sector in which it can achieve sufficient relative scale. But this sector also needs to be defensible and to have a future. The Holden Commodore platform peaked at 165,000 units in 2004 and the Ford Falcon at 105,000 units. Even if the leading global platforms were produced at somewhat lower volumes in 2004, compared to the projected 2020 volumes in Figure 3.4, the yawning gulf in scale is obvious.

As can be seen in Figure 7.9, local assembly of low-volume products, presumably at lower levels of local content, finally died out by 2002, apart from a curious revival with the Holden Cruze between 2011 and 2016. More about this last in Chapter 9. The large brick-shaded area contained a number of models, including the Laser,

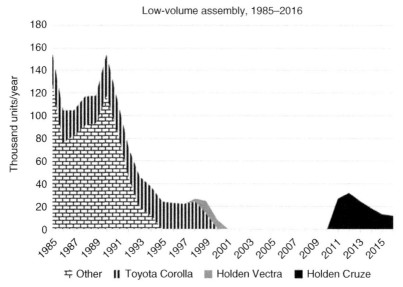

FIGURE 7.9 The end of low-volume assembly
Data sources: The Automotive Industry 1991, AAI, Key Automotive Statistics

Pulsar and Pintara/Skyline. It represents the running down of light-weight assembly of multiple models. This left only four models from four manufacturers in production.

## THE INDUSTRY DIED FROM OLD PRODUCTS, NOT HIGH LABOUR COSTS OR LACK OF GOVERNMENT SUPPORT

Even with this concentration, the automotive industry in Australia persisted for far too long with the production of unique legacy products at far too small a scale to be viable. It had established full design and development capabilities, as was often trumpeted in its defence, together with flexible production. But these could not of themselves overcome the cost disadvantages induced by such low scale. Remaining in large RWD volume cars long into the declining years of their life cycle doomed the industry. But the local industry could not afford to replace them with new, uniquely Australian products. The national icons – both products and manufacturers – became relics. Once Australians realised they had

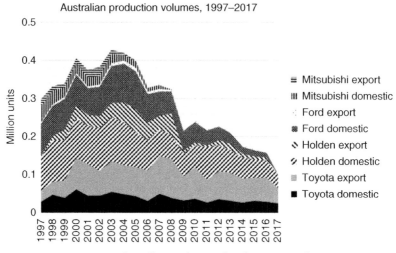

FIGURE 7.10  The collapse of Australian large car production
Data sources: Key Automotive Statistics, AAI yearbook 2017, Autopolis
estimates

a choice, they progressively deserted the local brands. Fewer sales
resulted in lowered revenues for the local manufacturers, which reduced
their already weak capacity to refresh and update their product lines,
which resulted, in turn, in lower sales. Figure 7.10 shows the results up to
2012: the government's Key Automotive Statistics ceased to be available
thereafter. Traditional large cars held their domestic volumes for quite
a long time but lost heavily in market share and eventually those
volumes started to fall. Their belatedly achieved export volumes were
never large enough to make up for those losses.

High Australian labour costs have often been invoked as a reason
for the decline of vehicle production in Australia. This is a contentious
issue, much tinged with political prejudices. The data in Figure 7.11 do
not show Australia as disadvantaged compared to the developed automotive countries, notably Germany, Japan and the United States. By 2012,
South Korean and Brazilian automotive hourly labour costs were catching
up, and Brazil has never been a competitive exporter. There clearly was
and is a major gap compared to Mexico, India and China. Thailand has

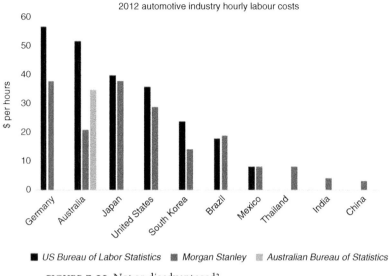

FIGURE 7.11 Not so disadvantaged?

become a major exporter to Australia, thanks to a Free Trade Agreement that failed to take automotive industry realities into account. Mexico has not been a factor so far. Neither India nor China has developed to any significant degree as exporters of vehicles to Australia. But it all depends very much on the strategies of the global vehicle manufacturers and the balance between local demand and production capacity in their different producing regions, plus trade agreements. The overwhelming disparity, though, is in the scale of operations. The weight here lies not so much in vehicle assembly as in components production, which today represents 80 per cent of the cost of light vehicles. This is discussed in Chapter 9.

Nor did the industry collapse for want of support by government. Figure 7.12 shows the history of the effective rate of combined assistance (tariff relief plus budgetary grants) to industry as a whole and to the automotive industry in particular. The rate of support was very high in early years, principally because of relief from high import tariffs. But it remained well above the average for all industry, right until the end, mainly because of assistance programmes specific to the industry, which we discuss in Chapter 10.

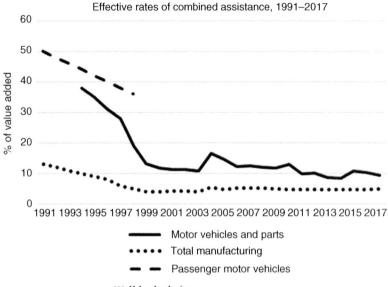

FIGURE 7.12  Well looked after
Data source: Productivity Commission Annual Trade and Assistance
Reviews

## THE FINANCIAL COLLAPSE OF THE INDUSTRY STARTED
## WITH FALLING VOLUMES, BEFORE THE GFC

Whatever the causes of the decline in production, the consequences
for the Australian manufacturers were dire. Figure 7.13 shows their
trading profits, split between manufacturing (the black portions of the
columns in the diagram) and other operations (imported vehicles,
parts, finance – the grey portion of the columns). By the early 1990s,
the vehicle manufacturers, by now well below their collective production peak of 400,000 units in 1980, were losing money on their manufacturing operations, as margins over variable costs dipped below the
level needed to cover fixed costs. The extra volume afforded by
exports, which passed the 100,000-unit mark in 2000, restored
a modest level of profit. All this was lost again as volumes collapsed,
first through loss of share on the domestic market from 2006. Note
that this took place *before* the GFC, which can therefore not be

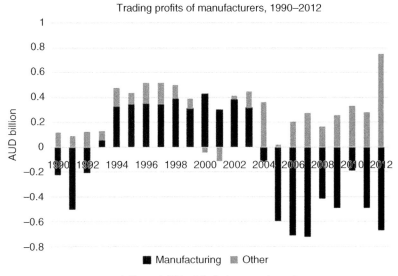

FIGURE 7.13  A financial black hole in manufacturing
Data source: Key Automotive Statistics Australia

blamed for it. On top of that came the fall in exports from 2009, which was indeed caused by the GFC, in which both General Motors and Toyota suffered heavily in the North American market, as noted earlier. It was only increased vehicle imports by these manufacturers that eventually brought them back to break-even in 2012. Australian light vehicle manufacturing had become a financial black hole. The losses were increasingly masked by the domestic manufacturers' own increasing level of car imports under their brands. This had the unfortunate side effect of weakening the association between those brands and iconic Australian cars, mostly for Holden, also for Ford but least so for Toyota, whose locally built Camry never was an Australian design. Both Holden and Ford had long held onto the idea that they were primarily Australian manufacturers, with importing cars a secondary activity. In contrast, Toyota had started as a pure importer in Australia, before adding manufacturing there, presumably in a bid to make itself appear more Australian.

## THE AUSTRALIAN AUTOMOTIVE INDUSTRY WAS COMING
## TO THE END OF ITS NATURAL LIFE CYCLE

These results, in volumes and value produced, and in lack of profits, all arose from an industry that rested on trying to prolong the life cycle of vehicles produced to outdated design concepts (large, mass-market RWD layouts), when the markets, both in Australia and abroad, had long since moved on – at least for the Commodore and Falcon. The small – and shrinking – size of these two operations could not, even in the best of times, generate enough cash flow to finance complete replacements. And why bother to do it in and for Australia, when global platforms were available? By 2010, it was obvious to the informed onlooker that Ford Australia would not be able to justify replacing the Falcon with something similar. Holden spent an average of 4.4 per cent of sales on R&D – a respectable ratio, given that manufacturers normally spend about 3 per cent, although this has been rising of late, with electrification and autonomous driving in prospect. The problem was the absolute figure, AUD 220 million per year. Almost all of this would be 'D', i.e., routine product updating and refreshing, and process improvement, rather than 'R', for real technical innovation.[2] Its total annual spend fell abruptly (by 60 per cent in 2009) following the GFC. This was surely not decided without the knowledge of GM and should have been an early indicator of the latter's withdrawal of support from its Australian subsidiary. Ford spent proportionately more, although on much lower sales, with the spend boosted by work done for parts of the group outside Australia. Removing that boost, there would have been no room for much beyond routine upkeep of the current product. Toyota's spend was negligible, reflecting its role as a satellite assembly plant for an already designed world product.

---

[2]    Lumping together expenses for R and for D is a statistical error perpetuated by the OECD in its reporting. They are fundamentally different activities, which should on no account be confused.

## THE COSTS TO AUSTRALIA OF LETTING GO
## OF THE INDUSTRY HAVE BEEN EXAGGERATED

Claims were made about the dire threat to employment that shutting down the industry would create. There would, of course, be a painful impact in the vicinity of the assembly plants, which were large employers, often of first-generation immigrants. Vehicle manufacturers have always been a haven for these, whether in Australia, Detroit or Europe. Some misleading statistics, citing 100,000s of jobs, were bandied about by some but these illegitimately included the considerable employment in the downstream sectors of the industry – from dealer sales staff to filling station employees – which would remain, wherever the vehicles were sourced from. These downstream, post-manufacturing activities typically employ 80 per cent of those working in the broader automotive sector. Of this 80 per cent, a quarter are in car distribution and sales and three quarters in service and repair. Over 75 per cent of those in service and repair work in the independent aftermarket. Employment in the manufacture of passenger motor vehicles and parts for them had reached almost 100,000 in the mid-1970s but drifted steadily down thereafter, with the occasional resurgence, for example, with the post-2000 export mini-boom. Fifteen years later, it was down to 40,000, which represented under 5 per cent of all employment in manufacturing, and a tiny proportion of the 12.5 million working Australians. As shown in Figures 7.14 and 7.15, the blow to the balance of payments had already been largely incurred.

The claims that it would represent the loss of a unique set of skills and of a continuing feeding of techniques into the broader manufacturing sector were in fact unprovable. A modest-sized and agile automotive engineering sector had grown up. But the economics of building smaller and smaller volumes of unique products in locations very distant from the main markets were not sustainable. This was particularly so in the much-less-discussed or visible components sector, which we address in Chapter 9. Two Australian icons of long standing were lost. But they had long since lost most of their devotees.

FIGURE 7.14  The trade balances
Data sources: DFAT, AAI

Nor could lack of government support be blamed. It was made available in considerable quantity but with too few strings attached. We
discuss this in Chapter 10.

Figure 7.14 shows the development of Australia's external trade
in all goods and in the automotive sector. Note the logarithmic scale,
which shows up ratios rather than absolute number differences.

Apart from an unsurprising deficit in the early decades and a sharp
drop in imports during the Great Depression, the country's overall trade
in goods has been fairly balanced. The effects of the accelerating and then
slowing minerals boom can be seen from the mid-1970s. In contrast, the
automotive sector has run a heavy deficit over the last thirty-five years.
The export-to-import imbalance ran at 5:1 in the peak years for vehicle
exports, 2003–4, but deepened again to 10:1 thereafter, as exports dipped.
The ratio in components has held steadier at around 7:1.

Figure 7.15 shows the relative significance for Australia of its automotive imports and exports. Automotive exports painfully crept up from

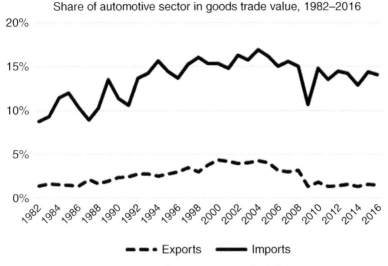

Share of automotive sector in goods trade value, 1982–2016

FIGURE 7.15  An endemic automotive trade deficit
Data sources: DFAT, AAI

2 per cent to almost 5 per cent of total goods exports, only to crash down again to 1.5 per cent, until production ceased. The share of the automotive sector in goods imports steadily increased from 9 per cent in 1982 to a peak of 17 per cent in 2004, before gradually declining again to 14 per cent in 2016, with a sharp downward blip after the GFC – showing that Australia was not totally unaffected by it. Any vestige of an import substitution strategy had long disappeared. The benefits of continuing to manufacture cars had become minimal.

## BREAKING OUT OF THE IMPASSE THROUGH A MASSIVE EXPANSION OF PRODUCTION WAS IMPLAUSIBLE

At the time of the Bracks review of the industry and its prospects in 2008, there were calls for a massive expansion of Australian PMV production, to 1 million units per year. Theoretically, this kind of volume, spread over three vehicle manufacturers, would have given them and the suppliers behind them the necessary scale and cash flow to ensure their survival. In practice, however, for Holden or Ford to try to emulate Toyota's export-led strategy would have totally depended on their parent groups' ability and willingness to absorb the exports into their overseas distribution networks and markets. Not all markets are easily open to such flows. China and India have high tariff barriers on CBUs. The EU has a 10 per cent external tariff, the United States 2.5 per cent, Japan none – but with a high consumer resistance to foreign imports. Besides which there is endemic assembly over-capacity in all the mature, developed, accessible markets.

## INCREASING EFFECTIVE SCALE THROUGH COLLABORATION BETWEEN LOCAL MANUFACTURERS WOULD HAVE REQUIRED FORCEFUL GOVERNMENT INTERVENTION

The task of the 2008 review was to look at the industry and provide recommendations as to how it might be made more successful and sustainable. As a result of Australia's small and highly crowded market place, it should have been obvious that a 'business as usual' approach was not sustainable in the long term. The three manufacturers were struggling to produce vehicles in the volumes required to amortise the sunk costs and the extensive design and engineering required to support their independent operations. That model might have worked – reasonably well – in a market the size of the United States or Europe, in which annual light vehicle sales range between 13 and 17 million units. However, it was unsustainable in Australia's 1 million unit/year market.

Autopolis proposed that the industry would benefit from taking a more 'Australia, Inc' approach. Appropriate collaboration between vehicle manufacturers and component suppliers at the technical and manufacturing levels could have allowed the industry to operate in a more sustainable manner. It could perhaps have created a vehicle anchored in Australian market requirements, such as an up-line SUV. Land Rover/Range Rover might, in fact, more logically have had a home in Australia than in the United Kingdom.

There were examples in existence around the world that illustrated the possible viability of the approach. The German, Japanese and Korean industries each had deployed elements of this proposal in various ways and at various times and under strong government guidance, and had gone on to build successful global enterprises. But this required the Australian industry to escape from its condition of frozen oligarchy, which would probably only have forceful government intervention, which was exactly what government had been backing away from.

## LOW VOLUME CONTRACT ASSEMBLY FOR EXTERNAL MANUFACTURERS WAS NOT A VIABLE PROPOSITION

Resumption of low-volume assembly of foreign vehicles at low local content would have made no sense. Holden's attempt to assemble the Cruze in limited volumes for the Australian market only, presumably to prop up activity at its Elizabeth assembly plant, made no sense (we shall discuss this more in Chapter 9) and led nowhere. Existing large MVPs may occasionally elect to have selected very low volume models designed and/or assembled by a specialist external firm. Examples of such firms include Magna Steyr (Austria), Valmet (Finland) and Pininfarina (Italy). This strategy can be beneficial for the large MVP since their main operations are not set up for low volume production – attempting to manufacture very low volume models would tend to disrupt their normal high-volume operations. A recent example is Jaguar, which is having its new I-Pace electric car assembled by Magna Steyr.

There was a proposal to have a small-volume assembler establish operations in Australia, with a view to designing and/or assembling vehicles for a large manufacturer on a small-volume basis. Any rational analysis however would suggest that this proposal is a non-starter. Australia's geographic isolation would make communications with the commissioning client difficult. The costs of relocating design and engineering personnel between the client head office and the new facility in Adelaide would be significant. Australian labour costs, while no higher than in many other centres, would certainly not represent an incentive for the plan to proceed. Other costs (real estate, power, plant and equipment, components, raw materials, etc.) would inevitably be higher in Australia than many other countries. Supply chains that are already in place in, say, Europe would need to be extended to Australia, which would require the active involvement and backing of the relevant suppliers. Inevitably the PMVs that resulted from such an arrangement would have limited appeal in an already small but crowded Australian market so the bulk of the output would be shipped back to the client's home market – in Europe, the United States or Asia – thus introducing yet more costs into the plan and making it still less attractive. It is difficult to identify a single significant benefit accruing to the operation that would have encouraged its establishment in Australia.

### LOW-VOLUME MANUFACTURING OF A RANGE OF LOCALLY DESIGNED VEHICLES USING NOVEL BODY STRUCTURES WAS ANOTHER SPECIOUS SUGGESTION

Another proposal envisaged the establishment of new kind of automotive manufacturing facility. The plan involved the deployment of new (to Australia) manufacturing techniques to make a range of cars including an SUV, a two-door coupe, a three-box sedan and an upline, luxury sedan. While the project appeared attractive initially, in-depth analysis showed it to be essentially flawed. The low-volume manufacturing and assembly methods proposed for this plan are similar to those deployed in other very-low-volume facilities in other countries. The cars produced in those facilities are both high cost and highly priced, which is acceptable if the cars are in the highly specialised, low-volume end of the market. However, the Australian venture relied on being able to use these high-cost, low-volume manufacturing techniques to produce a car that would sell in high volumes in the mainline 'D-class' segment (alongside Mazda 6, Toyota Camry, Honda Accord, etc.). Implausible assumptions were made about huge volume-driven productivity gains to be obtained by scaling up production.

The products were to be positioned as up-line entrants in the Australian market yet little attention had been paid to the extensive 'refinement engineering' that is required to make the difference between a mainline and up-line product – or even to be really competitive in the global mainline market, for that matter. Virtually no market analysis had been performed (or planned) to establish a real understanding of the needs or wants of the consumer public. It was assumed that the car would sell in high volumes purely because of its Australian design and manufacture credentials. That assertion was not supported by any analysis. There was an implicit requirement on the part of the proponents to gain access to the unspent portions of Automotive Transition Scheme funding, in order to make the proposal financially viable.

## RESTARTING MANUFACTURE OF AN EXISTING MODEL IN AN EXISTING PLANT WAS COMPLETELY UNREALISTIC

There was a proposal to use the existing Holden Elizabeth facility to continue to manufacture the traditional Holden Commodore models. There were a number of problems with this proposal, the first of which being the degree to which General Motors would cooperate with it. For it to be viable, General Motors would have had to provide open access to information such as:

- Design and engineering data
- Manufacturing data
- Testing and compliance data
- Spare parts supplies and data
- Diagnostic and repair data
- Model upgrade and development plans
- Marketing and sales data

Further, General Motors would have needed to allow use of and access to its brand names ('Holden' (presumably) and 'Commodore', etc.), its dealer and service network and its marketing resources. Whether General Motors would have been agreeable to such commitments was moot, to say the least. That consideration alone resulted in the plan's being highly problematic. Furthermore, the whole proposal was predicated on a belief that the Australian public would rush to purchase a by-then outdated and obsolete Commodore product (presumably

superseded at that stage by a newer, fresher, more modern 'real' General
Motors Commodore) even though they had largely stopped buying that
product in recent years anyway. The proposal appeared to be well-
described as 'courageous'.

All this was a sad end to a heroic effort to build a national
automotive industry, which for a time succeeded far better than
other such national projects in other countries. In retrospect, however,
the risks to it were evident long ago, because of the changes in the
industry outside Australia.

### IN SUMMARY, THE AUSTRALIAN CAR INDUSTRY HAD A VIGOROUS LIFE BUT THIS CAME TO ITS END

Australian vehicle assembly began prior to World War I on a very
small scale. Government regulations during World War I set the
scene for a nascent coachbuilding industry. In the late 1930s, the
Australian Government committed to full Australian car manufacturing. The fully integrated manufacturers established after World War II
continued to be flanked by a number of assemblers. After a rapid start,
Australian automotive manufacturing started to fall behind the world
growth trend from quite early on, resulting in a yawning gulf in the
scale of operations. The industry died from lack of scale, not from high
labour costs or lack of government support. The financial collapse of
the industry started with falling volumes, before the GFC. The
Australian automotive industry was in fact coming to the end of its
natural life cycle. The costs to Australia of letting go of the industry
have been exaggerated. Breaking out of the impasse through a massive
expansion of production was implausible. Increasing effective scale
through collaboration between local manufacturers would have
required forceful government intervention, which it had, in fact,
been backing away from. Low volume contract assembly for external
manufacturers was not a viable proposition either. Low-volume manufacturing of a range of locally designed vehicles using novel body
structures was another specious suggestion. Restarting manufacture
of an existing model in an existing plant was completely unrealistic.

# 8 Distant Children: Australian Vehicle Manufacturers and Their Foreign Parents

## FORD WAS FIRST TO ESTABLISH MANUFACTURING IN AUSTRALIA

Ford has a long history in the Australian automotive market. It commenced importing Model Ts prior to World War I and achieved remarkable market success. The car was simple, durable and, for its time, fairly powerful. Perhaps most importantly it represented remarkably good value against its (mainly English origin) competition. Ford Australia was formed in 1925 as a subsidiary of Ford of Canada, an arrangement that allowed Fords to be imported into Australia at the lower, 'British Preferential' rate of tariff. During the 1920s and 1930s it partnered with local coachbuilders to build bodies for the Model T and Model A chassis.

Ford's proposal in response to the Australian Government's call in 1944 for the establishment of an automotive industry was less generous than General Motors' – it called for significant financial investment on the part of the Australian Government (in return for an equity stake) and more restrictive protection measures. Ford established manufacturing and assembly plants in Geelong and Broadmeadows, Victoria; and Homebush, NSW. During the 1940s and 1950s it assembled several British Ford models including Prefect, Popular, Consul, Zephyr and Pilot – see Figure 8.1. The American Customline and Fairlane models were also assembled in Australia.

It took a major step when, in 1960, it commenced full manufacture in Broadmeadows of the XK Falcon (seen in Figure 8.2), which was a mild reworking of the equivalent US model. While this was a considerably more modern product than the Holden of the day (the 'FB') in terms of appearance, specification and performance, the initial cars were plagued

FIGURE 8.1 Ford Consul and Customline models, assembled in Geelong, 1950s
Source: State Library of Victoria

FIGURE 8.2 1960 Ford Falcon XK
Source: Tony Buckland

with front suspension durability and other problems, which negatively impacted Ford's – more specifically, Falcon's – reputation for the next four years.

FIGURE 8.3 The first Euro-styled Falcon – the 1979 XD
Source: Ilinga Books

The Falcon was in many ways the 'most Australian' of the cars manufactured and marketed by the local manufacturers in Australia during the 1980s and 1990s and into the twenty-first Century. From 1965 onwards, the Australian Falcon gradually moved away from the influence of the Ford parent company in terms of styling, design and specification. In 1979, European-influenced styling was adopted with the XD Falcon – see Figure 8.3.

With the exception of the 289, 302 and 351 cubic inch ('Windsor' and 'Cleveland') V8 engines, there were virtually no components shared with the US-based products. This isolation was useful for Ford Australia's marketing, as it allowed it to proclaim and emphasise the vehicle's uniquely Australian character. The inevitable downside of that arrangement was that Ford Australia was obliged to amortise the full design, engineering and development costs for the complete Falcon family over what were necessarily limited production volumes in a small market.

## BUT ITS CORPORATE CULTURE DID NOT GIVE ENOUGH
## SUPPORT TO ITS LOCAL SUBSIDIARY

From its inception, Ford Motor Company's management style tended to be highly autocratic and 'top-down' in nature. It led the global industry in the design and application of rigorous statistical financial measures across all of it operations. Its daughter companies in Canada, Europe, England and Australia enjoyed little real autonomy. In particular, Ford Australia was seen by Ford of America as somewhat of an unconnected outpost within the corporate structure. Ford Australia never achieved anywhere near the same level of acceptance within the Ford global network as Holden achieved within the GM global network. Thus, it had little chance of successfully emerging from its protected autarchic position, once the Australian market opened up to imports. Ford Australia did have a brief, ill-starred flirtation with the US market by way of its Capri model (Figure 8.4). The car was based on previous generation Mazda 323 mechanicals and featured a body designed by Ghia. Interestingly in view of its Mazda origins, its

FIGURE 8.4  1991 Ford Capri – an export miss
Source: Ilinga Books

FIGURE 8.5  1998 Ford Falcon AU – a market miss
Source: Ilinga Books

closest competitor was the first model Mazda MX5 (Miata). Exports to the United States commenced in 1991, but the Capri was plagued by reliability and durability concerns, including a major problem with the roof system. There were many delays in bringing it into production. Small volumes were sold in New Zealand and South Africa in its right-hand-drive version. The car never established a solid foothold in any market it contested and production ceased in 1994. The failure of the Capri in the US market damaged Ford Australia's standing in the eyes of Ford of America. Ford Australia was never permitted by Ford of America to develop an effective export programme, which further limited its volume potential and reinforced its overall isolation.

Ford Australia then suffered a string of market misses, commencing with the AU Falcon model in 1998 (Figure 8.5), which admittedly, was developed on a shoestring budget and combined obsolete mechanicals with an ungainly body style. The AU caused Ford Australia to lose significant market share: with the exception of the 'cops and cabs' market it failed to achieve meaningful success in the local market. See Figure 8.6. The decline, in fact, started in the mid-1990s. There was a short-lived bounce-back in 2003–4 but the fall accelerated sharply thereafter.

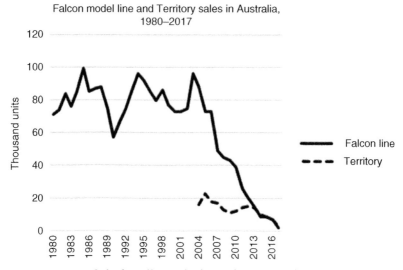

FIGURE 8.6  The collapse of Falcon sales in Australia
Data source: VFACTS

## AS A RESULT, FORD AUSTRALIA WAS STARVED OF DEVELOPMENT FUNDING FOR ITS FUTURE MODELS, PLACING A FURTHER DRAG ON ITS POTENTIAL SUCCESS AND ULTIMATELY LEADING TO CLOSURE

The Ford Territory (shown in Figure 8.7), released in 2004, was a case in point. A brilliant concept and design, skilfully aimed at the then-burgeoning SUV market, it was hobbled by a lack of development funding. Had it been engineered for left-hand drive and specified with a diesel option (Ford had access to world-leading diesel engines at the time, co-developed with Peugeot-Citroën and Jaguar) it could have been marketed in Europe with every chance of success. Even a tiny penetration of this huge market would have transformed its production volumes. Ford Australia's limited development budget combined with its isolated position within the Ford global structure effectively restricted the Territory to the Australian market and impli-citly, mediocre sales. Low sales volumes increased the unit cost of production above the break-even point and made any plans for invest-ment in new model lines totally impractical.

FIGURE 8.7 2004 Ford Territory
Source: Ilinga Books

In the final analysis, Ford failed in Australia because its products were becoming increasingly uncompetitive and unattractive with advancing age. It failed because the Australian public grew tired of its products and stopped buying them. Most importantly, it failed because Ford Australia's management never succeeded in building a solid position for the Australian operation within the global Ford network. It never managed to achieve meaningful backing from the parent company, so when it experienced a severe and sustained downturn in sales success in Australia, its head office turned off the life support. In May 2013, Ford announced that it would withdraw from manufacturing in Australia in 2016. Nissan had ceased local production long before. Mitsubishi Australia had given up production earlier, following the all-too-predictable failure of its attempt to create a new Australian model, the 380, on tiny volumes. Ford's throwing in the towel was widely viewed as the trigger for the end of Australian car production, even though its volumes were by then so small that the loss of them was not determining.

## GENERAL MOTORS MADE A MAJOR COMMITMENT
### TO HOLDEN

The Managing Director of Holden at the time, Laurence Hartnett, played a major role in brokering the agreement that was established between General Motors and the Australian Government in 1944. The General Motors proposal was accepted due in large part to the much-lower financial commitment required of the Australian Government, compared to Ford's proposal. GM effectively assumed all the financial risks of the venture. Until its new locally developed car was ready for manufacture, Holden continued producing bodies for a number of GM brands including Buick, Chevrolet, Pontiac and Vauxhall. The Holden 48–215 was first displayed to the public at Fisherman's Bend on 29 November 1948. Prime Minister Ben Chifley, shown with the new car in Figure 8.8, who had been instrumental in convincing

FIGURE 8.8  Prime Minister Ben Chifley and the 1948 Holden 48–215
Source: Neil Pogson, Holden Retirees Club

General Motors to design and manufacture the car, proclaimed its arrival by way of his famous line, "She's a beauty!"

It was released to a market that was just starting to experience the post-war prosperity similar to that being enjoyed in the United States. Demand for new cars was high, while supply of imported vehicles was still severely limited. Despite being heavily marketed as 'Australia's Own Car' it had in fact been largely designed in Detroit, based as it was on a pre-war Chevrolet Fleetwood design. It was equipped with a 2172cc straight-six engine producing 60 bhp (45 kW). The car was simple and rugged, and ideally suited to Australian conditions. At the time, the best selling cars in Australia were the Austin A40 Devon (four-cylinder, 1.2L, 40 bhp) and the Morris Oxford (four -cylinder, 1.4L, 40 bhp). Against those competitors, the Holden was larger, smoother, more comfortable and better performing. The Standard Vanguard of the day (four-cylinder, 2.1L, 68 bhp) more closely matched it in terms of specification but was significantly more expensive.

## HOLDEN ACHIEVED A MAJOR ADVANTAGE BY BEING THE FIRST FULLY INTEGRATED MANUFACTURER IN AUSTRALIA

Even if the car had been largely designed and engineered in the United States, it was still manufactured in Australia, initially in plants at Woodville (Adelaide), shown in Figure 8.9, and subsequently in Fisherman's Bend and Dandenong (Melbourne), Acacia Ridge (Queensland) and Perth. Note the very simple production facilities at Woodville, visible in the photograph. Holden eventually concentrated assembly at its large plant in Elizabeth, north of Adelaide. With local content initially around 60 per cent and increasing to close to 100 per cent over the next decade, it was 'Australia's Own Car' and was accepted as such by an adoring public.

During the 1950s, Holden dominated the Australia market, achieving up to 75 per cent of total market sales, with demand exceeding supply for many years. Even by 1960, the figure was still greater than

FIGURE 8.9  Holden production at Woodville, 1949
Source: Neil Pogson, Holden Retirees Club

50 per cent – reminiscent of GM's share of the US market at the time. Its products might have been technically conservative and somewhat un-refined, and their equipment specifications parsimonious, but Holden established a strong position for itself in the minds of the Australian public. Holden also developed a solid export market in the 1950s and 1960s, based on both CBU (completely built-up) units and CKD (completely-knocked-down) kits, i.e., complete cars disassembled. Holdens could be found in New Zealand, Africa, South East Asia and Polynesia/Melanesia. At the time, there were countless newsreel clips, shown at the local cinema, showing Holden FCs, FBs and EKs being driven onto waiting cargo ships. The 1960 FB is shown in Figures 8.10 and 8.11. In 1963, Holden produced its millionth vehi-cle, an 'EJ Premier'.

There was considerable national pride vested in the Holden product – Australia had established itself as one of very few car man-ufacturing nations, a list of which included the United States, Canada, Britain, France, Germany, Italy and Sweden. Australia's position as an advanced industrial economy was significantly fortified by its suc-cessful and growing automotive industry. Most importantly, Holden was able to drive local production scale and sourcing to a level that

FIGURE 8.10  Holden FB production at Woodville, 1960
Source: Neil Pogson, Holden Retirees Club

FIGURE 8.11  1960 Holden FB
Source: Neil Pogson, Holden Retirees Club

FIGURE 8.12 1977 Holden Kingswood HZ, with its US-inspired styling
Source: Neil Pogson, Holden Retirees Club

most of it competitors could not match. But it was ultimately reliant on a protected market, in its role as the national champion, as were SEAT in Spain and Fiat in Italy – with the attendant latent risks.

Driven by the oil price shocks of the 1970s, Holden replaced its long-standing American-inspired Kingswood model line-up (illustrated in Figure 8.12) in 1978 with the new, (slightly) smaller VB Commodore, involving a switch to a more European design, shown in Figure 8.13. Its exterior and interior styling were closely based on the Opel Rekord of the day, giving it a considerably more European flavour than the largely American-inspired vehicles that had preceded it. The drivetrain mechanicals, however, were largely a straight carry-over from the Kingswood models. The Commodore represented a significant change for the Australian market as it marked the start of the 'Europeanisation' of the Australian market. European style, dynamics and packaging were seen as the 'new normal' by the Australian consumer.

FIGURE 8.13 1978 Holden VB Commodore, with new European styling
Source: Neil Pogson, Holden Retirees Club

In 1982, Holden released the Camira which, as part of the General Motors innovative 'global platform program' shared styling and mechanical design with GM products in Europe and the United States, which appeared under a range of GM brand names including Opel, Vauxhall, Chevrolet, Pontiac, Oldsmobile, Buick and Cadillac. Early models suffered from poor build quality, which severely limited its market success. Australian production was discontinued in 1989.

As part of Holden's compliance with the Button Plan for the rationalisation of the Australian automotive industry, it commenced a model-sharing programme with Toyota in 1989, which was perhaps influenced by the NUMMI (New United Motor Manufacturing, Inc) assembly partnership between GM and Toyota in the United States. The Toyota Corolla and Camry models were rebadged as Holden Nova and Apollo respectively, while the Holden Commodore was rebadged as a Toyota Lexcen. Model sharing was not restricted to Holden and Toyota. Holden and Nissan shared the Astra/Pulsar from 1984 to 1989, while Ford and Mazda shared the Laser/323 and the Telstar/626 models in the 1980s and Ford and Nissan shared the Corsair/Pintara from 1989 to 1992.

The public appeared to be generally unimpressed with these schemes, however – typically, they saw through the ruse and consistently preferred the 'real' versions of cars to the rebadged ones. The Holden-Toyota model-sharing programme was quietly dropped in 1997. Whether an independent Automotive Industry Authority, mooted as part of the Button Plan but not implemented, might have been more effective than burcaucratic government intervention remains unresolved.

## HOLDEN STARTED TO MAKE THE CRITICAL MOVE FROM NATIONAL AUTARCHY TO BEING LINKED IN TO ITS GLOBAL PARENT IN THE EARLY 2000S

Particularly during the early 2000s, Holden established a strong position for itself within General Motors' increasingly global networks of engineering, manufacturing and sourcing. Peter Hanenberger, Holden's Chairman and Managing Director from 1999 to 2003, was instrumental in building Holden's capabilities and its profile within GM in body styling and design, and rear-wheel-drive chassis design. His work culminated in the development of the VE Commodore (Figure 8.14), which was released in 2005. Thanks to Holden's position within General Motors, the VE was selected for a number of export programmes to the US market, including the Pontiac GTO and G8, and the Chevrolet SS models. The Holden Caprice was adapted for the General Motors' Police Car programme. Holden was also successful in developing export sales to the Middle East and (albeit in low volumes) Europe and the United Kingdom.

## THIS UNFORTUNATELY EXPOSED HOLDEN TO THE CONSEQUENCES OF GM'S BANKRUPTCY, FOLLOWING THE GLOBAL FINANCIAL CRISIS

General Motors was severely affected by the Global Financial Crisis, which crippled the US market in 2008–10. GM declared bankruptcy in 2009 and was eventually re-formed by way of an extensive US Federal Government assistance package. GM was forced to divest itself of many of its brands as part of the plan: Oldsmobile, Pontiac, Hummer and Saturn in the United States and Saab in Europe all ceased operations.

FIGURE 8.14  VE Commodore SS
Source: Neil Pogson, Holden Retirees Club

Active consideration was also given to the sale of the Opel-Vauxhall
and Holden brands at this time. Opel-Vauxhall was nearly sold to
a consortium of Magna, the large Canadian components supplier, and
Sbrbank of Russia. GM backed off in the face of strong public pressure
against the deal in Germany.

The loss of the Pontiac brand and sales channel was particularly
detrimental to Holden as it had achieved impressive sales success
with its Pontiac G8 and GTO models. Between 2007 and 2009,
Holden had exported 41,000 G8s to the United States, which represented a significant increment to its Australian production volumes.
The export programme was abruptly terminated when Pontiac was
discontinued. Once General Motors had exited its bankruptcy and
returned to reasonable health in 2010, Holden attempted to rebuild
its export programme to the United States. The Chevrolet SS was one
result of the renewed programme and was still available in the 2016
model year in the United States. In 2010, Holden secured the contract
to supply its Caprice vehicles to various US state and city agencies for

service as a PPV – Police Pursuit Vehicle. The car was favoured because of its spacious body and trunk, the V8 engine and, importantly, its rear-wheel drive architecture. There was little else in the global GM portfolio that could match the Caprice in these aspects. Typically, the Caprices were used to replace the ageing Ford Crown Victoria models which had been the vehicle of choice for US police forces for decades.

## COMBINED WITH THE FALL IN THE DOMESTIC SALES OF ITS AUSTRALIAN PRODUCTS, THIS FATALLY COMPROMISED HOLDEN'S MANUFACTURING POSITION

By this time, Australian sales of Commodore were trending down as the dynamics of the Australian market changed, as explained earlier – see Figure 8.15. Consumers were expressing a preference for either smaller, lighter, more economical cars or SUVs. In an effort to counter this trend, Holden commenced production of the four-cylinder Cruze at the Elizabeth plant in 2011. But this was a marginal assembly operation of a non-Australian car, with lower Australian content than that of the Commodore. The resulting poor cost position was

FIGURE 8.15  The collapse in Commodore sales in Australia
Data source: VFACTS

reflected in the need for an early price increase. The Cruze achieved only mediocre success in the market, failing to make an impression on the sales of competitive models from Toyota, Mazda and Hyundai. It would have made more sense simply to import the Cruze. Seaborne transport of CBUs is very cost-effective – they are specialised bulk, in shipping industry terminology, carried in huge box-like ships, with the unique property of being able to load and unload themselves. Holden also imported the Captiva SUV and the Epica models, to further broaden its product the range, which by now mainly consisted of imports. It was perhaps also unfortunate that the formerly iconic Holden product brand was diluted by being applied to a diverse range of sub-standard, non-Australian models.

## THIS PUT AN INCREASING AND FINALLY FATAL STRAIN ON HOLDEN AND GM'S RELATIONSHIP WITH THE AUSTRALIAN GOVERNMENT

Holden's Australian manufacturing operations thus became increasingly unprofitable and their continuation depended on ongoing support from the Australian government by way of the ATS mechanism, which is described in Chapter 10. Relations between Holden and the government became strained at best, with negotiations on the continued support being conducted by megaphone diplomacy in the public domain during 2013. From its time in opposition, the clear stance of the government had been against public support of industries, particularly manufacturing ones. From the time of its election in September 2013, the government fervently pushed its agenda of withdrawing public assistance from Australian manufacturing industries. Other more favoured industries, such as mining and agriculture, escaped such scrutiny. In addition, the government was keen to curtail the supposed power of the unions, so support for manufacturing was doubly fraught.

Unfortunately, the government's politically inspired chest beating coincided with the negotiations with the remaining manufacturers, General Motors and Toyota, as to the nature of the ongoing assistance to be provided to the industry. During Parliamentary Question Time on

10 December 2013, the Federal Treasurer, Joe Hockey, challenged Holden to 'come clean with the Australian people' and be 'honest'. In effect, he goaded General Motors into leaving Australia. This was an unusual situation in the history of the global automotive industry, to say the least. There are many instances around the world of governments' actively encouraging investment in their local automotive industries. There are remarkably few instances of their turning it away. On 11 December 2013 – the day after Joe Hockey's speech – Dan Akerson, chairman and CEO of GM, reacted to the challenge from the Australian government and announced that General Motors would withdraw from manufacturing in Australia. He said 'The decision to end manufacturing in Australia reflects the perfect storm of negative influences the automotive industry faces in the country, including the sustained strength of the Australian dollar, high cost of production, small domestic market and arguably the most competitive and fragmented auto market in the world'.

## THE REASONS GIVEN FOR GM'S WITHDRAWAL WERE NOT WHOLLY COGENT

Taking his comments in turn, one would agree that the 'sustained strength of the Australian dollar' was an issue for consideration, although it was always going to be a temporary situation, driven at that time by the mining boom in Australia. It was always expected to – and did – return to a more natural level against the US dollar – around 75c – within months of the GM announcement. The more fundamental and lasting problem was the high level of competitiveness of the Japanese manufacturers and their products, with respect to cost, quality and levels of equipment. The low value of the Yen also played a part.

The 'high cost of production' was also a valid concern, driven by typically high costs of components manufactured in Australia. This is surely what drove the intention to reduce the local content: that of the Commodore was reportedly around 50 per cent (the level widely quoted in the media at the time – not helped by the fully imported engine and transmission), that of the Cruze was around 30 per cent and that of the 'Next Generation' Commodore – heavily based on the Opel

Insignia – was expected to be lower still, at around 25 per cent. This began to look more and more like lightweight local kit assembly, which cannot compete with CBU imports in an open market. The need to amortise Holden's fixed costs over declining production volumes would also have been an important factor. The labour costs and overall productivity of the Elizabeth plant were perhaps not the important issues that some politicians and the tabloid press tried to imply they were at the time.

The 'small domestic market' was a key issue for Holden and the other manufacturers. However, that was the very point of Holden's – and Toyota's – successful drives for export markets. Success with export programmes such as the General Motors Police Pursuit Vehicle programme demonstrated that the local manufacturers did not have to be bound by the constraints of the small local market – provided, of course, that their parent corporations supported them in accessing overseas markets. Similarly, the 'most competitive and fragmented auto market in the world', although a valid statement, does not represent any more of a reason to withdraw from manufacturing than not to compete in the market at all.

In conclusion, Holden came very close to establishing a sustainable role for itself within GM but this was fatally compromised by the GFC and the resulting cutbacks by GM in North America, as well as by its apparent willingness at the time to consider sacrificing overseas operations. Thus, Holden's manufacturing operations became even more dependent on Australian government life support, with a government ideologically opposed to this kind of subsidy and inclined to attack the unions. And this really was the signal for the end of the Australian automotive industry.

## TOYOTA ADOPTED A COMPLETELY DIFFERENT STRATEGY OF INTEGRATION WITHIN ITS GLOBAL NETWORK, WITHOUT A SPECIFICALLY AUSTRALIAN PRODUCT

Toyotas first appeared in Australia in 1958, when Thiess Holdings started importing Land Cruisers for use on the Snowy Mountains Hydro-

FIGURE 8.16  1959 Toyota Landcruiser
Source: News Ltd / Newspix

Electric project – see Figure 8.16. The rugged, simple Land Cruisers were well suited to the conditions in the Snowy Mountains area.

Local assembly of Toyota passenger vehicles commenced in 1963 with the Toyota Tiara (Figure 8.17), which was assembled at the Australian Motor Industries plant in Port Melbourne. AMI, a contract assembler of multiple brands, also assembled Standard, Triumph, Rambler and Mercedes Benz vehicles in the 1950s and 1960s. This was a typical colonial era multi-manufacturer low-volume, low-national-content assembly plant, of the kind that existed in South Africa during the apartheid years of isolation. The Tiara was subsequently replaced by other Toyota models, including Crown (Figure 8.18), Corona, Camry and Corolla, which were notably successful in establishing the reputation of Japanese cars in the Australian market. In 1994, Toyota moved its production from the AMI Port Melbourne plant to its own Altona plant (Figure 8.19).

FIGURE 8.17 1963 Toyota Tiara, assembled at AMI in Melbourne
Source: News Ltd / Newspix

FIGURE 8.18 1968 Toyota Crown, assembled at AMI in Melbourne
Source: Toyota Motor Corporation Australia

FIGURE 8.19  Toyota Plant, Altona, Victoria
Source: Toyota Motor Corporation Australia

They were mechanically simple, reliable and, by the standards of the day, well equipped. At a time when a radio or a heater was an extra-cost option for a Holden or a Falcon, Toyotas appeared to be lavishly fitted out.

As a result of the rationalisation forced by the Button Plan and following its own global manufacturing strategy, Toyota eventually ceased the manufacture of all but the Camry/Aurion model, concentrating on achieving economic scale with it. Toyota Australia has for many years been far more of an importing operation than a manufacturing one. Its high-volume products for the Australian market (including Corolla, Prius, all Lexus-badged models, Land Cruiser, Prado, Kluger, Hi Lux, Hi-Ace, etc.) are imported from either Japan or Thailand. Unlike Holden and Ford, both of which developed models exclusively for the Australian (and export, where possible) market, Toyota adopted a different manufacturing strategy – rather than designing and engineering specific and different models solely for the Australian market, it chose to manufacture a limited selection of its global products here. Design, engineering and development functions are highly centralised within the Toyota network, so that a Camry produced in Australia was more or less identical to one produced in the United States. There is virtually no engineering or development work performed in Australia.

This strategy was implemented from the start of Toyota's local manufacturing activities in 1963 to the end of production. Its key benefit was that its engineering and development costs were amortised over a far greater production volume than either Holden or Ford could hope for by way of their local production of Australia-specific products. The Toyota Camry had for many years been the highest-selling passenger car in the United States, with volumes of greater than 400,000 units per year for most years since 2000, compared to recent annual sales in Australia of around 30,000 units. It has also been a significant success in Middle Eastern markets, which have product preferences similar to those of the United States. If there is a downside to that strategy it is that the products manufactured in Australia (Camry/Aurion) do not display any 'Australia-inspired' design or engineering characteristics. Consequently, Toyota products tend to be conservative and bland in character. This, together with its relatively large size, caused the Camry to be withdrawn from sale in Europe, where it could not compete with BMW, Mercedes and Audi. Nevertheless, the cost benefit for Toyota by way of this global production strategy is significant.

Largely because of the recognised high quality of the cars produced in its Altona facility, Toyota Australia was successful in winning the right to export its vehicles. Commencing in 1986, Toyota built a successful export programme based primarily on shipping Camrys (Figure 8.20) to the Middle East market. At the peak of the programme, between 2005 and 2012, its export volumes ran close to 100,000 vehicles per year. The downside of the global product strategy was that Toyota's main competition for the 'right to manufacture' in Australia was in effect other Toyota plants around the world, rather than the other Australian MVPs. While the Altona facility was able to produce

FIGURE 8.20  The last Toyota Camry produced at the Altona facility,
Melbourne
Source: Toyota Motor Corporation Australia

vehicles to a high standard of quality and at a cost that was competitive
with other Toyota plants, it received support from Toyota to continue
doing so. Altona, in fact, did a notable job of training a very disparate
workforce, with many languages spoken, in applying the Toyota
Production System. If, however, for any reason the per-unit cost or
the quality of the cars manufactured fell outside Toyota's stipulated
standards that support could be withdrawn. In that event, the production capacity provided by the Altona facility could easily be replaced by
one of the many Toyota facilities located in other countries.

### BUT TOYOTA COULD NOT ON ITS OWN SUPPORT
### THE LOCAL SUPPLIER COMMUNITY NEEDED
### TO MAINTAIN ITS MANUFACTURING OPERATION

Toyota Australia's continuing viability as an Australian manufacturing
operation also depended significantly on the depth and breadth of its

local supplier community. Too much of a reduction in local content through substituting supply from Japan or elsewhere outside Australia would wreck the plant's competitiveness – the Cruze problem over again. Once first Ford and then, most crucially, Holden announced their intention to withdraw from local manufacturing in 2016 and 2017 respectively, it was inevitable that Toyota would follow suit. In 2013, Toyota announced that its Australian manufacturing operation would close in 2017. Unlike Ford, Toyota did not really 'fail' in Australia – rather the framework upon which Toyota had built its Australian operations collapsed. Nor did Toyota as a corporation let its Australian manufacturing operation down – it merely applied its normal rules of capacity allocation to it. Toyota, in fact, displayed a remarkable loyalty to Australia. But its Australian manufacturing strategy was a much more prudent – and reversible – one than that of its two main rivals.

## CHRYSLER ESTABLISHED AN IMPRESSIVE MODEL LINE IN AUSTRALIA IN THE 1960S AND 1970S – THEN ITS CORPORATE PARENT RAN INTO TROUBLE

Chrysler Australia started assembly (with some local manufacture) of Plymouth, De Soto and Dodge vehicles in 1954. In 1957, it released the Chrysler Royal, an Australia-only model, which was a mild makeover of the earlier Plymouth 25 products. It assembled the Simca Aronde and Vedette models from 1959.

In 1962 Chrysler commenced assembly of the Valiant 'R' and 'S' models (Figure 8.21).

In 1963, it commenced local manufacture of the AP5 Valiant (Figure 8.22) at its Tonsley Park plant, south of Adelaide (Figure 8.23). Typically, Valiants were more powerful, more glamorous and better equipped than their Holden and Ford counterparts.

The Chrysler Valiant Charger (Figure 8.24) was a locally-designed and -developed model which featured US-based 'muscle car' styling on a shortened Valiant wheelbase. It was produced from 1971 to 1978 and was the most successful Chrysler Australia product.

FIGURE 8.21 Chrysler Valiant R Series assembly at Mile End, Adelaide
Source: Ilinga Books

FIGURE 8.22 1964 Chrysler Valiant AP5
Source: Ilinga Books

FIGURE 8.23 Chrysler Plant, Tonsley Park, South Australia, 1963
Source: Ilinga Books

FIGURE 8.24  Chrysler Valiant Charger Prototype
Source: Ilinga Books

It was raced successfully and generally made a significant impression on the Australian market.

However, Chrysler Corporation (US), which had been very successful in the 1950s and 1960s, started to run into trouble in the 1970s. It had undertaken ill-judged forays into the European market, purchasing Rootes and Talbot, which had absorbed significant resources. It was generally unprepared for the gas crises that hit the United States in the mid-1970s and was forced to rush more fuel-efficient products (the 'K-Series' cars – Dodge Aspen and Plymouth Volare, etc.) onto the market in 1976. The engineering refinement and build quality of these vehicles was shoddy at best, resulting in massive warranty costs and consequential distraction within the corporation. Chrysler sold the remnant of its European operations to Peugeot in 1978 and came very close to total failure in the United States. In 1979, Chrysler appealed for and was granted $1.5 billion in federal loan guarantees, which allowed it to rebuild itself with new (and remarkably successful) products such as the mini-van (Dodge Caravan and Plymouth Voyager) and the Dodge Omni/Plymouth Horizon twins.

The troubles of the parent corporation represented the death knell for the Chrysler Australia. Starved of product-development funds, it was forced to rely on ageing product. It had been in a partnering arrangement with Mitsubishi Motors for much of the 1970s and, in 1980, Mitsubishi purchased the complete Chrysler Australia operation to form Mitsubishi Motors Australia Limited.

## MITSUBISHI MOTORS AUSTRALIA FELL VICTIM TO A TURBULENT CORPORATE HISTORY OUTSIDE AUSTRALIA

Mitsubishi assumed control of the Chrysler manufacturing facility at Tonsley Park in 1981 with the formation of Mitsubishi Motors Australia Ltd (MMAL). Chrysler had successfully manufactured the Valiant/Charger ranges in the plant from 1964 until the mid-1970s, when its lack of viable fuel-efficient models made it ill-equipped to respond to the gas crises. MMAL manufactured its Sigma, Colt, Magna, Verada and 380 models at Tonsley Park from 1981 until 2008.The first Magna, using a widened Japanese Mitsubishi Sigma base and equipped with a 2.6 litre engine, was unique. It was the most successful medium car in Australia in the 1980s (Figure 8.25).

In 2000 Daimler Chrysler purchased a controlling influence in MMC. The alliance was never successful, however – cultural differences between the Daimler, Chrysler and Mitsubishi factions were always a problem, preventing viable operation of the corporation. Mitsubishi Motors North America (MMNA) engaged in a particularly aggressive marketing campaign (known as the '0–0–0' plan) in the United States in 2003, which featured zero down-payment, zero per cent interest and zero payments for the first twelve months. Not surprisingly, the scheme resulted in significant sales growth for MMNA. Unfortunately, it also resulted in cars being sold to credit-risky buyers who had no discernible income and no assets – some owners had to park their new MMC vehicles alongside the bridge under which they themselves resided – and who then tended to default on the contract after the expiration of the initial grace

FIGURE 8.25  2000 Mitsubishi Magna TJ
Source: MMAL

period. The scheme was basically a pre-run for the Global Financial Crisis that hit the United States in 2008/09, as a result of similarly dubious marketing schemes applied to the real estate market. MMC suffered considerable reputational damage in the United States as a result of this debacle, from which it took many years to recover.

Coincidentally, MMC suffered from poor management practice in Japan during this period. Various MMC Fuso truck models suffered from catastrophic failures of their front wheel hubs, which would have been bad enough in itself, except that Mitsubishi attempted to conceal the failures and not recall the faulty trucks. It then further compounded the problem by concealing the whole sordid story from Daimler Chrysler, which was negotiating to purchase the controlling interest in MMC. When the facts eventually came to light, the Daimler Chrysler management were less than impressed.

MMC's financial and legal difficulties in both Japan and the United States from 2003 on came close to crippling the complete enterprise. As a result of those difficulties, Daimler Chrysler withdrew from the alliance in 2004.

## THE CORPORATE PROBLEMS OF MMC UNDERMINED MMAL'S PRODUCT PLANS AND LED TO THE CLOSURE OF ITS MANUFACTURING OPERATION

MMC's corporate problems during this period had the effect of delaying MMAL's plans for the development of the new 380 model (Figure 8.26) to replace its successful but ageing Magna. As a result of that two-year delay, the Australian public became bored with the Magna and its sales declined precipitously. By the time MMAL was eventually able to release the 380 in late 2005, the public had virtually forgotten about Mitsubishi as a brand, which made the 380's task close to impossible to achieve. This was fatal for MMAL, as the 380 development project had been key to a major expansion

FIGURE 8.26 2006 Mitsubishi 380
Source: MMAL

strategy for the Australian operation. It was intended to launch the Australian operation into international significance within the MMC network. MMAL had negotiated the rights to an export programme and it was to become a main engineering centre for the corporation. Plans included the development of a Long Wheelbase 'Diamante' version of the 380, which MMAL intended to export to North America and the Middle East – the 30,000 units exported under this plan would have allowed MMAL to achieve to achieve its designated 60,000-unit break-even point. It is possible to achieve this with a plant deliberately designed for low volumes, as demonstrated by Suzuki in Hungary, with a similar capacity.

As part of this manufacturing strategy, MMAL invested in a complete side-body press for the 380, an innovation that would have resulted in significant improvements in quality and productivity and reductions in cost. Again, Suzuki did something similar in Hungary. In an effort to defray the costs of this investment and increase the utilisation of the press, MMAL invited the other local manufacturers (Holden, in particular) to enter into some form of collaborative arrangement but none would entertain the idea. Had this plant-sharing plan eventuated in some form, it might well have represented a model for the development of a truly sustainable Australian motor industry – it would have helped the manufacturers achieve the required economy of scale that was so problematic with the traditional model of operation.

As it happened, MMC's global financial difficulties overran all these plans, first delaying, then effectively starving MMAL of development funding at a critical time in the 380 programme. The car was always less than it should have been, in many aspects. MMAL was never able to achieve anything like the 60,000-unit per year volumes required for break-even and hence never returned a profit on the 380. Production ceased in 2008 and MMAL reverted to an importing operation. It had always been a somewhat marginal player in the Australian market, not able to withstand the impacts of the poor management decisions of its parent company.

## NISSAN WAS THE FIRST OF THE REMAINING MAJOR
## MANUFACTURERS TO GO, POST-BUTTON

Nissan exited local production in 1992 (long before MMAL, even), primarily because of its largely pedestrian product offering in Australia. It was forced out by market pressure (lack of sales) rather than as a direct result of the Button Plan, although this certainly laid the groundwork for Nissan's exit. Nissan and its products were running into increasing difficulties in Japan at the time, as Toyota forged ahead of it. This was eventually to lead to Renault taking a 44 per cent stake in Nissan and control of the company, with Carlos Ghosn and his team brought in from Renault to turn it around. One of their first actions was to appoint a new European-trained design director, reporting directly to the CEO and not to the engineering director. This was yet another example of the Australian manufacturing subsidiary being pulled down by the failures of its parent.

## OTHER FOREIGN COMPETITORS NEVER ACHIEVED TRUE
## AUSTRALIAN MANUFACTURING AND WERE
## FORCED OUT

During the 1950s and 1960s, more car makers entered the Australian market. British and European firms commenced CKD (completely-knocked-down) assembly: BMC (Austin, Morris, Riley, Wolseley), VW, Renault, Rootes Group (Hillman, Singer, Sunbeam and Humber), Standard Triumph (Vanguard, Triumph), Land Rover, Peugeot, Fiat, Citroën, Mercedes Benz and Rambler all established assembly operations in Australia during the period. These were contract assembly operations, conducted by local companies, often assembling multiple brands, similar to the ones that existed in South Africa during the years of apartheid and economic isolation. They shut down as a consequence of the Button Plan.

## OTHER FIRMS MADE REASONABLY SUCCESSFUL FORAYS
## INTO THE VERY-LOW-PRODUCTION VOLUME MARKET

One such venture was Bolwell, which designed and built a series of sports cars in Melbourne, during the 1960s and 1970s. The best known

FIGURE 8.27  Bolwell Nagari
Source: Bolwell Car Club

and most successful of these was the 'Nagari' (Figure 8.27), which was the company's first full-production sports car. It was manufactured from 1970 to 1974 and comprised a fibreglass body on a backbone chassis that carried Ford suspension components and either a 302 cid or 351 cid Ford V8 engine. Some 118 Nagaris were produced.

### ATTEMPTS BY LOCAL ENTREPRENEURS WERE MARGINAL

No history of the Australian industry in the 1960s would be complete without mention of the Lightburn Zeta (Figure 8.28). Lightburn was a well-established manufacturer of washing machines and cement mixers, located in Adelaide. The Zeta was an interesting entrant in the 'bubble car' class, along the lines of various European makes in the immediate post-war period such as the BMW 'Isetta' (Figure 8.29). It came in 'Runabout' and 'Sport' versions and boasted a fibreglass body sitting on a rudimentary rubber block suspension system. The sedan had a Villiers 324cc 2-stroke engine and a 4-speed gearbox. Reverse motion was achieved by stopping the engine and restarting it in the

FIGURE 8.28 1963 Lightburn Zeta Runabout
Source: National Motor Museum, Birdwood, South Australia – CC
BY-SA 3.0

FIGURE 8.29 BMW Isetta
Source: www.myautoworld.com

reverse direction (possible by virtue of its being 2-stroke), which effectively gave the driver the option of four gears in reverse. A particularly courageous driver could therefore drive the car as fast in reverse as in the forward direction. A total of 400 Zetas were sold between 1963 and 1965.

Essentially, the failure of the Zeta was a case of the wrong car, in the wrong place, at the wrong time. Bubble cars such as the BMW Isetta succeeded in war-ravaged Europe for a while in the early 1950s when resources were scarce and consumer incomes were low.

By the mid-1960s, Australia was enjoying a level of prosperity it had never known previously. The public was generally of a mind to enjoy the prosperity – they were not inclined to return to austerity in any form. Just one aspect of that prosperous lifestyle was driving a relatively luxurious, glamorous American-style car. Especially at a selling price that was remarkably close to that of the newly released Morris Mini 850 of the time, the Zeta offered few benefits to excite a car-hungry public. While BMW went on from the 'Isetta' to ascend considerable automotive engineering heights in subsequent years, Lightburn did not.

## AUSTRALIA HAD LITTLE INFLUENCE OVER EVENTS IN THE WIDER AUTOMOTIVE WORLD

In seeking to create a 'real' automotive industry after World War II, as opposed to multi-brand contract assemblers, Australia had few potential partners – the Detroit Big Three. Eventually, it landed all three plus Toyota, the most powerful of the Japanese. GM and Toyota were to become two of the three global super-giants of the automotive industry. The Americans and their products were best suited to Australian driving conditions and the preferences of its motorists at the time. The future great changes in the world automotive industry would have been impossible to foretell. But, as the industry globalised and the giants emerged, Australia's power to bargain with them diminished considerably. Yet the Button Plan's drive to consolidate the industry and achieve as much scale as possible made sense. Had the United States not abandoned large RWD cars and retreated into virtual automotive isolationism based on light trucks, the outcome might have been different. As it was, Holden's special RWD role within GM might have worked, had there not been the GFC – which was not the fault of the automotive industry. Perhaps one of the Europeans could have been attracted, instead of Chrysler, Nissan or Mitsubishi. South Africa managed this, with BMW, Mercedes and VW all using it as a source of right-hand-drive versions of their largest volume models.

The Button-inspired attempts at platform sharing in Australia fell flat. They have generally done so throughout the world. One of the rare successes is the A-class platform shared by Peugeot, Citroën and Toyota in Europe, together with a shared assembly plant at Kolin in the Czech Republic, none of the brands being able to make the investment on its own. Even the sharing of relatively invisible engines and transmissions has generally been resisted or has not lasted, unless through an independent supplier, in the case of transmissions.

It is interesting to observe that in every instance since 1970 (bar one, namely Toyota) the failure of each of the Australian vehicle producers directly aligned with the failure or near failure of their respective parent companies. The withdrawals from Australia of Leyland, Chrysler, Nissan, Mitsubishi, Ford and Holden all demonstrate that linkage. (Toyota's withdrawal reflected the collapse of the whole Australian industry, rather than anything specific to Toyota itself.) This observation reiterates the degree to which the Australian vehicle producers were always minor players within their respective parent companies.

The Button Plan might have achieved a more lasting success had the local vehicle producers not had such an aversion to any form of cooperative approach to the Australian situation. Had they been able to take a more 'Australia, Inc' view to the industry they might have been able, together, to overcome the inherent constraints imposed by the small market size. Of course, no vehicle producer would follow such a course – no vehicle producer was Australian-owned or even Australian-managed to any great extent. None had the interests of Australia, or even the Australian industry, particularly uppermost in their corporate minds. Instead, even as the indicators all pointed to the looming catastrophic failure of the industry, the vehicle producers preferred to follow an approach more akin to MAD, the Mutually Assured Destruction of the Cold War.

### IN THE END, WHAT IS STRIKING IN ALL THIS IS HOW LITTLE CONTROL AUSTRALIA REALLY HAD OVER ITS AUTOMOTIVE DESTINY, IN THE FACE OF THE GLOBAL GIANTS

Ford was first to establish manufacturing in Australia but its corporate culture did not give enough support to its local subsidiary. As a result, Ford Australia was starved of development funding for its future models, placing a further drag on its potential success, and ultimately leading to closure. General Motors made a major commitment to Holden, which achieved a major advantage by being the first fully integrated manufacturer in Australia. Holden started to make the critical move from national autarchy to being linked in to its global parent in the early 2000s. This unfortunately exposed Holden to the consequences of GM's bankruptcy, following the Global Financial Crisis. Combined with the fall in the domestic sales of its Australian products, this fatally compromised Holden's manufacturing position. This put an increasing and finally fatal strain on Holden and GM's relationship with the Australian government, although the reasons given for GM's withdrawal were not wholly cogent. Toyota adopted a completely different strategy of integration within its global network, without a specifically Australian product. But Toyota could not on its own support the local supplier community needed to maintain its manufacturing operation. Chrysler established an impressive model line in Australia in the 1960s and 1970s – then its corporate parent ran into trouble. Mitsubishi Motors Australia fell victim to a turbulent corporate history outside Australia. The corporate problems of MMC undermined MMAL's product plans and led to the closure of its manufacturing operation.

Nissan was the first of the remaining major manufacturers to go, post-Button. Other foreign competitors never achieved true Australian manufacturing and were forced out. Attempts by local entrepreneurs were marginal. Australia had little influence over events in the wider automotive world.

# 9 The Australian Component Suppliers: Doomed by being so Sub-scale

PRIOR TO WORLD WAR I, SMALL ENGINEERING HOUSES
WERE ABLE TO HANDLE THE DEMAND FOR REPAIRS
AND REPLACEMENT PARTS

There were a number of engineering businesses that were able to service and manufacture replacement parts for the small volumes of cars that were imported to Australia in the pre–World War I period. The businesses had been established during the nineteenth century to service agriculture, mining and coachbuilding requirements. These business included foundries (T. Main and Sons in Jolimont, Victoria); tools and die makers (A. Flavell, Melbourne) die-casters (Lawrenson Diecasting Ltd, Sydney): engine makers (Kelly & Lewis, Melbourne; A. H. McDonald, Melbourne); gear makers (Richardson Gears Pty Ltd), spring makers (Davis, Shephard & Co, South Melbourne; J. K. Henderson, South Yarra; Pioneer Spring Co, Alexandria); tyre makers (Barnett Glass, Melbourne; Perdriau, Melbourne), lamp makers (Colonial Lamp & Accessories Ltd, Melbourne; Edwards Bros, Melbourne) and coachbuilders (Martin & King, Malvern, Victoria; Holden and Frost, Adelaide; T. J. Richards, Adelaide). In 1913, there were over 800 coachbuilders operating in Australia. In 1895, John Lysaght established the Sydney Wiremill and, in 1896, the Broken Hill Proprietary Company (BHP) was founded. Dunlop started the manufacture – by hand – of solid and pneumatic tyres in Melbourne in 1896. The great majority of these businesses were far from mass-production enterprises, however. They tended to be jobbing shops, producing replacement parts on a one-off basis, as required.[1]

---

[1]    A comprehensive history of the Australian Components Supply industry is to be found
       in *Beneath the Bonnet: a History of Australian Automotive Parts Manufactures since
       1896*, by J. D. Beruldsen, Longman Cheshire, 1989.

During this period, work was being done in both Europe and the United States in the area of precision engineering and manufacturing. This resulted in the ability to manufacture interchangeable parts in reasonably high volumes for either the original equipment (OE) or replacement parts markets. Among the automakers, Cadillac is credited with having pioneered this technology in the United States in 1903. In 1915, the BHP Newcastle steelmaking facility commenced operations. Gradually, the required components of Australian industry that would enable complete motor vehicle production were being put into place.

## A COMPLEX STRUCTURE OF TARIFFS ENCOURAGED THE VEHICLE IMPORTERS TO USE AUSTRALIAN-PRODUCED COMPONENTS TO REPLACE THE ORIGINALLY IMPORTED PARTS

The then-recently formed Commonwealth of Australia imposed its first tariffs applying to automotive imports in 1902, with a slight advantage given to imports from the United Kingdom. In summary, the tariffs were:

- Chassis: 0 per cent UK, 5 per cent general rate
- Bodies: 30 per cent UK, 35 per cent general rate
- Springs and axles: 30 per cent UK, 35 per cent general rate

The War Precautions Act had been enacted in Australia in 1914. In order to protect Australia's foreign currency holdings and control shipping capacity, one of its provisions was severely to limit the importation of CBU vehicles as well as some chassis and chassis components. The Act was repealed in 1920 and replaced with a new regime of tariffs. As intended, the tariffs had the effect of attracting the establishment of industries such as glass, wood, forgings, sheet metal, rubber, textiles and machinery presses. These businesses formed the foundation of the Australian automotive component industry. This was the start of Stage 1 in the local supplier sector development sequence described in Chapter 4.

It was in the interests of the local components manufacturers to maximise:

- The tariffs applying to imported parts – whether supplied as OE (original equipment, i.e., for building new vehicles) or for replacement – that could be manufactured in Australia.
- The extent to which locally manufactured parts could replace like components on imported vehicles – the so-called 'Deletion System'.

The Deletion System encouraged the replacement of parts imported as OE on imported vehicles by locally produced components. The overseas vehicle producer would agree to not ship certain components with the vehicle once a replacement agreement with the Australian component producer was in place. While local component producers strongly supported this scheme, the overseas vehicle producers were less inclined to look favourably on it. Consequently, those vehicle producers tended to 'delete' somewhat less than full value for the components they did not supply – American vehicle producers typically deleted 50 per cent of the value of the non-included parts while British producers offered only 10 per cent. Perhaps the British producers had lower margins in their pricing thereby constraining their capacity to be quite so generous, or perhaps they were less inclined to trust the manufacturing skills of the colonial outposts. Whatever the motivation, the reluctance of the British manufacturers to allow the full deletion value served to stifle the formation of local replacement parts manufacturing for longer than might have otherwise been the case.

### THERE WAS A STRONG GENERAL TREND — REINFORCED BY THE GREAT DEPRESSION — TO PROTECT THE LOCAL PRODUCTION OF PARTS

Parts imported as OE were generally not subject to duty while parts imported for replacement purposes attracted a duty of 45 per cent. Unsurprisingly, local producers tried to have the OE rule changed so as to apply tariffs on an increasing number of OE-supply components. In

1928, for example, they were successful in having the list modified to include spark plugs and, in 1930, springs. In 1929, in response to the Great Depression that was starting to dominate the global economy, the newly elected Scullin Labor government reflected the increasingly protectionist behaviour of Australia's main trading partners – particularly the United States – and increased the existing tariffs by 50 per cent. In the period 1937–9, there were Tariff Board inquiries on a range of parts including lifting jacks, radiators, car radios, brake and clutch linings and shock absorbers. In 1939, the Motor Engine Bounty Act took effect, resulting in a payment of 60 Pounds Kim, is this 60 Pounds or 30 Pounds (you made an earlier reference to the latter) ? for each motor engine produced in Australia. The combined effect of these measures was to encourage the establishment of local businesses to manufacture components – OE and replacement supply – for imported vehicles and eventually provide the foundation of the full local manufacture of vehicles in Australia. So local content was promoted, even before local production of vehicles – a kind of Stage 0 in our development sequence.

## FORD AND GENERAL MOTORS INCREASED THEIR LEVEL OF INVOLVEMENT IN AUSTRALIA IN THE 1920S, ENCOURAGING MANY LOCAL COMPONENT MAKERS TO ESTABLISH OPERATIONS

As discussed in Chapter 8, Ford commenced assembly of its Model T in Geelong in 1925. This corresponds to Stage 1 of the local supplier development sequence.

Firms setting up during the pre–World War II period to manufacture parts included:

- Pilkington Brothers (later, ACI-Pilkington) – glass
- Conqueror Cables (later, Ericson, Camelec, Pirelli, Repco Harness and Yazaki Australia) – cables and wiring harnesses
- Marsden and McCain (later, Bramah, United Kingdom)
- York Air Conditioning and Refrigeration (later, part of Borg Warner)
- Repco – formed as an IPO combination of Auto Grinding Pty Ltd, Replacement Parts Pty Ltd and Russell Manufacturing Pty Ltd

- Ediswan (later, Electronic Industries, Lugon Lamps, absorbed into Philips) – lamps
- Disco Manufacturing Co (later acquired by GM-H) – Firestone spark plugs
- Johns & McHales (later, Flexible Drives Pty Ltd, Flexible Instruments) – flexible drives, instruments
- British Tubemakers (later, Tubemakers Australia – steering columns
- American Rolling Mills (later, Commonwealth Rolling Mills – CRM) – steel
- South Australian Rubber Mills (later, Uniroyal, Bridgestone) – tyres

## WHEN GENERAL MOTORS-HOLDEN RELEASED THE FIRST 'HOLDEN' CAR IN 1948, IT ACHIEVED 60 PER CENT LOCAL CONTENT

The establishment of GM-Holden manufacturing encouraged many more firms to establish parts manufacturing during the 1940s and 1950s, including:

- Tecnico Pty Ltd (later, Bendix-Tecnico Pty Ltd), Bendix Corp Australia Pty Ltd
- Rainsfords Metal Products Pty Ltd – OE suppliers to GM-Holden in 1948
- Joseph Lucas Industries (the large UK supplier, particularly of electrical components) – coils, dynamos, etc.
- Coote & Jorgensen (later, Borg Warner) – transmissions
- Robert Bosch GmbH – electrical and electronic components
- Armstrong York (United Kingdom) – shock absorbers
- Smiths Industries – instruments
- Hitchin & Hallett Pty Ltd – exhaust systems
- Rubery Owen (later, ROH Industries) – wheels, transmission parts, brake parts
- Dunlop – batteries
- Castalloy Ltd
- British Automotive Industries (later, Girlock Pty Ltd, PBR) – brake systems, clutches
- Willi Kaufman Diemakers
- Diecraft – tooling for GM-Holden and Ford
- Champion Spark Plug Co
- Mintex Ltd (later Bendix-Mintex) – brake and clutch components

- VDO Instruments Australia Pty Ltd
- Brown & Watson (later, Hella Australia/Lucas, Hella Manufacturing Co)

The lists shown above are not intended to present an exhaustive record of the parts makers operating during these periods. Rather they do help to illustrate the depth and breadth of the industry needed to support full automotive manufacturing in Australia. This corresponds to the continuing Stage 2 of supplier base development. The presence of a number of established British, American and German suppliers reflects the need to import their expertise in their areas of specialisation. The presence of these (and other) suppliers paved the way for Ford, Chrysler and BMC to commence full manufacturing operations in the decade to 1965. In addition, by 1960, some fourteen companies were engaged in assembly (rather than full manufacturing) operations, from either CKD (completely-knocked-down) or SKD (semi-knocked-down) kits. Those companies included Daimler Benz, Fiat, Hudson, Rambler, International Harvester (IHC), Packard, Renault, Rootes Group, Rover/Land Rover, Simca, Standard, Triumph and Leyland (trucks). The vehicles resulting from these operations comprised varying – generally low – levels of local content. In contrast, by the end of the 1950s, Holden cars achieved 95 per cent local content, representing a remarkable achievement for the local industry in such a short time. This was characteristic of a country newly entering the automotive industry, imposing very high local content requirements behind strong protective barriers. Holden was in effect the National Manufacturer, a position similar to that of SEAT in Spain, although without the same degree of protection from competition.

## THE FIRST VEHICLE PLAN WAS INTRODUCED IN 1965, MANDATING 95 PER CENT LOCAL CONTENT – SUBSEQUENTLY MODIFIED IN LATER PLANS

Requirements for levels of local content are always part of national automotive industry development plans. They obviously have a considerable impact on the formation of a local component supplier base. In 1965, the first 'Vehicle Plan' was introduced for Australia. This was a rather complicated scheme, with three levels:

- 'Plan A': These vehicle producers were allowed duty-free entry of dutiable components once 95 per cent local content achieved – hardly a very generous concession! The initial manufacturers and their products under Plan A were:

  o  GM-Holden's Holden and Torana
  o  Ford Falcon/Fairlane and Cortina
  o  Chrysler Valiant
  o  Leyland Tasman/Kimberley, 1500, Marina, Mini and P76
  o  VW Beetle and 1600

- 'Plan B1': Vehicle producers could start at 40 per cent local content, reaching 50 per cent within 12 months and 55 per cent within a further 12 months.
- 'Plan B2': Vehicle producers that produced low volumes were able to run at lower local content than B1.

Despite the sound intention behind these plans, they still perpetuated a high level of fragmentation among the vehicle producers and low scale per model.

Gradually the restrictions on the importing of parts were loosened, as production volumes climbed. This is the start of Stage 3, in which local scale builds up. The Import Licencing Controls were abolished in 1960, allowing vehicle producers to import parts more easily; this was of particular importance to Ford and Chrysler since the Falcon and Valiant models were closely based on overseas designs as were a number of lower-volume, locally produced models including the Ford Cortina, Holden Viva, VW and BMC Mini. This was the beginning of specialisation, recognising that not all components could be competitively produced in Australia.

In 1966, the SV (Small Volume) Plan was introduced, setting local content levels for small volume assemblers and producers such as Rootes, Datsun, Toyota and Rambler. These are shown in Figure 9.1.

| Australian Production Volume | Required Australian Content |
|---|---|
| 1–2,500 | 45% |
| 2,501–5,000 | 50% |
| 5,001–7,500 | 60% |

FIGURE 9.1 Local content rules for low-volume production

In 1969, the 85 per cent content plan for vehicle producers building fewer than 25,000 units per annum was introduced, resulting in a complex structure of five 'plans' in place, which called for local content levels of 95 per cent, 85 per cent, 60 per cent, 50 per cent and 45 per cent, respectively. The inherent complexity of this system illustrates the downside of government policy that is subject to special pleading by various interest groups.

In 1973, the Whitlam government applied an across-the-board 25 per cent reduction to all tariffs. The Tariff Board and the newly established Industries Assistance Commission performed numerous reviews of the automotive industry. In 1974, the IAC commented that with four manufacturers and three assemblers the industry was inherently inefficient, lacking economies of scale and being too fragmented. It recommended:

- That vehicle plans be discontinued.
- The application of a single tariff rate of 35 per cent, progressively reducing to 25 per cent over seven years.
- That the duty on replacement parts be set at 25 per cent.
- The establishment of a single local supplier of major components with price competition to be provided by imports (implying many parts manufacturers would be allowed to fold).

It should be noted that these were only recommendations at this stage and while they were never implemented as such, they did reflect the government's realisation that a more rational approach to the industry was required.

Also in 1974, the Economic and Trade Committee recommended what was still a highly protectionist regime. Average local content was to be 85 per cent. A tariff of 35 per cent would be imposed while imports represented less than 20 per cent of the market, rising to 45 per cent once they exceeded 20 per cent. Commercial vehicles were to be treated similarly to passenger vehicles in terms of tariff rates and local content rules. Due to the political instability of that time, this recommendation was never enacted and, in an effort to appease the transport and rural sectors, successive governments allowed the commercial vehicle imports to retain a preferential tariff rate and no local content requirements.

The Fraser government revised the Vehicle Plan in 1976. This encouraged new players, including Toyota and Nissan, to establish manufacturing in Australia. It recommended the formation of a consortium to manufacture four-cylinder engines – the plan was promoted by the Australian Industries Development Commission (AIDC) and seriously considered by Chrysler, Toyota and Nissan. This was an attempt to force a degree of commonality – which is rare in the automotive industry, notably in engines. It also discontinued the Export Complementation Plan

In 1979, the Fraser government re-introduced export facilitation arrangements, which allowed a 5 per cent discount on local content rules. Vehicle producers on the 85 per cent plan could revert to 80 per cent local content with the remaining 20 per cent not subject to any duties. The 5 per cent was to be extended to 6.25 per cent in 1983, 7.5 per cent in 1984 and 15 per cent in 1987.

In 1982, the 'New Plan', which was still strongly protectionist, stipulated retention of the 85 per cent average local content plan. There was to be an increase in export facilitation for vehicle producers to 10 per cent in 1985, rising to 12.5 per cent in 1986 and 15 per cent in 1987. Export facilitation for components makers was to apply for up 20 per cent of OE sales value. Quotas and import licencing were to remain: 105,000 in 1985, rising by 4,000 units per year to 133,000 in 1992. Duty on in-quota vehicles was to be 57.5 per cent, while duty on above-quota vehicles would be at 150 per cent for 1985–7, phasing to 125 per cent by 1992. This plan was not implemented due to the change in government in March 1983.

The continuing changes to the Vehicle Plan demonstrated a growing realisation on the part of government that there was a need to make the industry more efficient at both vehicle producer and component producer levels. Also, that the local industry (again, at the vehicle and component producer levels) still needed protection from overseas competition. However, protection should not last indefinitely and needed to be scaled back as quickly as possible. Unsurprisingly, the vehicle and component producers saw it very much in their collective interest to have the levels of protection maintained or, if possible, increased. They spared no effort in lobbying the government for that outcome. An unpublished history of the Federation of Automotive Product Manufacturers (FAPM) was eloquent on these issues, which were a matter of life and death for its members.[2] This was not unusual in new automotive countries – the bargain struck was between vehicle and components producers prepared to invest where they would have preferred to import, against protection for those investments from import competition. Here was the seed of the future clash of intentions that eventually brought the local industry down.

## THE BUTTON PLAN RATIONALISED THE VEHICLE MANUFACTURING SECTOR BY REDUCING FRAGMENTATION, BUT WITH ONLY A LIMITED EFFECT ON THE COMPONENT SUPPLIER ENVIRONMENT

The Button Plan, discussed in greater detail in Chapter 10, was named after Senator John Button, the Industries Minister in the Hawke government of 1983–92. Introducing the Plan, Senator Button stated in respect of the automotive industry, 'the aim is for a more efficient and productive industry, with more rational structures.' The core elements of the

---

[2]    FAPM's *Fifty Years of Change and Progress*, 2008.

Button Plan, which was devised to achieve these outcomes, were radical and designed to flow through the whole industry, including both the vehicle manufacturers and component suppliers. The number of vehicle producers was to be reduced from five to three, and the number of models produced from thirteen to six by 1992. The local content plans were to be abolished. Import duties were to be reduced from the current 57.5 per cent to 5 per cent over time. Import quotas were to be abolished. But export facilitation was to be retained at 15 per cent. Importantly, a component of the Plan required the components industry to restructure itself and incorporate a greater level of collaboration and technology sharing.

The Button Plan achieved remarkable results within and for an industry that was inherently change resistant. Several model-sharing and component-sharing programmes were implemented between Holden and Nissan, Holden and Suzuki, Ford and Nissan and Holden and Toyota. GM-H (Holden Motor Company HMC) and TMCA merged to form United Australian Automotive Industries (UAAI). This reflected GM's and Toyota's NUMMI joint venture in the United States, which did not last long either. Nissan exited from automotive manufacturing in Australia in 1992. The AQAP (Automotive Quality Assurance Process) was established in an effort to lift the performance of the components sector and improve its competitiveness. The exports of components were significantly increased, examples including:

o Brake & Clutch Industries (ex-PBR/Girlock) – braking system for the Chevrolet Corvette
o ROH – wheels for Nissan
o Hella – headlamp reflectors for West Germany
o Robert Bosch – alternators for Daimler Benz and Isuzu
o Pilkington ACI – glass for Daimler Benz and Toyota
o Castalloy – inlet manifolds for Ford US, wheels for Nissan and Subaru
o Timken – roller bearings for Daimler Benz and Mazda

This marked the start of Stage 3 in the development scheme.

THE ABOLITION OF IMPORT QUOTAS AND LOCAL
CONTENT RULES WERE ABOLISHED AND THE
REDUCTION IN IMPORT DUTIES LEFT AUSTRALIAN
COMPONENTS PRODUCERS COMPETING FOR
A REDUCING SHARE OF A REDUCING MARKET

The removal of quotas and the rapid reduction in tariffs on imported cars inevitably led to a dramatic increase in the percentage of imported cars in the Australian market. The local vehicle producers were forced to compete for an ever-decreasing proportion of new car sales.

At the same time, removal of the local content rules encouraged the local vehicle producers to fit an increasing proportion of imported components to their vehicles.

So now the Australian component producers were forced to compete for an ever-decreasing proportion of the locally produced vehicles, which in turn, represented an ever-decreasing proportion of the total vehicles sold in Australia. The supplier sector in Australia was never able to reach Stage 4 of development.

GLOBALLY, COMPONENTS PRODUCERS HAVE TAKEN
ON A MUCH GREATER ROLE IN THE DESIGN
AND INTEGRATION OF MAJOR PARTS AND SYSTEMS

Figure 4.1 showed the increase since the 1950s in the share by value provided for a new car by component makers. Figure 4.8 illustrated the tiering system. Components producers, particularly at the 'Tier 0' and 'Tier 1' levels, tend to provide systems and sub-systems modules covering:

- Electronics/software systems
- Sophisticated steels/alloys development
- Sophisticated glass, rubber, plastics, paint, fabrics
- Engine and chassis control systems
- Drive train systems (hybrid/diesel/EV, etc.)
- Transmissions
- Suspension systems

- Braking systems
- Steering systems
- Dashboards and interiors
- Infotainment, HVAC systems

In order to defray the cost and technical risk implicit in the development of these major functions, the vehicle producers sought to outsource a large part of the R&D effort to the components sector. That innovation requires massive R&D spending on the part of the component suppliers. It is only the major global players – Bosch, Siemens, ZF, Visteon, Valeo, St Gobain, Hella, Denso, etc. – that can support the level of R&D spending required to be competitive. They generally perform the R (research), the choice and development of technologies and advanced engineering in their home locations. D (development) and applications engineering are conducted in close working relationships with their vehicle manufacturer customers. Where needed, applications engineering is decentralised, with the necessary designs provided or licenced to their foreign affiliates.

## THE INITIAL APPROACH IN AUSTRALIA WAS TO HAVE LOCAL FIRMS REPLICATE FOREIGN DESIGNS

The low-volume assemblers imported many of the components they required, sourcing only standard items and commodities from within Australia. As the fully integrated Australian manufacturers developed, under the constraint of high local sourcing requirements, they initially got local supplier firms simply to replicate the designs of components made abroad – as they themselves replicated their parent groups' designs for the vehicles they built in Australia. This is precisely what the Japanese transplants were to do much later in the United Kingdom. As in the United Kingdom, that worked well enough initially but the limitations of the local supplier base quickly became evident. The complaints of the transplants in the United Kingdom mainly centred around lack of engineering capabilities, of project management skills and of the ability of suppliers to seek out lower-cost sources for their own purchasing. In the United Kingdom, that eventually resulted in the transplants turning to established large European suppliers. Thanks to the freedoms provided by the EEC and the later EU (no tariffs or quotas, no local content requirements within Europe, no customs inspections), plus well-developed transport infrastructures, it was easy to extend the physical sourcing radius. This was self-evidently not possible in Australia, so sourcing had to remain local, except for easily transportable commodities. But it left the problem of lack of capabilities in the local supplier base.

## CHALLENGES TO THE SECTOR WERE EVIDENT IN 2000

A study of the Australian automotive industry conducted in 2001 by the French automotive industry research association Gerpisa, and based on a ten-year longitudinal tracking of the industry started in 1989, identified a number of challenges.[3] They observed a tendency on the part of the Australian government to focus mainly on macro settings in managing the economy, with inadequate attention paid to the individual characteristics of particular sectors – the theme of this book. The fact was that increases in local content requirements and higher tariffs undermined the achievement of scale, despite their good intentions. This approach was being reversed by the Button Plan, which aimed to rebuild scale through rationalisation, reduction of tariffs and, ultimately, of government support to the industry, in order to enable it to compete on its own. Over 500 companies were supplying the OE and aftermarket sectors in 1988/9, already few in comparison to the totals in other countries, but reduced even further to 300 whose turnovers exceeded $100,000 per year – a tiny threshold! There was a low level of specialisation, with many suppliers still selling multiple products. Already by this date only a handful of the top twenty suppliers were Australian owned, and there were fewer Australian-owned companies than a decade previously. Ford,

[3] Running on Empty? Innovation in the Australian Automotive Industry, W. Riemen & J. Marceau, *International Journal of Automotive Technology and Management*, Volume 2, Number 1, p.101–25 (2002)

Mitsubishi and Toyota – but not Holden – had significantly cut their number of suppliers between 1988 and 1999. Local content levels in 1989 reported as 85 per cent for the Ford Falcon, 77 per cent for the Holden Commodore, 76 per cent for the Mitsubishi Magna but only 69 per cent for the Toyota Camry. A very satisfactory quadrupling of automotive exports that took place between 1990 and 2000 was noted. But the report also cited the opinion of Richard Lamming, the MIT International Motor Vehicle Program's supplier specialist, that the future for the Australian supply industry was grim, on account of its small overall size, the increase in foreign ownership and the fact that Australian suppliers were increasingly being forced into the second tier. Whereas 78 per cent of companies in the 1989 sample had been Australian-owned, this had fallen to 57 per cent 10 years later, and quite a number of those originally contacted had disappeared, as the supplier base concentrated into fewer, larger firms.

## THE LOCAL SUPPLIER INDUSTRY WAS CONSTRAINED BY ITS OWN FRAGMENTATION AND BY DEPENDENCE ON PARENT GROUPS

There were some more or less positive aspects also. Australians loved large sedans – they were affordable and there was a lack of competing foreign products. This was a curious conclusion, in retrospect, and a strength that was rapidly to turn into a weakness. But the observation was accurate in that it was this ownership of their products that made the local manufacturers more than mere assemblers duplicating over-seas designs. Except, of course, for Toyota. Previous concerns with supplier quality and delivery performance had largely been overcome, although replaced by concerns about costs and technological capabil-ities. There had been a move away from many small companies who were technology takers, i.e., executing designs given them by their customers, to larger suppliers and sole supply, with many companies supplying all of the then-four manufacturers. There had been an injec-tion of Japanese production principles, first into the larger firms and then further into the smaller ones. There was now a clearer segmentation of the supply base into global module suppliers, systems developers and integrators, component specialists and standard parts suppliers. The supplier community had a strength in working with short production runs for a variety of model platforms but had a high dependence on licenced-in technology. There had been significant improvements in facilities by 2000 over the 1989 level, when more than half the companies did not have CNC machines at all and less than one-fifth used CAD-CAM, with the vast majority now so equipped. There were a few cases of Australian leadership, such as in body electronics within the Bosch Group. But a general drop in business spending on R&D in Australia was noted, following tax changes, and the same among component suppliers – all of $173 million per year spent by 119 of them. Tier 2 suppliers were by now mainly competing on cost. There were export difficulties for Australian subsidiaries, who were only able to access foreign markets via their parent groups. Very little work was done by local suppliers to improve on designs granted them through licences.

## OUR OWN WORK IN THE SECTOR FIFTEEN YEARS LATER WAS ONLY PARTLY ENCOURAGING

The apparent adaptation of the Australian vehicle industry was looking good at the time (2004/5) because of rising exports, of both CBUs and components. Australian suppliers were generating close to AUD 9.5 billion in sales at the time, of which some 60 per cent went to domestic original equipment customers, i.e., vehicle manufacturers – predominantly for vehicle production but some lesser proportion, perhaps 5 per cent, for spare parts supply to dealers. Some 15 per cent was exported, close to 25 per cent went into the domestic aftermarket and a small proportion into export aftermarkets. But there were also some serious indications of fragility in the sector: a loss of ability to control its own destiny; the national vehicles looking increasingly outdated and fragile in the marketplace; the Button Plan rationalisation not having been fully effective in the components sector; Australian components supply was less effectively integrated into the global automotive economy than vehicle production.

## SOME AUSTRALIAN COMPONENT PRODUCERS ACHIEVED LIMITED SUCCESS IN EXPORT MARKETS

The components trade balance over time is shown in Figure 9.2. Exports reached their maximum of AUD 1.8 billion in 2002 and plateaued thereafter, apart from a temporary dip following the GFC. The limited volumes achievable in the Australian market, particularly in light of the fact that many component producers supplied only one, or at most two, vehicle producers, implied that component producers could not hope to build a sustainable business – and one which was in a position to finance the heavy R&D expenditures required to keep them – or make them – competitive. Hence some local component producers realised that they needed to extend their markets beyond Australia in order to achieve the required scale for their operations.

Several local component producers did manage to achieve significant profiles in overseas markets. Either by way of exporting from Australia or by establishing offshore manufacturing facilities, a number of local component producers – including Air International, PBR, ROH and Schefenacker – developed successful export programmes during the mid-2000s. Those programmes were not enough to sustain those players, however, when the home industry started to fail. The component producers could not become big enough, quickly enough to stave off the looming collapse. It would have required considerable commitment and support from the parent groups of those that had one and been virtually impossible for those that did not, given the closed nature of the global supply chains.

Some twenty suppliers alone were responsible for the great majority of the sector's exports. A small number of companies had managed to break out of the laager and establish an international presence. The nature of the global automotive industry, with its limited customer sets and closed supply chains, meant that even foreign-owned Australian supplier firms did not have an open access to export markets. Imports continued to grow. An unspecified proportion would

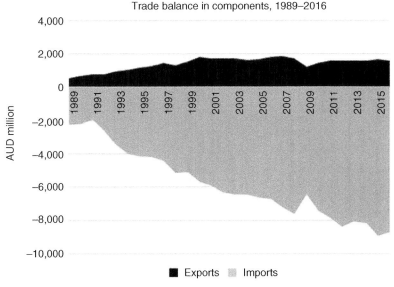

FIGURE 9.2 An ever-deepening trade deficit
Data source: AAI yearbook 2017

have gone into the Australian aftermarket, increasing with the growth of the parc of imported vehicles. But the magnitude of the imports suggests that the declared local content levels of vehicles may not have been quite as they appeared. The sales to manufacturers by a module assembler in Australia would register as of Australian origin – but how much of the components that went into it were really Australian? And so on back up the supply chain. There were frequent problems with trying to source certain specialist materials in Australia.

## THE SUPPLIER BASE HAD SERIOUS STRUCTURAL PROBLEMS

The component supplier sector was mixed in quality and its overall health, morale and competitiveness were questionable. There were structural maladjustments: the supplier base was too fragmented for the size of the Australian automotive industry, with unresolved issues of whether to accept single-sourcing and a single supplier per specialist

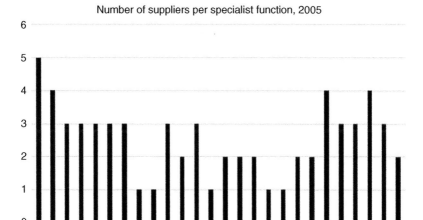

FIGURE 9.3  A still very fragmented supplier base
Source: Autopolis

field, in order to maximise effective production scale – the distance from achieving this is illustrated by Figure 9.3, which shows the number of different suppliers in different specialist functions. Too many suppliers, especially the smaller ones, had only one customer among the manufacturers. Despite rationalisation progress achieved at the vehicle producer layer as a result of the Button Plan, there was little consolidation in the Australian components sector. As late as 2008, many components producers still supplied only one or two of the local vehicle producers. Supplying only one or perhaps two vehicle producers in a small and diminishing market rendered the components producers' task of achieving real scale virtually impossible to achieve. The suboptimal scale of the component-producer–vehicle-producer market made life precarious for the component producers, in particular. In 2008, there were four major vehicle producers operating in Australia. Assuming each of those vehicle producers commenced a major new model development every ten years, and that a given component producer might have potentially supplied at most, two of those development programmes, this implies that the component producer could only hope to bid for a new major supply contract twice in ten years. If, for whatever reason, the component producer was unsuccessful in that bid, its very existence could be in jeopardy.

## THE QUALITY OF RELATIONSHIPS BETWEEN SUPPLIERS AND CUSTOMERS WAS NOT WHAT IT SHOULD HAVE BEEN

Relationships between the vehicle and components sectors and with government were clouded by mutual suspicion. Suppliers had varied views about their manufacturer customers, often negative and pessimistic. Holden was obviously critical to the whole survival of the industry but not liked for its management and project leadership style, or its pushing of global sourcing. Toyota was seen as far more measured, better organised and fair – but with a questionable long-term commitment to producing in Australia. Mitsubishi was viewed with sympathy and resignation as unlikely to survive – which of course proved true. Interestingly, Ford was seen as the most committed to Australia and the most Australian – this last quality was ultimately to prove the factor that precipitated its withdrawal and the start of the collapse of the industry. The manufacturers were in general rather disillusioned about their suppliers and their ability to function in the style of relationship required. Some were seen as capable and responsible but others as not properly in control of their businesses or their technologies and constantly requiring help.

The narrowness of the national market and the need to accept a stronger concentration of supplier power for the sake of scale put an exceptional premium on the quality of relationships and on mutual trust, which was far from universally present. The vehicle producers tended to behave as they were competing in any of the triad markets (Europe, Japan and the United States), in which there was always a fully functional, fully scaled market in operation. That was never the case in Australia. The vehicle producers held the bulk of the market power in the vehicle–component producer relationship. Component producers bid for contracts based on the vehicle producers' projected volumes over a say, three-year period. In many instances they were compelled to provide a 'cost down' of, say 40 per cent over that period. If the vehicle producers' volume projections were not realised – which was more likely than not given the dynamics of the Australian market – the financial basis of the component producer's operation could be jeopardised.

## SUPPLIERS TENDED TO BE COMPLACENT IN THE FACE OF MOUNTING COMPETITION, CONCENTRATING ON EXTRACTING ASSISTANCE FROM GOVERNMENT

The suppliers also felt that government support to them was often ineffective. As described earlier, there was a persistent background feeling of fear about the reduction of tariffs and the effects this would have on both the demand for Australian-built cars and on the Australian manufacturers' commitment to local sourcing. Many component producers were too slow to recognise the shift that was occurring in the industry. The combination of globalisation, the increasing technical complexity of cars, components and systems and the reduced transactional costs (shipping, tariffs, etc.) incurred by way of the importation of vehicles and components all conspired to undermine the foundations of the local components sector. No longer could the component producers hide behind industry protection barriers. No longer could they assume their customers would be willing to accept products that were less than state-of-the-art and uncompetitive (in world terms) on price.

In the early-mid 2000s, Holden was preparing for the release of its new VE Commodore. General Motors took a keen interest in the development of this model since it was scheduled to form the basis of Holden's export programme to the United States. GM became heavily involved in the design, engineering, procurement and manufacturing aspects of the project. It insisted on a more rigorous approach to procurement, in particular, than had previously been the case. Consequently the relationships with several component producers that had been developed over many years were jeopardised or destroyed.

The authors spoke at length with many component producers during this period. Largely as a result of GM's involvement with the procurement process, one supplier lost its long-standing contract to supply certain components for the VE. Understandably, the supplier was disappointed as well as blindsided by this outcome, commenting, 'But we've supplied GM-H since 1948 – why would they dump us now?' Unfortunately, the attitude underpinning this comment was widespread throughout the components sector.

Another components producer, which at the time supplied all four vehicle producers, took issue with the commercial behaviour of some of those vehicle producers and instigated legal proceedings against them. The litigation was successful, to an extent, but it totally soured the relationships with the vehicle producers, which represented the major proportion of the component producer's customers. It was a classic instance of winning the battle but losing the war.

Yet another local component producer lost a long-standing contract to supply to GM-H since the industry-dominant overseas competitor was able to offer a substantially lower price for, importantly, significantly enhanced technology and product functionality. Once again, the hitherto local supplier was totally blindsided by GM-H's preference for the imported product. At the time, the local component producer complained bitterly that GM-H should switch to an imported product over its locally made one.

Unable or unwilling as many local component producers were to fund the required R&D expenditure that might have resulted in truly world class products – products that could truly stand on their own feet against the best offered by the large global players – the members of the components-producing community resorted instead to devising ways to maximise their share of the various federal government industry assistance programmes – ACIS, ATS, etc. It was almost as if there was a dormant hope in the back of their minds that, magically, the industry would return to a 1950s state – all they had to do was keep drawing on the government funds until that happy nirvana might be achieved. This seemed to become characteristic of the industry as a whole.

## FOREIGN-OWNED COMPANIES TOOK OVER THE UPPER TIERS OF THE SUPPLY BASE

By 2000 already, the majority of components producers operating at the upper tiers of the industry in Australia were subsidiaries of the global majors rather than having originated in Australia. Figure 9.4 shows how this became very pronounced by 2005 and endured, although in reducing proportions, as the industry shrank over the next ten years. This is characteristic of Stage 3.

The advantage was that technologies perfected and designs developed overseas, together with process developments and management techniques, could be imparted by the parent groups to their Australian subsidiaries. The risks were that the foreign companies would look at their own sourcing options, whether from within Australia or from their other, larger operations over-seas, or that they could decide to leave Australia altogether. That some made the latter choice is evident in Figure 9.4 for the years 2010 and 2015, as the whole industry in Australia continued to shrink.

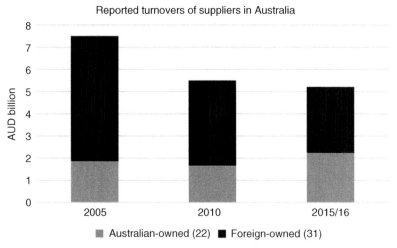

FIGURE 9.4  The predominance of foreign-owned suppliers
Data source: AAI yearbook 2017

## THE NEVER-RESOLVED UNDERLYING PROBLEM OF THE SUPPLIER BASE WAS INADEQUATE SCALE

The suppliers generally made enough profit to survive. Pre-tax profits as a proportion of sales for the sector normally fluctuated within a range of 4 per cent to 6 per cent from 1990 to 2016. Not princely rewards but adequate, by automotive industry standards, and – as throughout most of the automotive world – better than the profitability of the manufacturers in most years. All this despite the cost-down pressures. Pre-tax profits held up until the end, as Figure 9.5 shows. The remaining Australian-owned suppliers caught up with the foreign-owned.

The problem lay in the sub-scale nature of the whole sector. Figure 9.6 shows the average annual sales figures for those larger suppliers who filed accounts, separated into Australian- and foreign-owned. In 2005, the foreign-owned were on average 75 per cent larger than the Australians, although the gap diminished as the industry declined and more and more foreign-owned operations shut down. The average annual sales of the foreign-owned was AUD 170 million, that of the Australians AUD 100 million. Look back at Figure 4.2. The average sales of the top ten

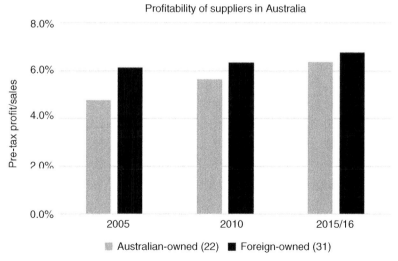

FIGURE 9.5 Still profitable – to the end
Data source: AAI yearbook 2017

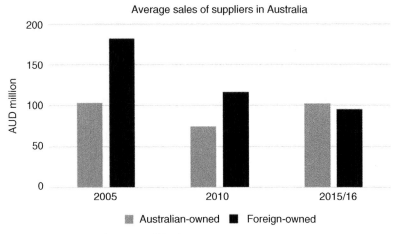

FIGURE 9.6  Too small by far
Data source: AAI yearbook 2017

global supplier groups was USD 22.5 billion, or AUD 32 billion, a 188:1 or 320:1 difference. Bosch Australia's sales in 2005, at the industry's peak, were AUD 930 million; those of its parent group, over AUD 60 billion. Of course, the full world sales of those large global groups is not the right measure, which would be production in each of their major regions. Even so, it would be a yawning gap.

We don't have a like-for-like comparison of unit costs between an Australian-built and a foreign-built car. Toyota would have had it for the Camry. But the Commodore and the Falcon had no direct equivalents being manufactured elsewhere in the world, so there could be no exact, item-for-item comparison, as was possible for the Turkish- and French-built Renault 12s. But the difference would have become substantial, once production of each dropped much below 100,000 units per year. And 80 per cent of that difference at the least would have originated in the components sector. Commodore and Falcon aged and sized themselves out of their domestic market and never found enough export sales to make up for the lost volumes. Their competition from the rising tide of imports was indirect but effective. Hence the constant threats by the Australian manufacturers to re-source parts from overseas, with the suppliers arguing that the comparisons were not fair, as they didn't

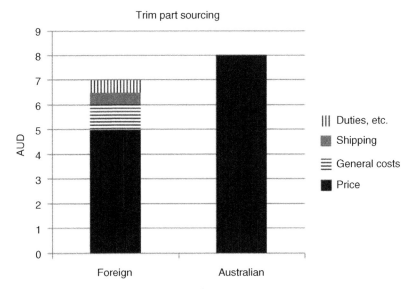

FIGURE 9.7  Not worth the effort?
Source: Autopolis

include the on-costs of resourcing from such remote locations. Figure 9.7 shows the results of such a comparison. The horizontal black line is the reference price, that quoted by the Australian supplier. The foreign price is the quote obtained by the customer. In appearance, an insurmountable advantage. The on-costs for duties and shipping were known. The argument centred on the general costs – the allowances that had to be made for extra handling, the inventory tied up in the lengthy supply chain, the risks of disruption. All this brings the gap down to fifty cents. And the shipping and general costs would explode out of all proportion, were the item a complex assembled module. An item exactly sequenced to the vehicle build schedule simply could not come from overseas. This is the penalty for Australia's physical isolation.

## REDUCING THE LOCAL CONTENT OF CARS BUILT
### IN AUSTRALIA DID NOT OFFER A SOLUTION

The consequence of all this is that local sourcing in Australia was expensive but needed in some part for any vehicle assembled there, and in large part if the vehicle is a uniquely Australian design. But it is not self-evident that it made financial sense to build a standard for-eign-designed vehicle in Australia by dropping the local content level and re-sourcing from abroad. The supply chains are just too long. When the scenario feared by Toyota came about, of a collapse in volume and many failures in the Australian supply base caused by the other manufacturers ceasing production there, it did not have an alternative but to shut down also. Why ship most components all the way to Australia to build cars, most of which are then exported? Simpler to build them in Japan, tapping into the huge supplier base there. Yokohama to Melbourne is 6,466 nautical miles, to which add Melbourne to Dubai (the Gulf Cooperation Council States were the largest export destination for Australian cars) 4,907, for a total of 11,373, whereas Yokohama to Dubai is 6,322 nm. The real competitor was not the overseas supplier shipping parts into Australia, it's the one shown in Figure 9.8, the parts being delivered in an imported car, into the heart of the local market.

In retrospect, the Australian components sector was doomed not ever to reach Stage 4, that of autonomous sustainable

FIGURE 9.8  The real competitor
Picture credit: Wallenius-Wilhelmsen

development, by a combination of unfavourable factors: too small a domestic market and production levels, with local vehicle producers failing to achieve sufficient export volumes (except for Toyota); a national base not in the accessible logistical periphery of a major automotive region; no local factor cost advantages. Removing barriers to entry into the Australian market and supporting the Australian automotive industry were fatally conflicting objectives. Chapter 10 describes the policy contortions involved.

## IN SUMMARY; THE SUPPLIER BASE WAS DOOMED BY THE REMOVAL OF PROTECTION FROM IMPORTS

Prior to World War I, small engineering houses were able to handle the demand for repairs and replacement parts. A complex structure of Tariffs encouraged the vehicle importers to use Australian-produced components to replace the originally imported parts. There was a strong general trend – reinforced by the Great Depression – to protect the local production of parts. Ford and General Motors increased their level of involvement in Australia in the 1920s, encouraging many local component makers to establish operations. When General Motors-Holden released the first 'Holden' car in 1948, it achieved 60 per cent local content. The First Vehicle Plan was introduced in 1965, mandating 95 per cent local content – subsequently modified in later Plans. The Button Plan rationalised the vehicle manufacturing sector by reducing fragmentation, but with only a limited effect on the component supplier environment. Import quotas and local content rules were abolished while import duties were reducing – consequently, components producers were competing for a reducing share of a reducing market. Globally, components producers have taken on a much greater role in the design and integration of major parts and systems. The initial approach in Australia was to have local firms replicate foreign designs. Challenges to the sector were evident in 2000. The local supplier industry was constrained by its own fragmentation and by dependence on parent groups. Our own work in the sector fifteen years later was only partly encouraging. Some

Australian component producers achieved limited success in export markets. The supplier base had serious structural problems. The quality of relationships between suppliers and customers was not what it should have been. Suppliers tended to be complacent in the face of mounting competition, concentrating on extracting assistance from government. Foreign-owned companies took over the upper tiers of the supply base. The never-resolved underlying problem of the supplier base was inadequate scale. Reducing the local content of cars built in Australia did not offer a solution.

# 10  From Consistency to Contradiction: Australian Government Automotive Policy

## THE AUTOMOTIVE INDUSTRY HAS HIGHLY DEVELOPED BEGGING SKILLS, WHICH IT DEPLOYS UNHESITATINGLY

The automotive industry's achievements have been enormous. It was arguably *the* industry of the twentieth century. It has perfected its products and the application of technologies relevant to them to an exceptional degree. They are a mainstay of contemporary society. The depth and breadth of its industrial organisation are extraordinary. It has been a leader in globalisation and scaled itself up prodigiously in the process. But the very skills and disciplines it has developed have become a limitation. It is like a vast army column marching along and, correspondingly, not especially agile. Its investments in its existing capabilities are so vast that it has adopted a defensive position. It too often casts itself in the victim position, blaming external forces and agencies for problems of its own making. While the nature of its products means it necessarily has extensive interactions with governments, it is too ready to cajole and threaten and to expect public support as a right. It is extremely adept around the world at dangling the carrot of new investment and brandishing the stick of threatened plant closures.

## THE GLOBALISATION OF THE INDUSTRY PUT ITS MANAGERS IN AUSTRALIA INTO A CONFLICTED POSITION

None of this was a problem as long as the Australian automotive industry remained essentially Australian, able to operate, to a large extent, detached from the rest of the world. Its managers could operate as Australians, in the interests of both their companies and of Australia. That changed as the industry globalised and the barriers protecting the Australian market were removed. Theresa May infamously said that citizens of the world are citizens of nowhere. The servants of the multinationals generally feel most attached to their employer. One country or another is just another posting. Their responsibility – and their loyalty – is to the corporation above the host country. It is in fact their responsibility to extract the best conditions and support they can from the host country. It is unwise to assume the contrary. 'Going native', i.e., arguing too much for the host country, can be seen as negatively today as it was in colonial administrations. Vehicle manufacturers have deeply ingrained cultures, which differ significantly from one to the other, and are too often inward-looking. Among the component suppliers, there was a clear difference between the views of often over-optimistic purely local firms and those of the local subsidiaries of global corporations. Very few Australian-owned suppliers achieved global status.

## THIS WAS A RECIPE FOR REGULATORY CAPTURE

Governments, naturally ever-sensitive to economic development and employment, easily fall prey to sectoral blandishments. Few ministers have significant business experience or an understanding of the workings of large multi-national corporations. They often have no formal grounding in economics. This tendency has become worse over the years, with the 'professionalisation' of politics. There is always pressure to be seen to do something, often coming from an opposition untrammelled by responsibility. Doctrinal conflicts are no help, either. It is difficult for civil servants, increasingly upstaged by 'political advisers' to hold the ring and maintain good sense and consistency in policy. This is a recipe for regulatory capture. The Australian automotive industry's mantra in this sorry affair was, 'Every government supports its automotive industry'. Successive governments fell for it.

## PROTECTION FOR FLEDGLING INDUSTRIES IS NEITHER NEW NOR UNIQUE TO AUSTRALIA

Since Federation in 1901, Australia has relied on a range of protection mechanisms to assist its fledgling industries to become viable, including tariffs imposed to protect them from the established international competition. It should be noted that many other countries' industries had been (and in some instances, still are) protected by way of tariffs and other devices. Australia was far from alone in imposing such protection mechanisms. But the combination of a small population, a small local market and geographic isolation has always presented Australian businesses with significant challenges.

## TARIFFS WERE AN INITIALLY EFFECTIVE BUT ULTIMATELY DESTRUCTIVE MEANS OF PROTECTING THE LOCAL INDUSTRY

Throughout the twentieth century, the Australian Government favoured the application of tariffs as its preferred protection mechanism. The first tariffs were applied in 1902 on all manufactured goods imported into Australia. Figure 6.15 showed the tariff rates that applied to the importation of motor vehicles from 1902 to the present day. Until 1974, the British Preferential (BP) rate applied to vehicles imported from British Empire (Commonwealth) countries. The Most Favoured Nation (MFN) rate applied to imports from non-British Empire countries. As can be seen from the figure, the rate was maintained at a variably high level from 1914 onwards, peaking at 57.5 per cent in the early 1980s. As a result of the Button Plan (described later) and subsequent policy adjustments, the tariff rate underwent significant reductions from 1988, falling to 5 per cent in 2010.

Certainly, the tariffs did provide the industry with some breathing space – sufficient to allow it to develop into a fully capable, reasonably efficient, close-to-world-class enterprise – in the global automotive context of the 1960s and 1970s. However, there were negative effects resulting from the tariffs. Consumers paid more for cars than would have otherwise been the case and manufacturers were able to produce vehicles that were not really competitive and sidestep the need to invest in improved manufacturing technology. Australian manufacturers rarely led the world in any aspect of vehicle design or production, usually adopting models, technologies and production techniques handed down from their respective overseas parent firms.

The Whitlam government, which had been elected in 1972, was the first Australian government to recognise the inherent negative effects of tariffs (and other protective structures) and to attempt to open the Australian economy to a degree of global competition. In 1974, the government unilaterally reduced the tariffs by 25 per cent, which sparked a considerable outcry from the established players in many industries.

## IMPORT QUOTAS WERE ANOTHER MEASURE THAT WAS NOT SUSTAINABLE

However, in response to constant pleading on the part of the local automotive manufacturers, in 1975, the Whitlam government imposed protective measures by way of a 20 per cent quota on imported cars. Once more this measure had unintended consequences: because of the limited supply, imported brands were able to increase the price of their vehicles, which introduced further distortions to the local market. As a result of the higher prices, the consumers' perception of the imported brands increased. They became more highly valued and sought after than the locally produced brands: for instance, as a result of those higher prices, Honda cars were able to be positioned in the local market as virtually 'a poor man's BMW', considerably above the level of the locally produced Toyota models, precisely reversing the market positioning evident in other, less-distorted markets. Of course, this phenomenon was unanticipated and far from the original intent of the scheme.

## THE EXPORT FACILITATION SCHEME (EFS)
### WAS AN EFFECTIVE SCHEME THAT SERVED
### TO BOOST THE INDUSTRY'S INTERNATIONAL
### COMPETITIVENESS

In 1979, the government announced its decision to introduce export facilitation measures into the Vehicle Plan. The decision represented a move away from the narrow objective that an 'all Australian car' should be produced locally, towards a greater emphasis on competitiveness, trade and world markets. This direction was subsequently confirmed.[1] The government's Export Facilitation Scheme (EFS) was the first policy measure designed to encourage the Australian industry to integrate into the global automotive industry, rather than being protected from it. The Government stated:

> In the last 12 months the Government has become convinced of the need for the Australian motor vehicle industry to become better integrated with the world industry and so enhance its long-term viability and competitiveness. ... Given the small domestic market for motor vehicles in Australia, the only real and effective way that the industry can improve its cost structure is through closer integration with the world industry.

Under the EFS vehicle manufacturers and component suppliers could earn credits for their exports and vehicle producers could use these credits to offset, to some extent, their duty on imports. The incentive to export more was being provided through import duty concessions. This encouraged the industry to specialise in what it produced most efficiently and to import components that Australia was particularly inefficient at producing. It enabled vehicle producers to use export credits to source components from overseas that were particularly costly to produce in Australia, and to reduce their effective local content below the prescribed 85 per cent nominal level.

---

[1] Commonwealth of Australia, Industry Commission, *The Automotive Industry, Overview, Recommendations and Findings, Report no 58*, 26 May 1997.

The local content rules in force at that time required that 85 per cent of the total wholesale value of domestic passenger motor vehicle production be sourced locally. If the local content requirement was met, participating vehicle makers were entitled to import, free of duty, vehicles or components equal in value to the residual 15 per cent of wholesale value of domestic production.

Under the EFS:

- Motor vehicle producers could earn additional duty-free entitlements (export credits) on the value of local content in their eligible exports. Export credits could then be used to import components duty free on a dollar-for-dollar basis, or sold or transferred to other vehicle producers.
- Automotive component producers could earn export credits on the value of local automotive content in their eligible exports. Those credits could be sold or transferred to vehicle producers.

Export credits could be earned on eligible exports, which were defined as:

- Specified passenger motor vehicles;
- Australian-produced OE components which were identical or similar to components used in specified passenger motor vehicles produced in Australia;
- Australian-produced OE components for use in vehicles, the export of which would contribute to the achievement of overall objectives of the Government's passenger motor vehicle industry policy;
- Products and services relating to the automotive products above – automotive machine tools, automotive tooling and automotive design, development and production services; and
- Products and services of emerging technology designed initially for use as OE components in vehicles other than passenger motor vehicles.

The original EFS was brought into effect in 1982 and was subsequently modified in 1985, 1987, 1988 and 1991. The modifications served to make the scheme more widespread in its application and beneficial for exporters and importers. Its beneficial effects tended to lessen, however, with the general reductions in tariffs brought into effect under the Button Plan. As the EFS was seen to contravene WTO rules, the scheme was discontinued in 2001 and replaced by the ACIS (described later).

There were several export programmes that can reasonably be seen to have been initiated and or nurtured by way of the EFS, including:

- The Holden Family II four-cylinder and 'High Feature' V6 engine export programmes, subsequently the growth in the export of Holden CBU vehicles to the Middle East and United States;
- The expansion of the Nissan casting plant, generating exports to Japan;
- The export of the Mitsubishi Magna wagon to Japan, subsequently the export of the Diamante to the United States;
- The export of the Ford Capri to the United States;
- The growth of Toyota CBU exports to the Middle East;
- Component exports by AAPL, Air International, Autoliv, Pacifica, Robert Bosch, ROH, and Schefenacker.

It is difficult to clearly separate the results of the EFS from other micro- and macro-economic changes that were at play during the period. However, the Department of Industry, Science and Tourism (DIST) reported that automotive exports increased by 18 per cent from 1984 to 1990, slowing to 12 per cent growth from 1990 to 1996, reflecting the reducing tariff rates during the latter period. These figures exceeded those for general exports, which increased by 12.5 per cent for 1984–1990 and 7 per cent for 1990–1996.

The EFS can be seen to have been one of the more effective industry-assistance measures deployed by the Government.

## THE BUTTON PLAN MARKED A RADICAL CHANGE OF GOVERNMENT POLICY TOWARDS THE INDUSTRY, WITH CONTRADICTORY IMPLICATIONS

The Hawke government was elected in 1983. Working with a number of well-placed industry personnel, newly appointed Industries Minister Senator John Button produced a plan for the automotive industry that for the first time sought to rationalise and streamline the industry and make it significantly more efficient and productive. The Plan was designed to operate at both the vehicle producer and components supplier levels. The number of vehicle producers was to be reduced from five to three, and the number of models produced from thirteen to six by 1992. The local content plans were to be abolished and import duties were to be reduced from the current 57.5 per cent to 5 per cent over time. Import quotas were to be abolished. Export facilitation was to be retained at 15 per cent. The Button Plan and its effects on the components supplier industry were discussed in Chapter 9.

As a direct result of the suite of protection measures in place at the time of the plan's inception, including high tariffs on imported vehicles, quotas and local content plans, there had evolved to be five automotive manufacturers operating in Australia – Holden, Ford, Toyota, Mitsubishi and Nissan – producing a total of thirteen models. One might have assumed that the high number of manufacturers and models was precisely the intended result of the protection measures. However, the proliferation of models inevitably resulted in only low sales volumes able to be achieved for each model, which in turn resulted in few (if any) of the manufacturing operations being financially viable. The Australian market was too small to support the local production of such an extensive proliferation of models.

The Button Plan was implemented in 1985, its aim being to make the motor vehicle industry in Australia more efficient through consolidation of resources, which would then allow import tariffs to be gradually reduced. To an extent, it can be argued that the Hawke government, of which Senator Button was a member, was following in the footsteps of the Whitlam government's attempts at making the automotive industry more open to global competition, by way of its (the Whitlam government's) 1974 reduction in tariff levels. It is interesting to note that in each of these instances, a Labor government, which might have been expected to adopt more protective strategies, actually introduced measures to move the industry to a more rational structure which was more open to global competition. By contrast, over many years prior to and subsequent to the implementation of the Button Plan, the conservative governments had tended to be more susceptible to the entreaties of the established industry players and facilitate a more 'business as usual' approach.

The Button Plan represented a rare attempt by an Australian government to force change in an industry when it was becoming increasingly obvious that the entrenched industry players neither saw the need nor displayed the willingness to review the operation of the industry as a whole and reshape it to make it truly sustainable. It was an exertion of power over the industry on the part of the government that would not be repeated – in a positive, constructive way at least – by any future governments during the life of the industry in Australia.

As a result of the Button Plan, the local industry would be exposed to increased competition from imported products, fostering improvement in local vehicles and creating the basis for a competitive export industry. The plan forced the reduction in the number of locally manufactured models to six. By 1992, the aim was to have three manufacturers each producing two model lines. Initially, the most obvious result was a flurry of badge-engineered shared models during the 1980s and 1990s: Holden and Nissan, Ford and Nissan, Holden and Toyota models were interchanged and sent out into the market. The public was largely unimpressed by the apparent deception, however: the 'daughter' models never achieving anywhere near the sales of the 'mother' models. Nissan was the first of the local manufacturers to withdraw from Australia as a result of the scheme, exiting in 1992.

The Button Plan succeeded in forcing significant change in the industry at the vehicle manufacturer level, though, largely in spite of the loud protests of those manufacturers who were typically not accustomed to Australian governments intervening so decisively. It achieved reductions in the number of manufacturers and the number of models produced by those manufacturers. As a result, the industry was placed on a more sustainable footing. But no effort was made to create Australian cars that could genuinely compete internationally in demanding major markets. There was no adequate product specialisation that might have compensated through premium pricing for the loss of relative production scale. While the Button Plan did establish a more realistic framework of government support, the leaders of the industry did not all play their role in transitioning their Australian operations from isolated outposts to viable participants within their global empires.

The Button Plan also marked a far-reaching transition from government leadership in the initial creation of an integrated Australian industry behind strong protective walls, encouraging consolidation under the pressure of progressively dismantling those walls. Interviewed as part of the second of the 1986 ABC *Quantum* TV programmes, Senator Button declined to identify who might be the survivor(s) or to accept any role in deciding that, stressing that this was a matter for the industry itself. There is an interesting similarity here to the fundamental change in US industrial policy in regard to the railroads described by Dobbin. The potential consequences for the industry were not faced up to, nor was the efficacy of continuing government support questioned.

## MUCH MORE RADICAL RATIONALISATION WOULD HAVE BEEN REQUIRED IN COMPONENT SUPPLY

Rationalisation would have benefited the supplier sector in a similar way to the manufacturer sector. At the conclusion of the Button Plan, the supplier level was still characterised by high numbers of firms operating at all tiers, many at sub-optimal volumes. Many of those firms had been formed in a highly protected environment, resulting in their persisting with uncompetitive manufacturing processes and uncompetitive products. As late as 2004, many Australian suppliers served one customer, not all four – a punishing level of fragmentation in an industry with such low overall production volumes. This was reminiscent of Europe twenty-five years earlier, when national vehicle manufacturers had a large number of small, national suppliers, who worked for manufacturer customers in other countries only in exceptional instances. Changing this situation, however, would have required a complete change of approach in the local vehicle manufacturers' sourcing strategies, with a general acceptance of single-sourcing, which has normally been anathema in the industry, particularly given Australia's history of industrial strife. To overcome this resistance would have required massive government intervention in the industry, which was not intended in the Plan.

## THE LUXURY CAR TAX (LCT) WAS A REVENUE-RAISING MEASURE BUT WITH A DISTINCT PROTECTIONIST FLAVOUR

In 2000, the Federal Government imposed the Luxury Car Tax, which applied a 33 per cent tax on the part of a car's price that exceeded a nominated amount. It was described by the government of the day as a social-levelling measure but its focus on one particular sector was suspect. After all, there were no equivalent taxes imposed on expensive wine, watches, yachts, works of art or five-star holidays. The LCT served as a protectionist measure for the local industry. Interestingly, the 'nominated amount' was set just above the price of the locally produced luxury variants of the Holden and Ford mainstream models – Statesman and Fairlane – respectively. Effectively, imported vehicles competing for the luxury market were forced to be significantly more expensive than the local models.

If the intent was indeed protectionist, it backfired as a measure. Generally, consumers' perceptions of car brands and models are based very much on their price – a more expensive car implies a better car and certainly, a more prestigious car. So a Mercedes E-Class (just one example) that, as a result of the imposition of the Luxury Car Tax was suddenly double the price of a Holden Statesman is obviously twice as good – and twice as prestigious – a car, as perceived by the average consumer. The unintended end effect of this price distortion was to effectively reduce the brand value and brand positioning of the local products in comparison with the imported competitors in the minds of the Australian consumers. The LCT was a classic 'own goal' on the part of the government and the local vehicle manufacturers that had advocated it.

This kind of measure is by no means uniquely Australian. The Italian and French governments imposed annual vehicle licence fees that were steeply progressive with increased engine size, in a blatant attempt to keep out large German cars. This was shot down by the creation of the European Union and Single Market. It has, however, crept back in the form of imposts related to $CO_2$ emission levels. Thailand stymied the prospects of Australian vehicle manufacturers (Ford, in particular), exporting their vehicles to it by similar measures, which had not been foreseen in the Free Trade Agreement. This demonstrated a poor level of knowledge on the part of the Australian negotiators as to how the world automotive industry actually functions.

### ACIS WAS A HUGELY EXPENSIVE BUT SELF-CONTRADICTORY COMMITMENT OF SUPPORT TO THE INDUSTRY ON THE PART OF THE GOVERNMENT

As announced on 22 April 1998, by the Honourable Tim Fischer, then the Deputy Prime Minister and Minister for Trade:

> The Automotive Competitiveness and Investment Scheme (ACIS) is a transitional assistance scheme that will encourage competitive investments by firms in the automotive industry in order to achieve sustainable growth. The Scheme will provide an incentive for industry to continue its progress towards global competitiveness and a self-sustaining future in the context of trade liberalisation and the globalisation of the car industry. It has been designed, to reward higher performing firms that are prepared to invest and be innovative.

The ACIS scheme was scheduled to commence on 1 January 2001 and run for five years, ending on 31 December 2005.

Eligible participants in ACIS included:

- Motor vehicle manufacturers;
- Automotive component suppliers with original equipment contracts;
- Providers of automotive design development and production services; and
- Automotive machine tool and tooling producers.

ACIS had two related sub-schemes. One rewarded motor vehicle producers for performance in production and investment in new productive capital assets. The other rewarded automotive component producers and service providers for investment in new productive capital assets and in technology development. The Scheme provided benefits in the form of duty credits to be redeemed on imports of eligible automotive producers. The credits earned through investment were transferable. ACIS benefits were capped at $2 billion overall and 5 per cent of a vehicle manufacturer's sales of eligible products or services in the previous year. There was a notional allocation of $1.3 billion to the motor vehicle producers and $700 billion to the automotive component producers and service providers.

Benefits under ACIS were calculated as follows:vehicle manufacturers were entitled to an expanded version of the duty-free allowance and an investment incentive applying to expenditure on new productive capital assets. The duty-free allowance was increased from its then-current 15 per cent to 25 per cent and operated under these rules:

- The basis for calculating value of production included engines and components of engines in addition to passenger motor vehicles (PMVs) and
- The value of production included all PMV sales;
- A duty-free allowance penalty was applied at 25 per cent of the value of production (at wholesale prices) to determine the value of eligible imports that could be entered duty-free;
- Benefits could not be claimed on engine or engine component production for internal use in the manufacture of complete PMVs in respect of which a production benefit was claimed;

- The investment benefit was calculated as 10 per cent of investment in new productive assets;
- Investment was calculated on the basis of a three-year moving average.

For component suppliers (and other eligible participants):

- The benefit was calculated as 25 per cent of investments in new productive capital assets plus 45 per cent of technology development expenditure;
- Both these values were calculated on the basis of three-year moving averages;
- Benefits could not be claimed on automotive design development and production services which are performed for internal use in the development and production of PMVs where a production benefit was claimed.

Similar to its predecessor, the post-2005 Automotive Competitiveness and Investment Scheme was a transitional assistance scheme intended to encourage competitive investments by firms in the automotive industry in order to achieve sustainable growth. On 13 December 2002, the then-Minister for Industry, Tourism and Resources, the Honourable Ian Macfarlane, issued a media release in which it was announced that ACIS would continue beyond 2005 to 2015. Although it had been intended to run for ten years with all industry-specific support ceasing on 31 December 2015, the ACIS scheme was subsequently superseded by the 'New Car Plan for a Greener Future' in 2008. A total of $7.2 billion was made available to vehicle manufacturers and component suppliers to help them to enhance their competitiveness. At the same time, a schedule for the reduction in import tariffs was specified – the tariff would reduce to 10 per cent in 2005 and then to 5 per cent in 2010.

Again, the policy was well-intended but not always well-administered. Effectively, the funding became merely a subsidy for the vehicle manufacturers' and component suppliers' normal operations. Whereas ACIS participants proclaimed loudly that the money was spent on 'R&D', in reality the vast majority was invested in 'D' (i.e., in normal operations, notably routine product renewals and the usual running modifications), rather than 'R'. It was in fact the intention to encourage 'D' from the Button Plan onwards and R&D was defined more broadly than in ordinary tax legislation for that purpose. the motor vehicle producers apparently hoped that 'D' expenditure would be included in the assessment of local content.

In its lobbying and public relations, the automotive industry throughout the world conveys a false impression of being a huge investor in research; for example, even surpassing the pharmaceutical industry in Europe. This is based on OECD statistics, which unfortunately lump R and D together. Some 80–90 per cent of the automotive industry's R&D spend is 'D', i.e., routine product and process improvement and replacement. This not illogical at all, as the industry has historically deployed new technologies very cautiously, given that it mass produces large and complex consumer durables to very high standards of cost competitiveness, reliability, safety, environmental protection, comfort and convenience of use. Even more so in Australia, which was mainly a production location, with little propensity to engage in real 'research'. The Productivity Commission's 2002 Review of Automotive Assistance said as much: exhibit B18 in that review shows much lower figures than those claimed by the industry, 'Based on the definition that would qualify for the R&D tax concession. Hence, it excludes product and process development and, as such, is significantly less than that which would qualify for ACIS funding'.

## IT PERPETUATED THE UNRESOLVED CONTRADICTION IN THE BUTTON PLAN

There was little accountability and transparency incorporated in the scheme. Equally, there was little value achieved for the public through the spending of the grant monies. Motor vehicle producers were encouraged to apply for grants for R&D projects such as the development of a new front bumper bar for one of the mainstream models, for which ACIS contributed a total of $22 million. Just how such expenditure would achieve improved industry competitiveness or a more self-sustaining industry was never clearly explained (or even understood, most likely) by the government. The allocation of support was based on accountancy-style mechanistic rules, which were not based on any degree of under-standing of the industry nor on the basis of any perceptive assessment of effective contribution to a defined strategy – because there was none, other than protecting existing operations. In sharp contrast to the Button Plan of the 1980s, the ACIS scheme appears to have been devised with little knowledge of the industry's modus operandi and little vision as to how it might be made more sustainable. The manufacturers and suppliers constantly and consistently sought increased levels of subsidies to support their 'business as usual' approach.

### THE NEW CAR PLAN FOR A GREENER FUTURE WAS ESSENTIALLY AN IRRELEVANCE, WHICH HAD LITTLE EFFECT

This Plan committed contributions of $6.2 billion to the automotive industry, applying from 2008 to 2020, aimed at helping the industry design and build more fuel-efficient, environmentally sustainable vehicles. The Plan included the $1.3 billion 'Green Car Innovation Fund', which commenced in 2009 and was cancelled in 2011.

Under this scheme, Holden received a grant of $149 million to establish the local production of the four-cylinder Cruze model, which had been designed and manufactured by General Motors in Korea. As suggested earlier, it is unclear what was gained over simply importing this model. This seemed like a retrograde step, given the previous abandonment of low-volume assembly, and more like a device to prop up volumes of activity in Holden's assembly plant. It is hard to imagine how this could be considered an innovative measure. In addition, Holden received $40 million to develop 'a range of fuel efficiency and carbon emission reduction technologies and features for future Commodores'.

Ford received $42 million to assist with 'the engineering and fitment of EcoBoost, direct injection, turbo-charged, four-cylinder for the Falcon'. The EcoBoost engine had been developed by Ford of Europe for use in its Mondeo and other models. Smaller and more efficient engines help reduce $CO_2$ emissions from a car of a given size and weight but this would not make that car much more attractive in a market in which cars were generally downsizing, which is the most effective means of reducing emissions.

Toyota's introduction (at a total cost of $100 million to the scheme) of local production of the hybrid Camry was also supported under the GCIF. The technology (both production and vehicle operation) deployed were taken from the previous generation of Toyota's US model range and therefore did not represent an Australian innovation. The hybrid Camry did rapidly become the vehicle of choice for cab drivers around the country because if its greatly improved fuel efficiency (in the urban/suburban environment), combined with the traditional Toyota virtues of reliability and durability. This programme yielded an identifiable improvement for the environment and some extra activity for Toyota's Altona assembly plant. But the volumes achieved were small and it was never clear why this was better than simply importing these cars.

## THE AUTOMOTIVE TRANSFORMATION SCHEME WAS A LAST FAILED ATTEMPT TO SHIELD THE INDUSTRY FROM CHANGE, AT THE EXPENSE OF THE TAXPAYER

In 2011, the federal government announced the Automotive Transformation Scheme (ATS), which was intended to assist the industry transition from its then-current state to some other, undefined future state. Its stated aim was to 'encourage competitive investment and innovation in the Australian automotive industry'.

The scheme was to apply from 2011 to 2020, providing $2.5 billion of capped assistance to motor vehicle producers and automotive component producers. In essence, ATS was a poorly devised and implemented instrument, put into place at the behest of the vehicle manufacturers, in order to provide a subsidy for them and the component suppliers, to help fund their operations. In the end, it provided the public with zero residual value from the investment of its money in the industry.

One telling aspect of the design of the ATS was the fact that the department administering the scheme (the Department of Industry) was not obliged to publish a list of those manufacturers and suppliers that accessed the funds, nor a list of their projects so funded. It was established as a 'legislated entitlement scheme' (rather than a grant scheme), which supposedly removed any need for accountability or transparency in its operation. Hence, the public was provided with no information as to how its monies were spent or distributed. The department did publish the 'ATS Regulations', which defined the scheme's rules and criteria for application. It also published annual 'audit reports', supposedly documenting the administration of the scheme but no list of recipients, projects and amounts granted was ever made public.

Like ACIS but unlike the Button Plan, ATS was designed without any clear, documented strategy for the industry or even any real understanding of it, particularly in its global context. Most importantly, there was never any attempt to define the survivable future state to which the industry was supposed to transition. In reality, it was purely a subsidy to the existing order of the industry, which was already fatally flawed and on its way to extinction. The ATS lost all relevance once the three local MVPs announced their respective decisions in 2013 to withdraw from local manufacturing by 2017.

## THE THAILAND–AUSTRALIA FREE TRADE AGREEMENT WAS A NOTABLE EXAMPLE OF AN AGREEMENT CONCLUDED WITHOUT ADEQUATE SECTORAL UNDERSTANDING

The Thailand–Australia Free Trade Agreement (TAFTA) was executed on 1 January 2005, after having been negotiated by the Ministers for Foreign Affairs and Trade. Its aim was to reduce restrictions on trade between Australia and Thailand, primarily by way of zeroing the tariffs applying to the bi-directional trade. At the time, Thailand's automotive industry was in its infancy. The Thai government was offering tax breaks and other financial incentives to actively encourage global vehicle manufacturers to establish assembly operations there. The Japanese manufacturers (Toyota, Honda and Mazda initially) were the first to take up the offer, setting up the assembly of vans and pickup trucks.

TAFTA applied a zero tariff to automotive trade between Australia and Thailand, which represented a major benefit for Thailand. It was inevitable that there would be a greater flow of vehicles from Thailand to Australia than in the opposite direction. Ford Australia should, however, have had a clear opportunity to export its Territory SUV to Thailand. Under the terms of TAFTA, it would have attracted a zero tariff and would have represented a very competitive offering in the Thai market.

However, along with TAFTA, the Thai government imposed an 80 per cent excise duty on cars with engine capacity greater than three litres. Since the Thai industry produced no vehicles of such engine size, the excise was clearly established as a protection against imported vehicles and was directly in contravention – certainly in spirit, if not in word – of TAFTA. This was a blatant example of a non-tariff barrier to trade. The Australian negotiators appeared to be completely blindsided by this development and were unable or unwilling to challenge the excise ruling. Ford Australia, and by extension, the Australian industry as a whole, were denied a significant export opportunity – an opportunity that might well have significantly improved the viability of Ford Australia's position within the global Ford corporation and within the Australian industry.

## THE LEVEL OF GOVERNMENT ASSISTANCE
### TO THE INDUSTRY WAS DELIBERATELY MISREPRESENTED

There was considerable debate as to how the level of government assistance to the Australian industry compares with other countries. In 2011, the Federal Chamber of Automotive Industries (FCAI) commissioned the Sapere Research Group to examine an OECD (2010) comparison of international assistance to the automotive industry. The Sapere report (Davey 2011) suggested that assistance to the automotive industry in Australia was relatively low by international standards. The report showed that the cost of assistance provided per head of population in

2009 was lower (at USD17.80) than any other country. This figure received considerable and generally uncritical airplay from a range of industry and political sources advocating an increased level of assistance in Australia.

However, once the assistance provided is set against the number of vehicles produced in the respective countries, which is far more meaningful than the per capita value, a completely different picture emerges. Furthermore, the Sapere study simply added all forms of assistance together for each country, assuming all schemes operated in an identical manner and selected a highly atypical year – 2009, at the peak of the Global Financial Crisis – on which to conduct its analysis.

When the Sapere estimates are adjusted for the nature of each country's budgetary assistance, and one-off effects are removed, the ranking of countries by their assistance levels changes dramatically, as shown in Figure 10.1.

Regardless of which analysis is the more correct, the fact remains that the assistance provided did not achieve its stated objectives. In essence, ATS funds were handed to the vehicle manufacturers and component suppliers by way of grants or 'access to funds'. There

| Country | Sapere report (Davey 2011) | Autopolis assessment | |
|---|---|---|---|
| | $US per capita | $US per capita | $US per vehicle |
| Australia | $17.80 | $17.75 | $1,885.00 |
| Canada | $96.39 | $2.00 | $28.00 |
| France | $147.38 | $2.97 | $100.00 |
| Germany | $90.37 | $14.33 | $206.00 |
| Sweden | $334.18 | $5.30 | $297.00 |
| UK | $27.99 | $0.56 | $22.00 |
| US | $264.82 | $5.41 | $166.00 |

FIGURE 10.1 Lies, damned lies and statistics

Data sources: Sapere/FCAI and Autopolis submissions to the Productivity Commission

was little real accountability or transparency, and little real progress was achieved towards a truly self-sustaining industry. The vehicle manufacturers seem to have regarded the grant monies as just another contribution to their bottom line. There is little evidence of any real innovation having been achieved which might have improved the industry's competitive position and chances of survival.

## CONTINUED GOVERNMENT SUPPORT APPEARED TO PROVIDE GOOD VALUE FOR MONEY, AS THE LOSS OF THE INDUSTRY WAS A BLOW TO THE NATIONAL ECONOMY

By one interpretation, the some $500 million per year provided by way of the Automotive Transformation Scheme appeared to represent a sound investment of public funds in avoiding closure of the industry. The losses from the ending of local vehicle production appear to be huge. Once the local production ceased in 2017, Australia suffered significant losses:

- Foregoing the export revenues of PMVs and components. In 2012, this figure was $3.71 billion, which was considerably lower than in previous years as a result of the Global Financial Crisis – the export programmes of Holden and Toyota in particular would have resulted in significant growth in this number.
- Importing vehicles to replace the locally produced sold in Australia. In 2012, this figure was $3.23 billion. Summing the loss of export revenues and the cost of the replacement imports, the total loss to the Australian economy by way of the shutdown in manufacturing is approximately $7.0 billion annually, using the 2012 figures.
- Suffering the significant social disruption caused by the loss of approximately 50,000 jobs at the vehicle manufacturer and components supplier sectors, along with the resulting increase in welfare payments. There will be some additional losses at providers of services to the industry. But it is important not to use the 250,000 number advanced by some, which includes the huge downstream sector (franchised dealers, garages, smash repairers, insurers, fuels distributors, etc.), which is indifferent as to the manufacturing origins of the vehicles all these actors support.
- Losing the advanced manufacturing know how and overall capability represented by the automotive industry.

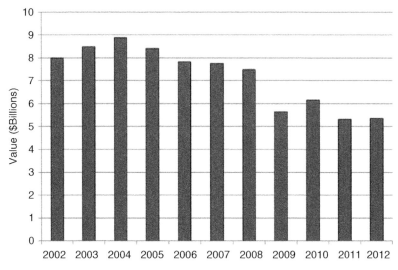

FIGURE 10.2 Value of local PMV and derivatives production, 2002–12
Data source: Automotive Statistics Australia

Figure 10.2 shows the value of local production of local PMVs and derivatives. Despite the decline, this was still a substantial number, at $5.37 billion in 2012, of which $2.14 billion was exported.

The value of exported vehicles and components (Figure 10.3) shows the successful Holden and Toyota export programmes leading up to 2008, and the effect of the 2009/10 Global Financial Crisis on those programmes. The true value to the economy of component exports independent of vehicles may have been overstated, depending on their own local content, which is not easily measured.

## BUT THE OPPORTUNITY COSTS OF SUBSIDISING THE AUSTRALIAN AUTOMOTIVE INDUSTRY REMAIN UNRECOGNISED

Simply supporting production, import substitution and exports is all very well but not if the businesses involved are inherently unviable and will require subsidy (which is what ACIS and ATS

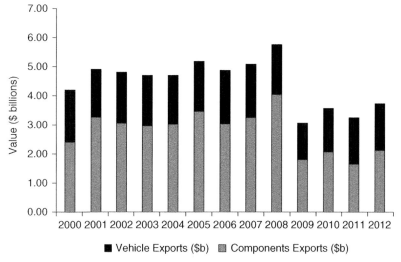

FIGURE 10.3 Value of vehicle and components exports 2000–12
Data source: Automotive Statistics Australia

were) indefinitely. This is social policy, not support to enterprise, and was exactly what government was seeking to avoid. The unanswered – and probably unanswerable – question is: what might have been achieved by using these huge amounts of public money to support businesses in other sectors, in which Australia could have achieved a comparative advantage and a durable position? Examination of the Productivity Commission's annual Tariff and Assistance Reviews shows the extent of the subsidies over the years – Figure 10.4. The drop-off from 2011 is noticeable, as the industry shrank. Cumulative assistance to the automotive sector for the sixteen years from 2001–2 to 2016–17 amounted to $23 billion, expressed in 2017 dollars. Given the sustained high levels of assistance in previous years, we may be looking at anything up to $100 billion (2017 values) since the start of the industry.

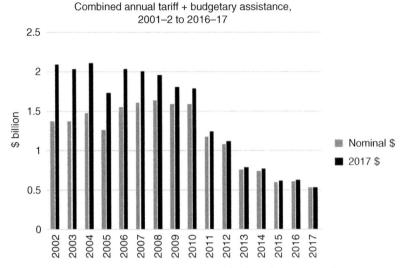

FIGURE 10.4 Assistance to motor vehicle and parts manufacturing
Data source: Productivity Commission Tariff and Assistance Reviews

## BEYOND THE BUTTON PLAN, AUSTRALIA HAD NO COHERENT GOVERNMENT POLICY OF SUPPORT TO ITS AUTOMOTIVE INDUSTRY

While the Button Plan was an attempt to force rationalisation upon the industry and thus to ensure its long-term survival, it was never taken through to its ultimate conclusion. Four vehicle manufacturers and four platforms were simply too much for Australia. The components supplier sector was rationalised to a certain degree, within Australia, and foreign suppliers were brought in. But this was never sufficient to ensure the competitiveness of the sector. ACIS and, most particularly, ATS were blatant, undiscriminating subsidies to a failing industry. ATS, in particular, was a misnomer: it should have been entitled APS – Automotive Preservation Scheme. The attempt to preserve the existing industry in aspic failed spectacularly. Australian taxpayers contributed billions of dollars to a dead-end scheme. The country is left with little but the headache and heartache of locally concentrated long-term unemployment.

## VERY FEW GOVERNMENTS HAVE MANAGED TO PROPEL THEIR AUTOMOTIVE INDUSTRIES INTO SELF-SUSTAINING FLIGHT

Could it have been different? The Japanese pulled it off, creating a huge national automotive industry off limited resources and a small national market base. The Japanese manufacturers were clearly helped in this by their own ingenuity, notably their application of lean production, which immensely improved their quality and productivity, compensating for their initial lack of scale compared to their established Western competitors. The Japanese manufacturers and suppliers also achieved much more cooperative relations than was common in the West. The sudden opening of the American market to their products, provoked by the vehicle downsizing forced on Detroit by Washington, enabled them to start globalising through massive exports from Japan, which continue to this day, supplemented by transplanting operations to both North America and Europe. All this was clearly part of a national industrial policy, strongly supported by MITI, the Ministry of International Trade and Industry. There was no hesitation in Japan about government support to industry. But MITI had a very clear idea of what sectors it could and should invest in.

South Korea, having achieved major international success from virtually nothing in shipbuilding and electronics, decided to do the same in the automotive industry. The cost was very high: unquantifiable and often occult financial support on a massive scale. Only one vehicle manufacturer, Hyundai-Kia, made it through as an independent to become a truly successful major global player. A ruthless rationalisation of the South Korean supplier sector was also carried out, which has resulted in the emergence of a small number of global players.

On a more modest scale, the British automotive industry, which had been almost wiped out by a combination of its own incompetence and haphazard government policies (in painful contrast to Germany or Japan), was saved from extinction in extremis by well-targeted government support to the establishment of transplant assembly plants in the United Kingdom by Nissan, Honda and Toyota. The then-UK Department of Trade and Industry developed a real understanding of what had gone wrong in the United Kingdom, of the global automotive industry and of the Japanese industry in particular. It developed strong relationships with the Japanese manufacturers and strongly supported them in establishing assembly operations in the United Kingdom as a springboard into the wider European market. It had to fight against strong German, French and Italian opposition to have UK-built Japanese cars accepted as European products, not subject to the Common External Tariff. The negotiated price was a commitment to the rapid achievement of 80 per cent European (and not solely British) content, thereby cleverly playing the European suppliers against the established manufacturers; and a voluntary 10 per cent ceiling on the Japanese MVPs' Europe-wide market share. So strong was the relationship that the DTI was even subsequently able to challenge the Japanese for their failure to hit the 10 per cent ceiling, as their products' performance and styling compared to those of their European competitors diluted their initial quality and cost advantage. Of UK vehicle production, 80 per cent is exported, principally to the rest of Europe – a situation that might change considerably as a result of Brexit.

Thailand has also managed to build up a substantial export-driven automotive assembly industry, playing on its low labour costs, protection of its domestic market by means of tariff and non-tariff measures (such as deliberately distorting internal vehicle taxation in favour of pickup trucks and against imports such as large-engine cars – thereby stymying the Thai–Australia FTA), and exploiting the potential of ASEAN.

No other country has achieved this kind of export success. Chinese manufacturers as yet export relatively little and the domestic market is protected from imports. The same applies to India. The

Russian industry has suffered from the country's economic woes, after an initial recovery from its slump following the end of Communism and the disintegration of the USSR. It is mainly foreign-controlled and exports almost nothing. Brazil has a long-established industry, largely under European control, but with a protected home market and only limited exports. Iran's industry has been cut off by sanctions against the country until very recently. Malaysia's continues to exist only thanks to strong protections and massive subsidies, without the benefit of being part of the production networks of large global MVPs in the case of Proton.

The common factor in the few successful cases have been: a clear understanding of the nature of the global automotive industry, which is a very difficult one in which to attempt to play; a feasible plan to establish a secure position in it for the fledgling domestic industry; and the willingness to enforce this, to commit the necessary resources to it and to change course when necessary.

## IN SUMMARY, GOVERNMENT INTERVENTION LOST ITS EFFICACY, ONCE PROTECTIONISM WAS ABANDONED

The automotive industry has highly developed begging skills, which it deploys unhesitatingly. The globalisation of the industry put its managers in Australia into a conflicted position. This was a recipe for regulatory capture. Protection for fledgling industries is neither new nor unique to Australia. Tariffs were an initially effective but ultimately destructive means of protecting the local industry. Import quotas were another measure that was not sustainable. The Export Facilitation Scheme (EFS) was an effective scheme that served to boost the industry's international competitiveness but depended on continued protection. The Button Plan marked a radical change of government policy towards the industry, away from protection, and with contradictory implications. Much more radical rationalisation would have been required in component supply to ensure survival. The LCT was a revenue-raising measure but with a distinct protectionist flavour. ACIS was a hugely expensive but self-contradictory commitment of support to the industry on the part of the government. It perpetuated the unresolved contradiction in the Button Plan. The New Car Plan for a Greener Future was essentially an irrelevance, which had little effect. The ATS was a last failed attempt to shield the industry from change, at the expense of the taxpayer. The Thailand–Australia Free Trade Agreement was a notable example of an agreement concluded without adequate sectoral understanding. The level of government assistance to the industry was deliberately misrepresented. Continued government support appeared to provide good value for money, as the loss of the industry was a blow to the national economy. But the opportunity costs of subsidising the Australian automotive industry remain unrecognised. Beyond the Button Plan, Australia had no coherent government policy of support to its automotive industry. Very few governments have managed to propel their automotive industries into self-sustaining flight, and this has required ruthless protectionism and strong intervention.

# 11 Government Support Policy and Sectoral Analysis: Lessons Learned

## THE LIFE CYCLE OF AN INDUSTRY AND ITS RELATIONSHIP WITH GOVERNMENTS

The previous chapters tell of the rise and fall of the Australian automotive industry, placed in the context of the history of the global industry, and of the role of governments:

- Australia followed the same life cycle path to intensive motorisation as other countries. It had a fast-growing car market that also underwent a massive internal shift in product preferences, as Australian society changed, away from the ageing traditional Australian-made large cars to more modern and cheaper small imported cars and SUVs. There are indications that the proprietary channels of the industry may have been used to try to protect the domestic products.
- The industry in Australia went through its own life cycle from early craft production, to assembly, then to fully integrated manufacturing. Production volumes rose rapidly at first but then fell away over a long period, as the Australian market moved away from the local industry's products. The belated attempts to boost exports to compensate for this loss of volume failed. The industry had a persistent problem with lack of relative scale, which fatally exposed it to foreign competition, as the protective barriers around the Australian market were dismantled.
- The creation and development of the automotive manufacturers in Australia was a huge endeavour. The shake-out intended by the Button Plan was never fully effective. The relationships between the manufacturers in Australia and their parent groups, and the loss of independence of the former created a major problem. The financial collapse of the light vehicle industry, despite generous government support, was primarily caused by lack of scale, not labour rates. Various rescue schemes were proposed but were all implausible.

- A full local supplier sector was created, behind strong protective barriers. Limited exports were achieved and there was a huge growth in imports of components, as barriers fell and a growing number of local suppliers were acquired or replaced by global groups. Only partial rationalisation was possible and resulted in a failure to achieve internationally competitive scale

- There was a reversal in relative power between companies and government. The Australian government initially successfully induced the creation of a full manufacturing industry, and protected and supported its development. Its policy towards the industry changed fundamentally with the Button Plan. There was a loss of control as barriers were dismantled, the industry lost its hold on its domestic market, and went into decline. Government's role was reduced to that of being a life support machine for a dying patient.

Building an entire industry more or less from scratch, creating products that were popular and loved for a long time, and keeping all of this going for seventy years was quite an achievement. But, like everything else, it followed a life cycle was born, matured, aged, declined and finally died. Three score years and ten sounds in a way normal. Could it have gone on longer, perhaps as long as the wider automotive industry itself? In Chapter 7, we concluded that the alternative tracks proposed towards or after the end were dead ends. But there might have been better alternatives, had they been pursued earlier.

## A FAILURE OF INFORMED GOVERNANCE AND DECISION-MAKING

The impression that comes out of this history is of a progressive loss of control by the Australian government over its own automotive policy, as options for the industry narrowed. In order to make the industry truly competitive, decisions would have had to be taken in favour of possible major changes of course, not the default of minor tweaks to the existing one. A different strategy, in other words: a new plan. This did not happen. We contend that government lost its grip, through want of a proper understanding of the structures, mechanisms, dynamics, relationships and capabilities of the automotive industry in Australia, set in the broader context of the global automotive industry. But it was the local industry that should, first and foremost, have been aware of its own problems, informed government of them, and proposed alternative courses of action, including the support needed to help effect the changes.

This was not for want of reviews, which happened in weighty form and more than once. We now examine the quality of the most recent of those reviews, which informed the decisions that were taken about the industry – or not taken. We look at the reports that resulted from four such exercises:

- The Industry Commission review of the industry of 1997
- The Productivity Commission Review of Automotive Assistance of 2002
- The Review of the Australian Automotive Industry of 2008
- Australia's Automotive Manufacturing Industry, Productivity Commission 2014

## THE INDUSTRY COMMISSION'S 1996–7 REVIEW OF THE INDUSTRY WAS WIDE-RANGING BUT INCONCLUSIVE

In 1996, the Treasurer tasked the then Industry Commission (later the Productivity Commission) with a wide-ranging enquiry. This was duly conducted, with many documentary inputs and discussions with involved parties, within and outside Australia. The 1997 report of the Commission is substantial (501 pages) and fascinating to read, containing a treasure trove of information.[1] It is comprehensive and covers most aspects of the Australian automotive industry and its position and prospects in the wider automotive world. The arguments are clearly presented and the writing style is clear and direct. The purpose of the report is to make recommendations to government about regulations and tariffs that are recognised as having major guiding impacts on the national market and industry. The Commission comes to clear and explicit

---

[1]  Commonwealth of Australia, Industry Commission, The Automotive Industry, Overview, Recommendations and Findings, Report no 58, 26 May 1997.

recommendations on future regulations, tariff settings and support to the industry, consistent with an end objective of achieving a self-sustaining and internationally competitive Australian automotive industry that will survive and prosper in the long term. This had to be reconciled with the other and potentially conflicting objective of allowing Australian buyers of new cars freer access to them on more competitive terms. In short, making the difficult trade-offs between continued protection of the industry and lower import tariffs for the benefit of consumers.

## THE REPORT COMPLETELY MISREAD THE IMPLICATIONS OF THE FLOOD OF IMPORTED CARS

From the standpoint of more than twenty years later, and with all the benefit of hindsight, it is the forward-looking chapter 10 of their report, Potential for Further Development of the Industry that is of particular interest. We quote the summary at the end of that chapter:

> The Commission is cautiously optimistic about the future of the Australian automotive industry. This optimism is based on:
>
> • domestic consumers' strong and growing demand for upper medium sized vehicles;
> • local manufacturers' dominance of that sector of the market;
> • strong anticipated growth in exports of vehicles and components; and
> • the scope for local producers to improve productivity, including through increasing volumes to take advantage of economies of scale.
>
> However, the current structure of the industry, with four independent vehicle manufacturers and over 200 component manufacturers is not sustainable without substantial exports.

Given the subsequent decline and collapse of the Australian automotive industry, it is appropriate to ask whether this reading was accurate, given the knowledge available at the time. Our view is that it was not, as the enquiry did not dig deep enough into the reality of the industry's situation and prospects, and that an optimistic bias was introduced, with some information dismissed or not given sufficient weight. The Commission itself did, after all, have to publish a dissenting minority report.

We now know what was to happen to consumers' strong and growing demand for upper medium sized vehicles (large RWD passenger cars and their derivatives): it collapsed – as shown in Figure 6.10. Could that have been foreseen in 1997? Figure 11.1 takes that chart and removes the then-future years from 1998 onwards and shows shares of the market by class of car, rather than absolute volumes. A similar chart for the years 1988 to 1996 appears in the report, which attributes the increase in these imports to the increased availability of small cars following the end of import quotas, their increased popularity, and the cessation of low-volume assembly of small cars in Australia. The emphasis was thus placed on the fact that they are imported, not on the reasons for their popularity.

SUVs, people movers, sports cars and upper large cars were negligible factors in the market in those years. Large cars did indeed gain market share. In the twenty years from 1977 to 1997 it went up from 37 per cent to 41 per cent. Some of this was attributable to Toyota

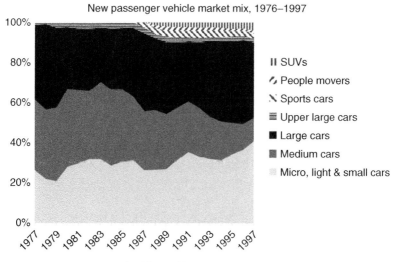

FIGURE 11.1 A highly visible invasion
Data source: AAI yearbook 2017

Camrys and Mitsubishi Magnas receiving six-cylinder engines and being promoted to the large car category but this would not have changed the conclusion that large cars had at least held their own. But the slightly disparagingly termed micro, light and small cars went from 26 per cent to 44 per cent of the market: a huge gain. Their relative market share, compared to large cars, went from 70 per cent to 109 per cent. They captured 70 per cent of the market's growth in units sold over those twenty years. This was a highly visible development, a veritable tidal wave, a seismic shift in the Australian new car market. Yet the Commission concluded optimistically, writing about the domestic large car producers: 'Their ability to retain market share would appear to be relatively sound, provided that Australian business consumers and fleet managers retain a preference for the 'big sixes', these vehicles are produced competitively, and the secondary market stays strong' (p. 302 of the report). While the report implicitly recognised the heavy reliance on the fleet market for demand for the large RWD sedans, it clearly missed the canary in the mine – what happens when the fleets change their purchasing patterns? What happens when the restrictions on choice on the part of the fleet clients are removed (as indeed happened during the early 1990s with the increasing availability and take-up of 'user-chooser' novated vehicle leases) with the result that the source of approximately 80 per cent of purchases of locally produced, large RWD vehicles looks elsewhere for their vehicle purchases? The report did not attempt to analyse the demand for the large RWD vehicles with any degree of understanding. Rather, it assumed that the 'business as usual' case would persist. It even went on to recommend an early cut to the 22.5 per cent of the import tariff on small cars, in order to help younger Australians with their car purchasing. This was giving away the industry's future by encouraging first-time buyers to look elsewhere.

## THE RIGHT QUESTIONS WERE NOT ASKED ABOUT THE MARKET AND OF CONSUMERS

No one asked why so many Australians were going for these nasty little Asian econoboxes, rather than wanting robust Australian cars.

Consumers seem not to have been asked – no surveys, no focus groups. Not even car magazines. Not even dealers, who, for all their limitations, do know what sells and what doesn't. Yet the reasons were clear: cheaper, more reliable, more compact (often with a far better ratio between internal space and external bulk), less thirsty cars. No mention of the increasing proportion of female buyers or of their preferences. The industry was extensively consulted. AFMA (the Australasian Fleet Management Association) was interviewed and identified the importance of mandatory buy-Australian policies of government fleets and a continued preference in private fleets. No one looked at the precedent of the large fleet sector in United Kingdom, long-established for tax reasons and long reserved to national vehicles – the Cologne-built Ford Granada had to be given honorary British citizenship for the purpose (an early case of a golden visa). National buying preference was dropped and a flood of imports resulted. There was no acknowledgement that national preference in the Australian fleet market was an artificial barrier, potentially insecure, the industry's Maginot Line. Satisfaction was expressed that private customers could buy de-fleeted Australian large cars in the secondary (i.e., second hand) market but there was no realisation that it was against these that the econoboxes in part competed, which would depress residual values, upset the fleets' depreciation calculations and lead to pressures for discounts on new large cars. Implicitly, the micro-light-small car market segment was treated as some sort of separate business. 'We don't compete with people like those', was the implication.

## NO QUESTIONS WERE ASKED ABOUT RELATIVE COST POSITIONS OR EXPORT MARKETS

Moreover, these small cars were imports, jumping over a 22.5 per cent tariff wall. How could they do this, yet still be so competitive? The not-so-secret weapon of the Japanese manufacturers, and of Toyota in particular, which first deployed it, was lean production. The story of this is told in the celebrated book that emanated from MIT's

International Motor Vehicle Program.[2] It describes in considerable detail how lean production works and the results it achieves for vehicle manufacturers, including charts comparing assembly plant productivity in hours required to build a vehicle and quality in assembly defects per 100 vehicles (pp. 85–6). The differences in performance are considerable: a US-owned plant in the United States took, on average, 50 per cent more hours and produced 50 per cent more assembly defects than a comparable Japanese-owned plant in Japan. The authors didn't attempt to compare costs. But replicate that productivity difference back up the supply chain and a Japanese-built car could well have had a unit cost 20–25 per cent less than that of an American-built one. Assume that an Australian plant performs like an American one and one can see how the imports could leap over the tariff wall. In fact, there is exactly such a chart in the Commission's report, showing assembly in Australia in 1993–4 taking twice as many hours as in Japan. It noted a 14 per cent improvement in Australia since 1988–9 and offered to have MIT update the analysis. Toyota agreed, provided the others did also. Ford and Mitsubishi refused – perhaps wisely. The conclusion drawn in the end is the one quoted above, about the scope for improving productivity, including through increasing volumes to take advantage of economies of scale – tempered by the comment that industry was not sustainable without substantial exports. On what scale? Of what products? To be sold where? To whom and by whom?

## OPPORTUNITIES TO RE-ORIENT THE INDUSTRY WERE MISSED

The Commission's task was not given the task of developing a strategy for the industry. But it could have questioned more deeply and recommended that plausible plans be required of the key participants, in return for continued government support. The conclusion might have been to pursue the same course. Or to force a further and

---

2    *The Machine That Changed the World*, James Womack, Daniel Jones, Daniel Roos and Donna Sammons Carpenter, Rawson Associates, 1990.

more radical consolidation, or a collaboration around a common Australian platform and derived products, positioned in less exposed segments of the domestic and international markets. Or to withdraw support. This would have required in-depth knowledge and analysis, not just consultations. Much of this information could have been obtained from the industry at the time, especially given the degree of its obligation to government. It appears that the Productivity Council did not dare ask for, and the vehicle manufacturers and component suppliers did not see it in their interests to proffer, any particularly insightful information or advice.

## THE PRODUCTIVITY COMMISSION'S 2002 REVIEW OF AUTOMOTIVE ASSISTANCE WAS ANOTHER MAJOR AND WIDE-RANGING INVESTIGATION THAT LED TO NO REAL CHANGES

It came at an apparent high point for the industry. The slide in volume of Australian cars in their domestic market had halted. Exports were taking off. See Figure 7.4. There were some grounds for optimism, it seemed. The review was given a considerable scope and, once again, the resulting report was detailed and weighty. Its whole focus was on how best to adapt support to the industry in a way that would encourage it to pursue greater competitiveness and reduced dependency, rather than on perpetuating the status quo. A worthy objective indeed but which needed to be based on whether and how an independently survivable end state could be reached. No definition of such a state was provided. The question of whether it was in fact achievable was not asked. The emphasis was on policy settings rather than the realities specific to this industry – just the failing identified in the Gerpisa report, cited in Chapter 9. There was a great deal asserted based on optimistic readings and too much reliance on consultation and evidence from interested parties. The descriptions of how the global automotive industry functioned may have appeared convincing to the lay reader but were, in fact, too much based on superficial reading and reproduction of publicly available analyses. Reading the report now, with the industry having collapsed, cruelly reveals much wishful thinking. A detailed review and criticism of the report would be far too long to be contained within this book. But it is worth commenting on the summary of key points provided in the report (the report's words are italicised, the authors' comments are shown in normal text):

- *In recent years, the automotive industry has transformed itself to become a major exporter and innovator. It has also greatly improved its productivity and the quality of its products. But it can do more to become truly internationally competitive.* More realistically, the industry can be viewed as having belatedly sought exports, in order to make up for its weakening grip on its domestic market.
- *It was a marginal exporter, by world automotive industry standards.* Calling it a 'major innovator' label was highly questionable. The Australian industry did indeed update and improve its products, but these remained too much based on increasingly superseded packages. Nothing was achieved which restored their appeal in the domestic market or made them original and strongly attractive to overseas customers. Substantial money was spent on R&D – at least relative to the size of the industry and compared to other industrial sectors in Australia – but there was not remotely enough of it for re-centring the industry in its markets. Again, the problem was of scale – simply not being big enough to generate the cash flow to support the massive reinvestments needed. Productivity and quality did indeed improve considerably. But these were qualifying factors, minima required to play in the game at all, not differentiators which allow market breakthroughs. The continuing gap in competitiveness (which is a multi-dimensional thing in this industry) was acknowledged but never defined. 'It can do more' was neither a measurable objective nor a plan.
- *This transformation has been influenced by reductions in tariffs, which have exposed the industry to increased international competition and also reduced costs for consumers and increased their vehicle choices.* Consumers indeed obtained access to more models of cars at lower prices and often higher quality, thanks to tariff reductions. Clearly, there would have been less incentive for the Australian automotive industry to up its game, had there not been this opening up of the Australian market. The implication here was that Australia had been able to have its cake and eat it – a better deal for both its consumers and its automotive industry. In

reality, the industry had not transformed itself fundamentally. The tariff reductions were in fact its death knell, because they were not accompanied by any effort to make it reposition itself and its products into any kind of sustainably defensible global niche, perhaps through developing a premium price positioning to compensate for low scale. There were some suggestions made about this but the industry was not challenged to come forward with concrete proposals. It was all very defensive and incremental.

- *ACIS support and a lower $A have both been important in helping the industry adjust to lower tariffs.* A weaker Australian dollar clearly alleviated the symptoms of distress but did not remove its causes. The report itself admits that it was far too early to judge the impact of ACIS support. The nature of the programme and hindsight suggest that ACIS was not transformational to any significant degree. It surely helped the industry to carry out the necessary running changes to its products and to modernise its processes, so as to catch up with the rest of the world. But no more than that. It is interesting to note the report's analysis of financial profitability, which held up. But being profitable is not enough if you are too small to keep up with the reinvestment requirements. Rover in the United Kingdom didn't fail because it didn't make profits but because it was too small to finance the vast investments required to keep up with the global industry's relentless product cycles. It's Net Cash Flow (cash generated from operations less reinvestment requirements) that matters, not reported profits. And especially in this industry. The report displayed no understanding of the economic and financial realities of the industry.

- *The industry has developed some key strengths, including its ability to respond quickly, innovatively and cost effectively to small volume market opportunities.* We read and heard this argument made many times over. Holden and Ford Australia clearly could engineer and design complete products. The Ford Territory was a fine example of measured innovation, derived from an existing platform, using very limited resources. But, on the whole, the Australian automotive industry was not able to respond quickly, innovatively and cost-effectively to the needs of its own small but growing and increasingly demanding domestic market. Rather, it continued with multiple competing manufacturers, each able to afford only infrequent and light product renewals, in a competitive environment of accelerating change. The idea of a new industry model actually appears in the report but is dismissed as impracticable: *'The recent report of the South Australian*

*Automotive Task Force (headed by Graham Spurling) concluded, among other things, that: there is a particularly strong case for some sort of cost sharing/rationalisation of very capital-intensive facilities such as those associated with engines and/or alloy castings, sheet metal stamping and tooling. ... a unique Australian industry model is required based on strategic alliances rather than the perpetuation of Australia's historically fragmented supplier base.'* (Graham Spurling had been the MD and CEO of Mitsubishi Motors Australia from 1980 to 1988. It was MMAL that proposed the sharing of a large motor body side press with other Australian Vehicle Producers; in particular Holden.) This seemingly modest proposal was in fact an invitation to take the Button Plan to its ultimate goal: a fully rationalised and competitive industry. Button sought to increase effective scale by reducing the number of producers and models built but was silent on the matter of how far to go to achieve viability. Given the size of the Australian market, the realistic share any one product could achieve, and a sensible estimate of its export potential, it should have been obvious that there was only room for building one uniquely Australian model family. There was no sense in having four manufacturers competing for this model, generating cash flows too small ever to allow it to be fully renewed – which ultimately condemned it to a slow death. Furthermore, Spurling's recommendation of avoiding duplication of investments could have been extended to the whole supply base, by accepting a single supplier in each category, once again maximising effective scale, cash flow and ability to innovate. This option could have been considered as a properly costed and evaluated long-term plan – to be compared with the alternatives of continuing on the existing multi-player and multi-product track, or closure. A proper strategic review of the industry was needed. It was not carried out.

- *A serious weakness is the adversarial workplace culture that continues to be evident in some parts of the industry. This has restricted the industry's capacity to implement just-in-time and other best practice processes essential to its long-term viability. While regulatory changes may help, better communication and greater cooperation between firms, their employees and unions are the key to improved workplace and industrial relations outcomes.* This was clearly a matter of the greatest seriousness, a deadly threat to the industry. Lamentable industrial relations, along with too many producers building too many models on too small a scale, in the face of protective tariff barriers potentially disappearing with entry into the

EEC was exactly the situation in the British car industry forty years earlier, so graphically portrayed by Graham Turner in his book, *The Car Makers*.[3] Here was a clear precedent, which ended with the virtual liquidation of the British car industry. Regulatory change by itself would indeed have been most unlikely to solve the problem. But a sector-specific collaborative solution might perhaps have been devised, in conjunction with a clear strategy for the industry along Spurling's lines.

- *Although assistance to the automotive industry will decline again in 2005, it will still be well above that for most other Australian industries. Further assistance reductions would benefit consumers and keep pressure on the industry to continue to improve its performance, as well as being consistent with Australia's APEC commitments.* The assistance was large enough to create distortions in the Australian economy by favouring one particular sector, yet too small to foster the changes needed in that sector, because too thinly spread and not tied to any clear outcome.

- *To meet the twin objectives of establishing a clear path to lower assistance and giving the industry time to adjust, a decade of policy certainty is desirable.* Policy certainty over a sufficiently long period continues to be the reasonable hope of the automotive industry everywhere to this day, given its long and heavy investment cycles. But the policy has to be one that leads to a viable future. 'Time to adjust' suggests incrementalism, when what was needed was a change of course.

- *Of the tariff options, there would be advantages in providing for a pause at 10 per cent from 2005, before reducing to 5 per cent in January 2010 and keeping this rate until 2015. This should be supported by retaining ACIS as a transitional mechanism, largely in its current form, until the end of 2010.* In other words, no real change.

- *These options do not envisage changes to government purchasing preferences for locally made vehicles or to the penalty tariff on used cars. The potential benefits of such changes at this time, appear not to warrant the additional uncertainty that would be created for the industry.* Maintaining national preference in government buying could not protect the industry's whole market position, especially when the commercial fleet preference for locally produced vehicles was in massive retreat. On the other hand, adopting the New Zealand policy of allowing unconstrained

---

[3]    *The Car Makers*, Graham Turner, Eyre and Spottiswoode, 1963.

imports of used cars would indeed have undermined the whole new car market.

- *Continued actions by government to improve access to overseas markets and to advance microeconomic reform are important for the industry's long-term future.* It would have been more important to secure firm commitments to export from the manufacturers, as part of an agreed and government-supported strategy, given their control over distribution.
- *The Commission's options have been designed to minimise the potential for disruptive change to the industry. Nevertheless, diverse pressures for adjustment will remain. As for other industries, any pronounced or regionally concentrated adjustment could warrant specific measures to assist affected employees or regions.* Disruptive change was exactly what was needed. Assistance to those affected by it would, of course, be required, particularly if a Spurling-type course involving much more internal cooperation was to be pursued.

Given how generous the government had been in its support over decades and that it was prepared to continue with it, it could have imposed far more direction on the industry and extracted far more commitment from it. This would have required a much more pene-trating investigation into the industry itself and less initial emphasis on policy settings as a kind of end in themselves.

## THE 2008 REVIEW OF AUSTRALIA'S AUTOMOTIVE INDUSTRY WAS MORE OF A REVIEW OF OPTIONS FOR SUPPORTING THE INDUSTRY THAN OF THE INDUSTRY ITSELF

The report's timing was unfortunate, coming as it did just before the GFC pushed GM into bankruptcy and caused it to pull the plug on Holden's prospects in the US market. Once again, the scope set for the review was wide-ranging, distracting attention from the industry's condition and prospects. The existing course for the industry – sub-scale and keeping three manufacturers and a weak supplier base in business – was not questioned. Perhaps it would have been too risky to do so. There was no review of the strategy or exploration of credible alternatives. Much of the analysis consisted of repetition of available information, without delving deeper to discover the reality of the industry's situation. The summaries of findings (paraphrased and condensed here) are revealing for their incoherence:

- Chapter 2: *outlook for the Australian automotive industry. The need to expand exports in order to achieve competitive scale* – no explanation given of how much expansion is or of how that will be achieved. *Manufacturers and Tier 1 suppliers in Australia competing for investment resources with subsidiaries of their parent groups in other countries, 'nevertheless, the Australian automotive industry continues to be globally competitive'* – in flat contradiction with the previous statement. *The vulnerability of Australia's Middle East market to Chinese, Thai and Indian competition, and to a preference to smaller vehicles, 'on the other hand, there is also the opportunity to expand Australia's market in the Middle East and North Africa, including in Libya'* – securing the industry's future via exports into marginal and exposed markets. No use was made of commercially available registration databases, which allow precise analysis of markets, product segments and competitive positions. *The downsizing trend in Australia, 'nonetheless, encouraging signs … such as plans to locally produce the Ford Focus and Toyota Camry hybrid'* – when assembly of models at low volume and with low national content had been discouraged under the Button Plan and had ended.
- *Chapter 3: the global automotive industry. Continuing expansion of production but shifting towards emerging economies* – caused by the shift of growth to new but closed markets. *Significant excess capacity and consequent pressure on profit margins* – an unfavourable environment for expanding exports from Australia. *The shift in the balance of output towards developing countries, with intensified cost-cutting and competition for new investment in the industry* – the problem identified in chapter 2 of the report, which should logically have come after chapter 3 *The resulting increasing strain on manufacturers' profit margins. The consequent effects on suppliers, with sourcing from fewer and larger ones, switching to lower-cost sources, and cost-down pressures* – fatal for a low-volume supply base (again, this should have come before the discussion of the Australian industry, as an important scene-setter). *Continued concentration of advanced design and engineering capabilities in*

*advanced industrial countries but with some emerging in China and India* – this implied a role for Australia, whereas these facilities are in fact usually in the central locations of the global automotive groups

- *Chapter 4: current Australian automotive policy arrangements. ACIS underwriting the profitability of many firms, thus keeping marginal ones in business and inhibiting scale-seeking rationalisation* – a perhaps unintentionally candid admission that ACIS was a subsidy to the existing order, rather than an incentive to change. *The industry receives substantial support from the Australian government* – to what end? *Tariff support equates to nearly $2,000 per new vehicle manufactured here* – a colossal level of subsidy, in flat contradiction to the later assertion pf the FCAI (Sapere report) that Australia gave less support to its automotive industry than did other countries. *A significant fall in assistance over the last two decades, with a move away from high tariffs and quotas* – but still very high.

- *Chapter 5: international automotive policies and assistance arrangement. Most countries impose tariffs on automotive imports, sometimes flanked by non-tariff barriers, foster the development of their automotive industries and offer investment incentives* – Chapter 5 of this book explains the role of different countries within the global automotive industry. *Australia has the fifth most open market, as measured by tariff rates* – earlier (p. 9, table 1.1) the report suggests that the low import tariff (10 per cent) is responsible for Australia's low production-to-sales ratio (39 per cent), while the same table shows the Czech Republic and Slovakia with the same 10 per cent tariff (the common EU one) with enormous production-to-sales ratios. It has little to do with the tariff and everything to do with the role the country's automotive industry plays within the global scheme of things (again, see Chapter 5 in this book). Parenthetically, this raises an interesting question: can one even speak of an Australian or Czech or Slovak automotive industry? Or should it be 'the automotive industry in Australia'? Who owns it? Who controls it? *The emerging automotive manufacturing countries are particularly active in providing up-front support to vehicle producers* – so was Australia, at the time of the creation of its industry, behind strong barriers.

- *Chapter 6: innovation. The level of automotive industry R&D expenditure has plateaued in the last few years, that in the total manufacturing sector has grown significantly* – note the simplistic use of R&D expenditure as a proxy for innovation, which in turn needs some definition in the context of the automotive industry. Perhaps there was a dearth of worthwhile projects. *Australia's provision of government R&D assistance funding to its automotive industry relative to GDP is similar to that of most other countries* – but is the absolute mass too great or too small, given the circumstances of the industry? *ACIS needs to be re-targeted to encourage further growth in automotive R&D* – to what ends? *Numerous examples of spill-overs to other sectors* – mainly advanced by the automotive industry itself, with little independent evidence. *Australian automotive component producers provide the skills and knowledge to allow the truck assemblers to supply the growing resources industry* – this assumes that assembling trucks locally makes more sense than importing them and that the mining sector cares about where they come from.

- Chapter 7: *market access. The need for a comprehensive international trade agreement with deep cuts to automotive tariffs and harmonisation of trade rules* – the strong and not the weak players would stand to gain from this. *Sign FTAs with economies with high trade barriers and where Australia can develop a competitive advantage* – which are these, in the automotive world? *Extend funding to initiatives such as Team Automotive Australia* – it makes good sense to coordinate approaches and pool resources in foreign trade representation but beware of trying to by-pass the management hierarchies of the global automotive groups. *Appoint an ambassadorial figure for the industry* – subject to the same caution about by-passing. More important is what Australia can offer.

- Chapter 8: *environment. A number of findings and recommendations* – not clear what special relevance they had to the Australian automotive industry itself. *Green Car Innovation Fund, $500 million, potentially doubling* – almost every government has some version of this, it was not made clear what concrete role Australia could play. Pre-setting the total invites marginal projects, the level should have been set after a review of proposals and selection of plausible projects. This also attached to ACIS as a whole

- Chapter 9: *restructuring the Australian automotive industry. A major employer* – which says nothing about its viability. *The need for a substantial increase in productivity growth* – to what levels and how? *Skills shortages in particular categories, lower educational qualifications at suppliers than at manufacturers* – solutions? *Continuing restructuring and consolidation, effect on changes in range and value of products and on the employment and skills base* – what changes, precisely? *Global integration, bigger is better, quality of management, particularly in smaller firms* – all real challenges but what solutions? *The Australian Government should contribute to a short-term automotive restructure fund, to assist in improving economies of scale, enhance management capabilities, internationalise production to build capacity and demand, and enhance long-term sustainability* – devise the strategy and plan first, decide on government support later.

- Chapter 10: *vehicle safety.* An important subject to which Australia has made important contributions and can surely contribute more, but not central to the survival of its automotive industry.
- Chapter 11: *future automotive assistance arrangements. A new Global Automotive Transition Scheme to replace ACIS, with three funding options presented and one recommended, with further details on the forms of funding, and on the eligibility of projects and recipients, and the establishment of an Automotive Industry Innovation Council to bring together motor vehicle producers, component suppliers, unions, research and academic organisations, and government.* This is a reflection of the belief on the part of economists that 'innovation' is some kind of Tabasco sauce that will bring any dull dish to life. It was acknowledged that 90 per cent of R&D spending in the industry is on routine product and process improvement. This, while necessary, would not be sufficient to transform the industry. How much would need to be spent by and on the industry to put it back into the product mainstream and whether this could plausibly yield enough sales volume and income, profit margins and cash flow for the industry to become self-sustaining without endless government support, are simply not addressed. This incrementalism and 'get-there-itis' do not constitute a strategy for survival.

## THE PRODUCTIVITY COMMISSION'S REPORT OF 2014 IS AN ASTOUNDINGLY DISINGENUOUS DOCUMENT

The report represents a complete volte-face, and an after-the-event admission that all the support given to the industry was pointless.[4] The report's own summary of key points will suffice here:

---

[4]    Australia's Automotive Manufacturing Industry, Productivity Commission Inquiry Report No. 70, 31 March 2014.

- Australia's automotive manufacturing industry is undergoing significant change.
  - Motor vehicle producers in Australia have not been able to survive in the highly competitive global and domestic automotive markets.
  - Ford, Holden and Toyota have announced they will cease local manufacturing before the end of 2017.
  - Component manufacturers face ongoing adjustment pressure and rationalisation.
  - It is estimated that up to 40,000 people may lose their jobs as a result of the closure of the motor vehicle manufacturing plants and the rationalisation of firms in the supply chain. It is likely that job losses will be staggered over several years.
  - Decades of transitional assistance to automotive manufacturing firms ($30 billion between 1997 and 2012) has forestalled, but not prevented, the significant structural adjustment now facing the industry.
- The policy rationales for industry-specific assistance to automotive manufacturing firms are weak and the economy-wide costs of such assistance outweigh the benefits.
  - The Automotive Transformation Scheme should be closed after Ford, Holden and Toyota have ceased manufacturing motor vehicles in Australia.
  - Component manufacturing firms are currently set to receive over $300 million in industry-specific assistance between 2014 and 2017. There are both efficiency and industry equity arguments against extending assistance beyond that already committed, or introducing new assistance programmes that would advantage component manufacturers ahead of other firms that face adjustment pressures.
- The labour market in Australia is dynamic – many employees lose their jobs in any one year and many people who are jobless are hired. In the year ending February 2013, about 355,000 people were involuntarily retrenched across Australia.
- Retrenched employees face costs associated with job search and training, and some will have lower paid or less secure jobs once re-employed. Loss of employment is particularly challenging for older people, or those with poor English proficiency or lower skill levels.

**(cont.)**

- – While retrenched manufacturing employees may take longer on average to find re-employment than employees retrenched from other industries, within a year about two-thirds are likely to be re-employed on a full, part-time or casual basis.
- – Adjustment pressures are likely to be concentrated within particular regions, such as North Adelaide, parts of Melbourne and Geelong. Some affected regions already have relatively high rates of unemployment and social disadvantage.
- • Governments should ensure the appropriate resourcing of the delivery of generally available welfare, training and employment services for all clients in regions placed under pressure by automotive manufacturing retrenchments.
- • Providing adjustment assistance to retrenched automotive manufacturing employees at a level that exceeds the assistance generally available to other jobseekers raises efficiency and equity issues.
- – Governments should consider ways to better target assistance to retrenched employees who are likely to encounter the greatest difficulties finding re-employment.
- • Regional adjustment funds, infrastructure and defence spending and industry support programmes are costly and ineffective ways to facilitate workforce adjustment.

The flagrant contradiction with previous reviews in content and tone needs no further emphasis. For all its efforts and spending on supporting the industry, the Australian government was unable to prevent its ultimate collapse. It was a very sad ending to something which had been a genuine source of national pride, and into which many, many people put their efforts and their hearts. The industry in Australia in the end went through its life cycle from birth, to growth and success, to decline in the face of outside forces beyond its control, and to final disappearance. It was a brave attempt to enable Australia to escape from being merely a supplier of commodities to the world.

That it ultimately failed only reinforces the country's need to find such domains in which it can establish durably successful competitive positions. Even when one such is achieved, there can be no guarantee that it will last forever. Industrial policy has to be dynamic.

## WHAT LESSONS CAN BE DRAWN FROM THIS PARTICULAR STORY?

Governments have an over-riding duty to ensure the security and prosperity of their countries, within the means at their disposal. Given that resources are limited, this may require alliances, in the case of security. In the case of prosperity, comparative advantage and achievable scale come into play. Some countries and sectors within their national economies have profited greatly from globalisation, others have suffered. There are choices to be made between material gain and independence. These choices are, of course, philosophical and political. Making them wisely requires sound information and understanding to enable a proper comparison of options, and detached and objective appraisal of these and their implications.

We were not particularly fingering Australia or its automotive industry in writing this book. Conveniently, we were familiar with both, and we could look back over the whole life cycle. Our views on the global industry did not derive from our work in Australia but certainly helped to inform it. We have sought to provide a rational explanation for what happened, within the limits of the information that we possessed. It would be interesting to look at market structures in more detail, notably the sales of Australian-type large RWD saloon cars and their derivatives; or at just what the unit cost differences were for comparable products (whether cars or components) between Australia and other producing countries. All this should have been known within the industry. Government and its agencies should have been able to access it, given their generosity towards the industry. This is also a poignant example of the power of global corporations over national governments. The only remedy for that, the means to redress the imbalance of power, is adequate information and sufficient understanding. Know your adversary or partner. That the automotive industry is particularly strongly structured, disciplined, scale-seeking, oligopolistic and adept at lobbying made the need particularly strong in this instance. But that need is by no means limited to dealing with this particular sector. The problem will recur.

And this is the heart of our argument, going well beyond one sector and one country. This is but one of innumerable instances of governments and their agencies falling prey to economic actors through failure to inform themselves properly, or to face up to the evidence presented to them. Raw information is not enough, it must be correctly structured and interpreted, and further information sought if necessary. The reviews described in this chapter are full of raw information – sales and production volumes in Australia, trade statistics, etc. – but no-one looked below the surface. Anyone in the business would have identified the shrinking appeal of the traditional Australian car. But the connexion was not made. Further afield, any-one in Detroit and other impoverished areas of the United States could see houses being sold to those who could not afford to repay the mortgages, which were re-packaged through securitisation and sold to unsuspecting investors by unscrupulous financial agencies. There was even a joke about a Detroit bar owner selling the bar bills of local alcoholics in this fashion. We are not quite at the extremes of the South Sea Bubble offering of shares in A Venture Whose Purpose Will Be Announced Later. Nor are we totally removed from it. The super-sonic Concorde, based on the false premise that the demand for air travel increased with speed (it was in fact because of reduced seat-mile costs). The Brexit referendum. The permanent triumph of hope over experience.

Some terms from the reviews cited above stick in the mind: policy settings, econometric modelling, productivity, innovation. They are part of the stuff of macro-economics, hugely bandied about and less understood. Businesses do not operate in 'the economy' as a sort of all-encompassing black box but within specific sectors of it, which have their own very distinctive and particular sets of market structures and segments, drivers of demand and product or service responses, technology enablers, production structures, distribution and retailing channels, and competitive dynamics. This has somehow been neglected, left to languish in the middle of the spectrum that reaches from grand and often untested (and untestable) macro-economic theories to the behavioural economics of the individual (otherwise known as perceptive market research). There is a failing here on the part of the economics profession. But equally, on the part of the clients for advice. It is not enough to gather the conventional information, to consult the industry, to ask for spontaneous submissions, to listen to the grandees. Someone has to ask the hard questions.

Simply blaming politicians is itself a cop-out. They have to balance multiple and often conflicting imperatives, and to make difficult decisions, often under unhelpful partisan pressure. Industry leaders should be the first to ask themselves and their organisations the hard questions, in their own interests. Internal and external advisers ought to speak the truth to power but there are obvious risks involved. Informed, sufficient and dispassionate analysis can help greatly.

# Index